D0941210

The *seventeen* Book of Etiquette and Entertaining

Also from *seventeen*

THE SEVENTEEN BOOK OF DECORATING

THE SEVENTEEN BOOK OF YOUNG LIVING

Enid A. Haupt

EDITOR-IN-CHIEF OF
SEVENTEEN MAGAZINE

The *seventeen* Book of

DAVID McKAY COMPANY, INC. NEW YORK

THE SEVENTEEN BOOK OF ETIQUETTE AND ENTERTAINING

COPYRIGHT © 1963 BY ENID A. HAUPT

All rights reserved, including the right to reproduce this book, or parts thereof, in any form, except for the inclusion of brief quotations in a review

Seventh Printing, October 1965

LIBRARY OF CONGRESS CARD NUMBER: 63-10778

MANUFACTURED IN THE UNITED STATES OF AMERICA

VAN REES PRESS • NEW YORK

Contents

Introduction:

My dear young friend,
This is your book. It has been planned to help you deal confidently and competently with the many situations you will face — and need to know how to manage — as you pass through the impressionable and swiftly-changing teen years.

I think it is extremely important to know how to manage the daily give-and-take of living, working and playing with other people. It is an essential part of education. No one likes to feel awkward or unsure or ill at ease. I think it is especially sad to hear a young person — so intense of feeling, so sensitive, so vulnerable — say ruefully, "Oh, I made the worst blunder — I had no idea what was expected of me — no one ever told me — if only I'd known."

Knowing what good manners are and knowing the kind of behavior that is expected of you helps you to be more comfortable. Even more important, and this is the heart of good manners, it helps you to put other people at ease. The inner security that marks a whole man or a whole woman comes from integrity, self-respect and confidence. Just as laws have developed as part of our civilization, certain codes of ethics and behavior have evolved, too. Good people, in whatever era, have always respected standards of right and wrong, have never wavered between kindness and malice. There is no "new breed" of human being. Even at this formative age of your life, you may not know what you want to be—but you know what kind of person you don't want to be.

I hope the guide lines in this book will help you find your way more surely, more swiftly down the larger and the small unknown paths that lie ahead. As you live and love these wonderful years, finding your way to maturity, founding your own family, remember how much the world depends on what your generation can contribute.

I hope that the spirit of this book will help you achieve the dreams, the high standards and the high hopes that each of you holds in your heart.

Most sincerely,

Enid A. Haupt

The *seventeen* Book of Etiquette and Entertaining

1. Nice People: THE HABITS THEY HAVE

nice (nīs), *a. Pleasing, agreeable, delightful, good, kind, considerate, or the like*

Nice people have good manners. Good manners are part of a good personality. Parents and teachers emphasize manners. Columnists write about them. Thinkers think about them. Ralph Waldo Emerson, perhaps the most cheerful positive thinker of the nineteenth century, offered many little sugared maxims on manners—including these, for example:

> Manners are the happy way of doing things.

> Good manners are made up of petty sacrifices.

We think that good manners come from the heart, that they're the sum of the adjectives describing the word "nice" at the top of this page. *Pleasing, agreeable, delightful, good, kind, considerate.* "You couldn't ask for a nicer friend." "She's as nice as she can be." "He's the nicest boy I've ever met."

We don't think good manners blossom from a quick study of the "correct" things to do. (One could be a walking etiquette book and—like Mr. Darcy in *Pride and Prejudice*—still be far from pleasing, kind or considerate.) The rules help you to be more agreeable because they serve as guides that indicate a way of doing things with grace and good taste—guides that you respect because you want to be both pleasing and pleasant to others.

Few of us could remember *all* the rules (that's why libraries put etiquette books on the reference shelf), but each of us can have manners that are very winning. It takes some alchemy that nice people know—a brew of kindness, considerateness and common sense. And the more you use all these habits, the more they become a part of you, until you no longer have to think of them.

The kind of thoughtfulness that makes you nice to have around is all part of being

Nice on the inside Like the courteous French, who appreciate that even buying paper clips can be a pleasant experience, you try to leave the other person with a cheerful feeling after you've gone. The kind addition of a few polite words—*"Good morning* . . . May I have a box of paper clips, *please* . . . *Thank you"*—unquestionably makes you feel more amiable. But think also of the difference in the salesperson's day—and how your kindness can buffer the people-are-no-good effect of a rude encounter later in the day.

The point is that you're not haphazard about courtesy, reserving it to lavish on people you like and want to have like you. All in your day—the elevator man, the bus driver, your little brother's best friend, your grandmother's bridge partner, the man who runs the shoe-repair shop—are treated to the same cheerful manners. Your universal goodwill may be the reason you're one of those sunny people whom everyone is glad to see, who's invited to every party, who can always be counted on to round up a needed committee, who can get the impossible done quickly (such as an emergency shoe repair five minutes before closing time).

Your friends like you because you can keep a promise and a confidence, because you try your best to live up to that difficult ideal of finding something good to say about others and smothering the urge for character dissection that starts, "You know, the trouble with Harry is . . ." They like you because you're forthright: what you have to say (glad, mad, sad) is said to the person involved, not to people on the fringes. If you accept a responsibility, you carry it out to the best of your ability—even when you find the job is not much to your liking after all. When you borrow something, you return it soon and in good condition. If you make a mistake (and who doesn't?), you try to overcome that human tendency to palm it off on someone else. If you owe an apology, you make it quickly and try to offer some kind of reparation to someone—being particularly helpful or agreeable, or just not criticizing for a while, or, if the break is material as well as emotional, getting the racket restrung or the china mended. If you're on the receiving end of both the hurt and the apology, you say, "Oh, do forget about it"—and, outwardly at least, you forget about it too.

Older people like you because you're friendly but respectful. You stand up when an older person (anyone from voting age on, man or woman) enters a room and *always* when you are introduced. You say, "Yes, Miss Smith"; "No, Mr. Brown"—rather than a flat yes or no. If you offer to get something for a woman your mother's age, you simply ask, "May I get it for you, Mrs. Brown?" —not being oversolicitous, not implying that she is aging too rapidly to endure the strain. You don't repeat adults' conversation—whether you hear it at home or somewhere else. You don't criticize another family's house, happiness or hospitality—and you don't abuse their hospitality, either by overstaying your welcome or by making their place your home away from home.

The very old, who often have a great kinship with the young, appreciate your interest, your ability to listen. They like your eagerness to compare the important happenings in your life with theirs—the excitement of the first big dance, the first stirrings of romance, making the team, an election, a hero's parade. The very small thoughtfulnesses of remembering to telephone, to mail a clipping, a card, a snapshot—all enrich their lives and yours too.

Children, the most critical group of all, like you because you laugh with but never at them. You don't talk about them in front of them as though they weren't right there. You are young enough to remember that—once past first grade—the savor has left the compliment of "how much you've grown," that all that's left is a measure of discontent at having grown too much or not enough. You remember to tell his mother how nice little Bobby was at your sister's party (particularly important if he was horrible, because she will be grateful and nicer to Bobby and the shock of this turn of events may surprise him into being a better boy). You don't tease, bribe or play favorites. If you have a favorite, you take that child on special outings; but in a group he's as good as anyone else but no better (after the first big hug, of course). And you never trick children into doing your work or running errands for you; if you want a hired hand for some reasonable job, you first work out a reasonable reward with the hand's mother.

Your dentist, your doctor—and any other expert in your life—appreciate you because you are on time for appointments and break them only with good reason and with as much advance notice as possible. Once there, you are truthful in discussing how you are. (Fib, and the doctor will either see right through you or, in doubt, be forced to do a battery of costly tests to discover the fib.) During an examination or treatment, you are composed and, when necessary, you make an honest effort to be courageous. (You may not succeed, but the doctor needs both the courtesy and the encouragement of that honest effort on your part.)

Teachers, clergymen, instructors, coaches like you because you listen, try to get the message, respect both their position and their knowledge. Whether you're the star Bible student or the star player, you know that you need direction, that you have to work to achieve excellence. You realize you wouldn't be the star if there weren't a group to shine from. If you're just in the group, you do your part well and support the star by being a good team-worker.

Those who serve you like you—waiters, bus drivers, salespeople, repairmen, porters, maids, cleaning people—because you give your order or your instructions quietly and clearly, you say please and thank you. If you are entitled to a protest or a criticism, you make it firmly, courteously and preferably privately—with the intent of improving the situation rather than reproving or letting the steam out of your temper or disappointment.

Celebrities—from the local hockey star to the movie hero appearing in person at the big theater—are grateful for your thoughtfulness too. They're glad to meet you, to give you an autograph, because you don't crowd, scream, try to cadge such souvenirs as buttons, snips of hair and fragments of clothing. They appreciate your enthusiastic applause when they're performing . . . almost as much as they appreciate your self-control in not staring, pointing, commenting about them in a loud voice or blocking their way when they're *not* performing.

Another quality about pleasant people is that they're

Nice on the outside They're easy in social situations and they know how to put others at ease. They're good hosts and delightful guests. Learning to be introduced—to shake hands, to respond courteously and take part in a conversation—starts in early childhood (often reluctantly!). Learning to introduce others starts with the first friend you make outside the sheltered world of your family—a milepost in growing up. Knowing what's expected of you makes this small part of growing up much easier.

In all introductions you follow three simple rules:

1. introduce the younger person to the older
2. introduce the less important person to the more important
3. introduce the male to the female

Regrettably, you can't depend on these three rules. As a wildly complicated example, suppose you are helping your mother with a large New Year's Day open-house party:

The young, new assistant minister of the Community Church comes in and you say, "Good afternoon, Mr. Black. Do you know my aunt, Mrs. Larramie? She will take you to my mother, who is in the next room." You walk over to your aunt and say, "Mr. Black, this is my aunt, Mrs. Larramie. Aunt Emma, Mr. Black is Dr. Brown's new assistant."

This breaks rules 1 and 3; it keeps rule 2

As you leave them, you see the new school principal—who has just moved next door—coming in and you corral your older sister to take him to your mother, saying, "Dr. Maynard, this is my sister Julie, who is home from college."

This breaks rule 3; it keeps rules 1 and 2

At this point your grandfather comes up with Mrs. Brown, your minister's mother. You say, "Mrs. Brown, this is Dr. Maynard, who has just moved next door. Grandfather, this is Dr. Maynard—my grandfather, Mr. Gibbons."

This breaks rule 2; it keeps rules 1 and 3

This breaks rule 2; it keeps rule 1

Mr. Black, the young, new assistant minister, joins your group and your grandfather says, "Mr. Black, do you know Dr. Maynard? This is Mr. Black, who has just come to the Community Church."

This breaks rules 1 and 2

As you, Mr. Black and Dr. Maynard head for the tea table, your little sister bounds into the room. You introduce her first to Mr. Black and then to Dr. Maynard.

This breaks rule 3; it keeps rules 1 and 2

Just as you are saying good-by to a departing guest, two young people ring the bell. They are your twelve-year-old cousin Mary and Dr. Maynard's college-age son, who has just won the state indoor tennis championship. You're fairly certain they have not met, so you say, "Mary, do you know Bob Maynard, our new neighbor? Bob, my cousin Mary Larramie."

This breaks rules 1 and 2
it keeps rule 3

If, about now, you are thinking glumly that the only situation you can rely on is boy meets girl, you are right. There was a sound reason for the rule-breaking at your imaginary open-house party—and the reason was based either on respect or on common sense. It is a mark of respect to present others to a member of the clergy (of any age)—even though the others are ladies (of any age) or older men. It is a matter of respect to introduce your older sister or your younger sister to a man of stature, such as the school principal, Dr. Maynard. It is a matter of common sense to introduce the college tennis star to your young cousin Mary—and she will appreciate your courtesy in treating her as a grownup. *Good cliché*—the one about rules' being made to be broken!

First names or not?—another decision you base on respect and common sense. In your own group you introduce Bob Maynard to your sister Julie Gibbons because they will use first names in talking to each other. You introduce your sister Julie to Dr. Maynard using her first name because he will call her Julie or Miss Gibbons as he wishes. You don't use first names in introducing one adult to another (as a matter of respect), even if you call the person by his or her first name—a stepmother or stepfather, perhaps, or a friend of your parents who doesn't like being called "*Aunt* Shirley." A stepmother is introduced as "my stepmother, Mrs. Thomas." To be remembered: if your mother has remarried, be sure to say "my mother, Mrs. *Willard*" distinctly.

oh, no!	*ah, yes!*
phrases like "Joe, meet my sister" . . . "I'd like to acquaint you with my sister"	phrases like "this is" . . . "do you know" . . . "I've wanted you to meet" . . . or, very formally, "May I present Sally Smithers?"
responses like "pleased" . . . "charmed" . . . "delighted" . . . "happy to make your acquaintance"	sincere, spontaneous responses like "I'm so glad to meet you!" . . . "I've been wanting to meet you. Sue has told me so much about you!"
to an older person: "Hello" . . . or "Hello, Dr. Maynard"	to an older person: "How do you do, Dr. Maynard"
to a contemporary: "Hello"	to a contemporary: "Hello, *Bill*"
calling an older or more distinguished person by his first name	waiting for the older or more distinguished person to ask you to call him by his first name
forgetting to introduce people—or assuming everyone knows everyone	saying "Do you know Sally Smithers, Joan?" And, if she doesn't, completing the courtesy with "This is Joan Blake, Sally"
a girl remaining seated when introduced to an older or more distinguished person	the lady rises
a boy remaining seated when introduced to anyone	a gentleman of any age stands up, barring plaster casts, infirmities
any guest at a party remaining seated when introduced to another guest (unless seated guest is much older or one of those distinguished persons)	rise, not only as a gesture to your hostess, but also because it's much easier to shake hands at the same level
saying "pardon my glove" as you shake hands	say nothing about it. A girl is expected to keep her glove on. A boy pulls the glove off unless it would be awkward (if he had his left arm full of tennis rackets, for example).

To jell it all down you introduce people to the person to whom you are deferring.

No name at all? It does happen: you don't always remember a name. Best bet is to let the other person talk and listen attentively; perhaps the talker will drop a clue to his identity or perhaps your memory will suddenly click. If you find you have to introduce the person, say, "I'm terribly sorry, but your name escapes me for the moment. . ."
If you greet someone who seems to be groping for your name, introduce yourself with some kind of identifying tag line: "Good afternoon, Dr. Maynard; I'm Kate Dodd, a classmate of Marilyn's."

Launching a conversation It helps if the introducer has given you both a logical starting point, such as "Mother, this is Laura Hastings; she's in the Art Club with me." If she adds one of those compliments which make an introduction ghastly ("Laura paints better than anyone in the whole club"), smile and say, "Thank you, and aren't you nice to say so!" Try your best not to agree smugly or mutter, "Oh, those old paintings; they're *nothing* really." If you are a serious painter (or student or athlete or musician) and realize soberly how far you still have to go, it's your privilege to acknowledge the fact with some words like "but I've got a long way to go" tacked on to your thank-you.
two notes on giving compliments

- it's great to tell Jane you like her dress (we once heard a clergyman charge his congregation to pay four different people a compliment every day for the next week), but do tell her when you're not with other girls—unless, of course, you want to admire every dress in the group.
- one compliment means more than a flood of them—which either embarrasses or waters down the effect till it's meaningless.

Once launched, most conversations will run on cheerily if you remember to
- listen sympathetically and interestedly
- ask pertinent questions
- avoid monopolizing the conversation
- think before you speak
- have the discipline to avoid tactless or cruel comments, whiplash wit
- pay attention—so you don't have to interject "what" too often
- say "I think that . . ." rather than make positive statements
- look for topics of mutual interest: "I ski; do you?" "You don't think Mr. Conant was talking about *our* school, do you?"
- let a reflective pause happen now and then, rather than keep the conversation going relentlessly

- draw out the other person's opinions, interests and ideas, rather than hold forth at length about your own
- discuss, analyze, dissect a subject, if you will—enthusiastically, determinedly, heatedly, *but never in anger.* And end the discussion on a friendly note: "I realize I may be all wrong, you know. . . ."
- turn a conversation that's becoming bitter, using any number of softening devices. The shock element: "*Oh, my word*—I forgot my brother's birthday. Excuse me for changing the subject, but what can I get him right now?" The hold-out-a-lollipop switch of subject: "I'm *starved;* wouldn't anyone like a vanilla frosted?" The temporary peace: "Well, we can't solve the problem today. Let's eat/dance/get home for all that homework . . ." The classic tension-breaker: "Oh . . . has anyone read any good books lately?"

TABOOS FOR TALKERS

- *never* criticize unjustly or destructively. It's true you must criticize sometimes if you are the leader, president, chairman of any group. Try to make the criticism only to the person involved—privately—and with the intention of improving the situation: "Jerry, I think it would be much better if you would concentrate on the sale of tickets and let the decorating committee do its job. Would you do that, please?"
- *never* ridicule or make fun of another person's mannerisms, eccentricities, shortcomings, taste, looks, clothes, possessions, relatives, friends, pets
- *never* wave these conversational red flags: "You *always* . . ." "The trouble with you is . . ."
- *never* gossip or repeat gossip (a disease that can become chronic and highly infectious to others; males catch it too)
- *never* ask personal questions. These include asking why your family doesn't belong to the club, what's the matter with your little sister who has to repeat second grade, is your mother a real blonde, is your brother ever going to marry Anne, how much insurance your father has, why don't you go on a diet
- *never* indulge in speculative talk about money. This includes wondering how much money someone's father paid for a house, what salary someone's father probably gets, how much someone paid for a dress, the amount of someone's allowance, whether someone's family can afford to live the way they do—and so on and on
- *never, never, never* be as funny as you can, especially at someone else's expense
- and NEVER dispense wholesale criticism of anyone's politics or religion . . . or of any racial, political, religious or national group *as a group*

This last "never" reminds us that good people are also

Nice clear through—with a built-in loving-kindness that makes them shun any opportunity to think, speak or act in a way that would damage another person's tastes, self-respect, pride, self-confidence, loyalties. In other words, good people are big people rather than little people. Little people are prejudiced; they're actually frightened of people, traditions and things that are "different," and it's easy to recognize them by their overpositive opinions and dislikes, slurring remarks, sweeping condemnations. When their prejudice is directed at contemporary furniture, modern music and madrigals or the Method method of acting, you can shrug it off as lack of culture, lack of knowledge, lack of interests. When the prejudice slashes into deeper loyalties, it takes compassion to understand and not be angry with the biased offender. Both time and the goodwill of the majority of people eventually educate the prejudiced.

As a teen you can build better understanding in many ways right in your own corner of the world. Here are a few ways that mark you as nice clear through:

1. *You don't exclude people from your group merely because*
   - they are newcomers and don't belong
   - they come from a different social background, whether it's higher or lower
   - they go to private school and you go to public school—or the reverse
   - their parents are separated or divorced
   - their speech or their clothes are different
   - their parents have more money or less than yours
   - their race or religion is different from yours
2. *You don't make other people's loyalties a subject for fun by*
   - telling dialect stories. Let the Scots tell the jokes about Scottish thrift, for example; then it's funny. (The great comedians turn the laughs on themselves.) It's not so funny to a Scot when someone of another group pokes fun at his group's supposed eccentricities or shortcomings.
   - telling hilarious tales about two clergymen—or deacons, nuns, rabbinical students or *anyone*—who belong to a faith other than yours. If you honestly think the story is choice and not disrespectful, switch it to your own religion.
3. *You don't make broad statements condemning any group of humans as a group*

   To be avoided also are statements, such as the following, that would reflect on a group or profession: "She's not like most . . ." "He's very nice, really, for a . . ." "Some of my best friends are . . ." "Isn't that just like a . . ."
4. *You use the honorable term for members of a race or religion that's foreign to you*—rather than a slang term or an abbreviation. If you are a Mixo-

Lydian member of the Druid faith and wish to refer to yourself as a Mixo, a tree-kook or whatever, go right ahead; at least the lack of respect hurts only your own group. (And you might become pretty unpopular with your own group, come to think of it.)

These four points about the good manners that make nice people stand out in a crowd lead us directly to a bigger subject (and also to the next chapter!) because nice people are also very nice to have around.

Let us also consider some of the plain but important points about nice people—who are

Nice to have near To describe the matter candidly, they are attractive physically—clean, scrubbed, fresh, well-groomed, neatly put together. You can be fairly sure the physical attraction comes from good maintenance of the human machinery, maintenance to keep it in tune and cycling properly.

What makes for physical attractiveness?

sleep eight, ten hours—whatever amount gives you that fine feeling of weightlessness when you walk, of comfortable ability to enjoy the day and take control of its events. As an occasional plus, the mental and physical boost of a round-the-clock sleep.

rest another matter than sleep. Rest in terms of short breaks during the day, during evening homework—a brisk walk, a cat nap, an escape into something good to read, playing with your pet, throwing a ball to your young brother. To achieve relaxation, do the opposite of what you've been doing, such as getting outdoors if you've been inside; curling up by the fire if you've been outside; taking a long hot bath in cold weather.

control the daily bath, frequent shampoos, faithful tooth-brushing and mouth-washing. Daily application of a deodorant. Nails scrubbed. Hands washed often and always before meals. Hair brushed and combed. For a girl, fuzz-free underarms and legs. For a boy, a shaved face (nickless with the right razor) kept healthy with an antiseptic lotion. For both, wash your face and scrub lavishly twice a day—and rinse, rinse, rinse.

care the twice-a-year sojourn at the dentist's, the annual check with the doctor, the weekly step on the scale—followed by immediate measures if it registers an alarm signal.

discipline exercise for good general health and buoyancy, for modifying figure problems or increasing skills in sports, dancing. The determination to eat a proper diet and to resist such pay-the-piper treats as fried foods, rich desserts, nibbling (see page 11).

SEVENTEEN'S DAILY FOOD GUIDE

- a quart of milk (skimmed, whole, nonfat dry or evaporated)
- two or more servings of fruit (fresh, frozen or canned), one of which is tomato or citrus
- two or more servings of meat, poultry, fish or eggs; occasionally alternate cooked dried beans, peas or nuts
- at every meal, a form of enriched or whole-grain bread, cereal or flour product; butter or margarine
- two or more vegetables (fresh, frozen or canned)—one leafy green or yellow—plus one potato
- six or eight glasses of liquid a day —milk, water, fruit juice, coffee or tea
- sweets, but moderately

If blemished skin or overweight disturbs you, strictness about eating habits can be very rewarding:

- choose meats, poultry, fish, eggs that are *anything* but fried. Let them be broiled, roasted, baked, poached—but not sautéed, braised, cooked on a griddle or fried.
- learn to love the fresh taste of hot or cold fruit and a plain cookie rather than those wickedly attractive pies, cakes and whipped-cream desserts
- avoid chocolate, cocoa, nuts, peanut butter, rich cheeses

approved nibbling Lettuce, carrot and celery sticks, water cress, radishes, raw cauliflower, dried fruit (apricots, prunes, peaches, raisins)

A further point about nice people: they are

nice to look at In the early years of this century, the young were often prodded to *"stand up and have some style about you!"* Today—somewhat less clearly—you are prodded to "project an image" to the world. One way of projecting an attractive image is to carry the human body with style—to stand, sit and move with verve, pride, elasticity, grace. (Yes, grace for boys too: you'll never see it demonstrated more perfectly than in a broken-field run in a football game or a dazzling play on the basketball court.) You might review the following image-wreckers and see whether any of the suggested repairs are in order for you:

image-wreckers	repairs
walking at a tilt—shoulders hunched forward, head leading. One tends to do this in a hurry (you won't get there a second faster, though your head may) or in a gloomy mood (projecting the gloom does little to cheer you).	1. let the top of your head pull your spine straight and stretch it so you feel, look taller—the way strings pull a puppet out of a heap 2. resolve to get there with some style—handsome if late, handsome if morose
flapping arms or hands. This will pass when you're grown. Complete coordination is difficult when arms or legs are still a little long for the rest of one's body or when one's frame is still girdled with that cushioning regrettably described as "baby fat."	1. time 2. slow but steady training: carry things at arm's length without swinging your arm—a package, a bag, a tennis racket, for examples
shuffling feet—bad enough when walking but maddening on the dance floor	1. pick them *up* and put them *down* 2. consider the type, fit and age of your shoes. Are they foreign to the needs of your feet even though the kind everyone wears? 3. survey the way others use their feet—athletes particularly, actors and actresses, dancers
collapsing into a chair and assuming a shape like a blob of putty	1. ease into the chair; it will live longer 2. sit *up,* not down, so you retain a human figure
sprawling when seated. Only those under the age of six months look charming with legs and arms spread like a starfish.	1. keep legs as parallel as possible whether both feet are on the floor or ankles or legs are crossed memo: ❦ boys—and girls in pants sit less formally ❦ a girl in a short, straight skirt looks prettiest with knees, legs, ankles together; even crossed ankles take on a pretzel quality with this kind of skirt

image-wreckers — repairs

hunchback climbing—as though there were an invisible pack on the back—whether on stairs, a ramp, a hill

1. thighs and legs are meant to do the work and carry the body upward
2. odd item: make sure you breathe as you climb. One reason climbers hunch forward is to gulp in oxygen for air-starved lungs.

scrambled descent on stairs, ramp, hill

1. here, too, thighs and legs are meant to do the work and the upper part of the body should be borne down—rather like a moving column
2. means to grace:
   - turning the knees slightly inward
   - making each step on the ball of the foot rather than the whole foot
   - watching where you're going *without* watching your feet

ramrod posture—with knees locked, back stiff as a board, head, neck and arms held rigidly

1. take a deep breath and, as you slowly let it go, try to ease every muscle, counting down from the headbone to the anklebone
2. work consciously toward a more fluid carriage—so you have the flexible living erectness of a tree that sways in a stiff wind rather than the deadwood look of a telephone pole

slumped posture—that discouraged effect of hanging head and drooping shoulders above a rib cage and waist—now without identity—that sink into the abdomen to form one long blob from neck to hipbone

1. fatigue doing this to you? Perhaps you might review the makings of physical attractiveness on page 10. A fatigue posture indicates something is wrong. If a week of proper sleep, rest and exercise doesn't help, do discuss the matter with your doctor.

image-wreckers	repairs
	2. slumped posture can also be "all in your head." Teens, as you well know, are somewhat mercurial about being glad and/or sad. When your mood is down, make sure your posture is still nice for others to see; there is no point in everyone's getting depressed.
	3. exercise is a marvelous tonic for slumped posture, whatever its origin, and especially if it's the outward sign of a blue mood. Not exercise of a penitential variety you dislike, but one you really enjoy—playing the drums, twisting, skating, raking leaves, swimming—so the sense of feeling happily tired will replace the fatigue.

What goes on the human frame is another factor in being nice to look at. Obviously, clothes should be pressed, spotless, with the buttons on and the shirttails in (if that's where they're meant to be). They should also be compatible with you, each other, and the day's activities. Examples of incompatibility would include

warring colors—while all colors are supposed to be friendly if used correctly, it takes years to develop the blending talent of a Gauguin. So if you have florid skin and red hair, it is expensive to keep trying different shades of red sweaters when nearly all blues and greens are becoming to you—or, if your suit is lilac, to wear red shoes when your only clean blouse is an emerald print.

your cue: wear becoming colors, whether or not your choice is the greatest fashion of the moment. One color and a contrasting color (or a neutral) make a better effect than mad mixing.

incongruousness—sneakers and gym socks with an afternoon dress, saddle shoes with a navy suit, a straw hat in the fall (more about special clothes for special occasions on page 161)

your cue: get things ready ahead of time; if in doubt about your choice, ask a parent or older friend *inappropriateness*—slacks when everyone else is wearing a dress or suit, party clothes at a picnic, a little black dress when shirts and skirts or shorts are in order

your cue: ask your hostess (or his/her mother) what to wear

Methods of enhancing the human frame—which also affect that image of you—need to be properly controlled

- *the haircut*—the one you got (or the one you didn't have time to get) can make the difference in your looking well-groomed. It's hard to say if a poor haircut looks worse than hair that's obviously in need of cutting—so it's wise to find and stay with a hairdresser or barber who cuts *your* hair satisfactorily.
- *scent*—whether it's his after-shave lotion or your cologne (soap, talcum or hand lotion), scent should be fresh, pleasant but not asphyxiating. If the kind you like is fresh and pleasant, there's no problem of when you may use it. (Maybe you remember the amusing Q.-and-A. ad that asked if it's all right to wear a special perfume when washing the car. The answer: "Certainly. Especially if you want help!") Girls who adore sultry fragrances do well to limit this kind of indulgence to late-afternoon and evening parties. Are you one of them? Be sure your beau likes the scent; if he doesn't—and you like him—use a few sultry drops in your bath (luxury indeed) or wrap the bottle tightly in that transparent plastic wrap and store it away for the next beau.
- *nails*—those that are not bitten are more desirable, particularly when neatly filed and scrubbed. Girls with dragon-lady fingernails—whether or not they're delicately pink or brilliantly red—meet with far less approval from two majority groups: males of any age, adults.
- *make-up—ladies only*—Those words exclude more than boys; they also exclude girls who are too young to use make-up *and* girls who—unlike ladies—use so much make-up that it calls attention to the camouflage rather than to the girl. If you start using make-up too early—before most of your friends do, before your family and your world in general think you should—you look as though your family doesn't care about you (a smack at your parents and also at their pride in you).

  When, with approval, you start wearing make-up, keep in mind that the purpose is to make you look prettier. A soft shade of lipstick, a dab of cream on the lashes, and a flick of pressed powder are all you need during the day. On greater occasions, you'll probably start using a base make-up and face powder. And if yours are the too light kind of eyebrows and lashes, you may want to bring them out with a little brow pencil and mascara.

Also important on the list of agreeable qualities is being

nice to listen to Even the words others want to hear least—"It doesn't fit" . . . "He's taking Cici to the dance" . . . "It's not a very good report" . . . "Good-by" . . . *any* kind of advice—are more palatable, produce a better reaction when said distinctly and cheerfully in a voice that has some sound of music to it. (More about how to achieve this on page 124.) Since a voice can have both sound and fury—meaning, in this case, a tempestuous level of noise—a deliberate effort should be made to speak loud enough for the immediate listener to hear you but softly enough not to distract those who aren't concerned with what you have to say. No trilling in the snack bar, no shouting across a crowded street or in the bus, no counterpoint of gossip and giggles at any performance—play, movie, concert, assembly, group TV watching.

2. Nice To Be With: IN YOUR HOME AND NEIGHBORHOOD

If you're nice to have around, people generally want to have you around. That means you're popular, and the longing to be popular is one of the keenest desires of the human heart. There are many "secrets" of popularity, but the important one—the one that's often overlooked—is that to be truly popular means to be beloved. You can lavish money, presents, rewards of all kinds on others and still not be beloved (leaving you with a very hungry heart). You can go along with the crowd for good or for evil, for better or for worse. You can be the girl who has everything material but who has nothing.

How to be beloved? It's a personal matter between you and other people. It means always being nice, thinking of nice things to say and smothering the desire for the final word or the cruel jibe that may seem brilliantly fitting. It means being nice for your family to live with, nice for your roommate and, eventually, the person you marry to live with. It means being nice for other people to be with, in and out of school, doing paid or volunteer work, at church, at play.

Perhaps you know the quip that advises, "If you don't have enough manners to go around, save the few you have for those at home." Sad and true, for home—the place we learn manners—is where they are forgotten the quickest. It isn't just remembering to say please and thank you. There are basic qualities that make you

NICE TO LIVE WITH

you respect privacy You have a vigorous opinion about your own right to privacy—and you're entitled to it; you also make a kind and deliberate effort not to interfere with your family's privacy. Your mother's, father's, brothers' and sisters' mail is theirs and only theirs—as are their diaries, appointment books, checkbooks, bankbooks, piggy banks! Their telephone calls are not always casual, and you tactfully disappear if you realize the conversation is really not meant for you to hear. You try, try, try to convince your younger brother that listening in on the extension phone is vexing, snooping, practically dishonest—even though he thinks it's a vastly clever trick.

You knock on any closed door in your house before entering. Actually you knock on a closed door anywhere.

You ask before you borrow things large and small—your mother's stockings, the family car, your sister's pen, your brother's baseball jacket.

You keep family secrets secret: the major ones, of course, like your father's business being in a shaky state—that's obvious and instinctive—but the gossipy ones too, the kind that would really make awfully good stories, such as your mother's adding the $159 to her checking account instead of subtracting it and subsequently being overdrawn at the bank . . . and the whiz of a battle your sister had with her beau. You know that your gossiping is not loyal and that it might magnify the stories far beyond reality and really hurt the ones you love.

Overpersonal questions are as out of bounds with your family as with friends. When you see a subject is getting touchy, you change it—no teasing, prying, playing Little Miss District Attorney.

you're accommodating, another comfortable quality—frequently just a matter of timing, too. Take the evening you have to eat dinner early because of a play rehearsal: you try to tell your mother the day before and *not* the day of the rehearsal. Ideally, you prepare your own meal.

Or if you'd like to bring a friend home for dinner, you ask in advance (unless yours is one of those easy households where the rule is "The more, the merrier" and "There's always room for one more").

You try to make your telephone calls at hours when your parents don't expect the phone to be free for them. If your friends call at the wrong hour, you chat briefly and ask if you can call back when the timing's better for your family.

if you lose the choice—whether it's a television show or where the family will go on vacation—you're a good sport about it and you don't spoil the fun for the others by quietly whining about how good the other show or the mountains would have been.

you're equally fair about not playing any instrument so loud that you disturb others. If you have to practice a piece at fortissimo level, you choose a time when the house is relatively empty—not, for example, the hour when your father has just sat down to read his evening paper. When the telephone rings for *anyone* in the house, you turn down the radio, television or phonograph. When you've finished watching or listening, you turn the thing off! (There is nothing more vexing than to have someone wander out of a room, leaving a machine going full blast—especially when it's a record player that doesn't shut itself off and the record keeps playing over and over and over and over.)

you don't use your family Meaning Daddy as a bank, Mother as a maid, older sister as a source to supplement your own stock of clothes or perfume, older brother as a date bureau. When someone in your family does a favor for you, you are grateful—verbally—and try to return the favor as best you can.

you help take care of the house Your own room, *of course.* No reasonable mother will expect you to keep it as impeccably neat as a show window—

but you keep yours presentable enough so the door need not remain closed. (Besides—if it's orderly, it looks pleasanter, it's more restful and you can find things in it.)

While the kitchen is really your mother's domain, she probably loves to have you and your friends in it. Things you remember that make you welcome: not to raid the refrigerator of everything planned for dinner; to clean up after whipping up a snack; to do the dishes, pots and pans; to wipe off the counters and sweep the floor if it needs it.

You tidy up any "shared" room when you've finished with it. Records, magazines, newspapers are put away; pillows are plumped; furniture goes back in place; ash trays are emptied; soiled glasses and dishes are taken to the kitchen and washed—or at least left to soak. If you use the dining table to spread out fabrics and dress patterns—or the galleys for the school paper—you clear it off before dinner, or before going to bed if the project is an evening one. You leave the porch, the garden, the car in order too. If you share your room with a sister, you keep your part of it looking fit so she won't die of shame if one of her friends comes in. Maybe you're the lucky one who has her own bathroom and you can choose any time for your eye-shadow experiments or diary-writing in the tub. Shared or not shared, you leave the room orderly—the basin wiped clean of spilled make-up, crumpled tissues and other debris of grooming; the towel folded on the rack, the rug straightened, the top back on the toothpaste tube, the comb and brush free of straggles of hair.

you lend a hand around the house. Since she can rarely hire it any more, your mother probably needs all the help she can get from the family. There's a special kind of pleasure in volunteering help when the pressure is mounting (to run a load of clothes through the washer or fix the dessert or whatever). But the hardest to do—because they're without glory—are the expected jobs: tidying up after yourself, doing errands willingly, faithfully doing any chores assigned to you. Chores *are* tedious, but they keep a household organized; maybe you can relieve the monotony by swapping or bartering: "Stevie, you empty the wastebaskets this month and I'll teach you to dance."

MONEY MANNERS

you manage your money (And we think everyone in the family should have some no-strings-attached money of his own to spend as he pleases.) You probably have an allowance; perhaps you supplement it with earnings from a part-time job or baby-sitting. Whatever the amount, you live within it (*not* like a girl we knew who was always wishing she had enough money to have a budget) and regularly feed an emergency fund, even if the best you can do is a dime a week. (At a year's end, with dimes, you'll have five dollars, assuming you've been able to resist "emergencies" that often seemed less urgent after a few hours' cogitating.)

If you find you're not managing well, perhaps you should keep a record for a week of the income and outgo of your funds. One of the two major money problems seems to be not having enough to survive on—which, regrettably, often telescopes into the second major problem of consistently overspending and having to negotiate a loan or an advance to get through the week. (Don't feel you're alone in this problem; Alexander Hamilton, among others, faced it his entire life.)

If you honestly haven't enough money and depend on an allowance for what you do have, talk out the problem with your parents—much better than brooding about it in secret. A quiet, friendly discussion of your expenses and needs, supplemented with an unrancorous comparison of your friends' allowances, might win you a raise. If the family budget is already strained—or if your parents feel your friends' allowances are out of line—take the verdict with good grace. As an alternate proposal, see if they are willing to let you take on a part-time job or money-making project—for after school, Saturdays or during the Christmas or spring holidays. Possibilities:

where	*you might*
a bookstore or specialty shop or a department store	fill orders, wrap and address packages, sort and check incoming stock, fill shelves that are depleted, sell
small business firms	type, run the mimeograph machine, answer the telephone
clubs, organizations	be a receptionist; man the telephones; provide baby care during a bazaar or special event of some kind; bring Christmas-card lists, mailing lists up to date
grownups—friends, relatives, your parents' friends, your friends' parents	help with children's parties—plan games, entertainment; help with food
	help with grownups' parties—there are always dishes, glasses, silver that need special washing and polishing
	help with children during the day
	start an errand service for the busy, the ill, the aged—returning library

books, shopping for presents or the hundred and one little necessities from the dime store

care for pets: walking, washing, even obedience training if you know how

coach classmates, younger children in school subjects, sports

do portrait sketches (easy way is to ask for a photograph)

if you overspend, look closely at that record of a week's spending. Study every penny of it. Circle the items you could have done without or postponed till the next week, the frivolous purchases and the bad buys. Try a system: Put the money you must have for school lunches, transportation, church in one envelope—and don't use that money for anything else. Put the balance of your money in another envelope (minus that small sum for your emergency fund). Resolve to make *not one* spur-of-the-moment purchase; buy the item a day later, if you still want it—and if you're sure you won't need the money for a possible trip to the lake or a birthday present.

Appreciate that learning to handle money is a good skill to acquire—not just for now but for your future happiness as a working adult and as a homemaker or breadwinner.

you abide by the rules However much authority irks, you face the fact that you will be subject to some kind all your life. Right now you may feel thoroughly overdirected ("Be home by eleven" . . . "You're too young to date/have a black dress/wear lipstick/smoke/learn to drive" . . . "I don't want you seeing that boy again!"), but you realize that neither scenes nor secret disobedience help modify a parent's point of view. More than that, you realize that your willingness to talk out your differences amiably is a sign to your parents that you are growing up and perhaps could have more freedom.

GRACE NOTES

Saying "Yes, Mother" or "No, Daddy" instead of a flat "yes" or "no"

Letting your parents go through doors first

Letting your father ring for the elevator, push the floor button, ask for directions, give the order to the waiter

GRACE NOTES

Remembering not to slam doors, crash up and down the stairs, bellow from room to room

Being on time for meals—and nicely dressed: if hair must be wound up in curlers at mealtime, it's turbaned with a pretty, unwrinkled scarf

Making mealtimes pleasant—never the time to quarrel, coax parents for a permission

Keeping scenes behind the scenes—and away from members of the family who are not involved

Not being an informer—or your brother's or sister's keeper (called tattling in toddler days)

Never teasing to the point of tears

Picking up your possessions instead of leaving them strewn in the path of the rest of the family

Not plaguing everyone with your dieting woes; to quote the poet, you diet quiet

Introducing new friends to your family—and excluding even the best of friends at times when your family obviously wants to be by itself as a family

Bringing your date in to talk briefly with your family—making conversation possible with some opening wedge, such as, "Dad, Jim's father is a lawyer too. . . ."

Taking a bit of time to make friends with your family's friends of all ages, not to monopolize, but as a "courtesy of the house"

Letting parents direct household employees and do the criticizing if need be

Being as courteous to employees as with the mother of your favorite beau or friend

Never demanding out-of-line favors from part-time or regular household helpers—such as asking a mother's helper who is busy with the children to drop everything and press your dress—but thanking her enthusiastically if she volunteers

Letting employees have privacy too—with their rooms, possessions, mail, phone calls, friends, day-out activities . . . and about their own eccentricities, which are not sources of conversation for your friends

Speaking of employees by name—"Hannah, our cook," rather than "the cook" or "the help"

Thoughtfulness goes beyond the grace notes, though. It includes listening to your mother talk about the garden club . . . making a special point of asking your father to come to a school function . . . offering to play canasta with your grandmother . . . teaching your little sister how to fix her hair . . . helping with invitations, your mother's committee paper work, the family Christmas cards.

And not wrecking the family's traditional Christmas plans by planning a date with your best beau: it is far better to bring him into the family party or transfer the date to another evening.

Thoughtfulness extends, too, to the visits you make to friends or relatives who are ill: Be sure to find out about the best hours to visit and never make a surprise of it . . . bring a token gift . . . enter smiling, sincerely . . . sit down in a pleasant, relaxed fashion, as you do when you go somewhere to enjoy yourself (and seat yourself on a chair, not the patient's bed) . . . make the small-talk lead yourself instead of putting the burden on the person you're visiting . . . leave the moment you see the patient growing tired or restless . . keep your word about any favors or future visits you've promised.

3. Nice To Be With: AT SCHOOL AND COLLEGE

In the bigger world outside your family, there are rules that make you nice to be with:

At school You are respectful and considerate to your teachers, whether they are male or female . . .

- you say "Yes, Miss Smathers" or "Yes, Mr. Darrell," rather than "yes" or "uh-huh"
- you're silent when the bell rings for class to start
- you do your homework on time, ask for extensions only when necessary (bad habit to get into, anyway)
- you do your homework neatly—in pen or typed, except, perhaps, math and lab reports
- you pay attention in class: while the subject may be massively boring to you—or you read the book under discussion as a small child—you at least look bright and interested. (Teaching is a give-and-take operation, and an alert class makes a teacher more interesting.)
- you understand *thoroughly* that note-passing, letter-writing, doodling and whispering to friends are unacceptable classroom activities
- when you are desperately bored—and it happens to us all occasionally—you maintain your manners and air of interest by taking notes to stay awake. You can always take them in French—or list clichés or idiosyncrasies of speech. Or you can work on a tangent—observing the way the teacher presents the subject, trying to work out the outline she must have used. Or even look out for mannerisms—hers or those of members of the class—making notes for "business" in the school play or that short story you've been meaning to write
- you take part in class discussions but try never to interrupt a classmate
- you wait your turn to speak and remember to be brief so someone else will have a turn
- you take pity on the class show-off, realizing that most show-offs parade their learning because they want attention and know few ways to get it
- when a teacher explains a point to you, in class or out, you thank her
- when you're quite at sea about a point the rest of the class already understands, you wait till after class for an explanation—rather than hold up everyone while you have your problem solved in detail
- you treat all school property as if it were your own (and your father, the taxpayer, probably feels it is!). Books, lab equipment, the gym, the washroom, the furnishings, the walls and the grass—all are yours to respect and care for

- at school functions—concerts, lectures and such—you are mindful that you represent your class, your school and your family, and you listen courteously, especially when enthusiasm is more than you can muster
- on field trips, ditto. And you're never guilty of the mammoth field-trip offense of wandering off from the group to explore far corners of the museum or factory or whatever—or dropping out of earshot of the tour leader for a good girl-to-girl talk
- in the cafeteria you don't cut into the line, shout or whisper (the staff may think you're snickering about the food and some sensitive soul in the line may be cut to the quick, thinking he's the subject of your whispering). You don't save places by turning chairs over. You don't trip others by letting your possessions straggle into the aisles. You don't pop bags, blow the wrappers off straws, throw papers on the floor, carve your initials on the table

Orientation This elaborate word has nothing to do with the mysterious East; it's merely a telescoped way of describing the process of getting acquainted with new people in a new situation. Many schools and colleges have an "orientation week" before classes officially start so that newcomers have a chance to meet a few people and to find their way around the school and campus. During this time—or the first days at school—get to know all the people you can, remember their names, be sociable, and be slow to plunge into firm friendships. Because you are new and eager to settle down into a comfortable routine, your judgment about people may be hasty. Possible mistakes you might make include wanting to make friends only with girls who are most like you and shutting out girls who are "different." Or confiding the entire story of your life and hopes to a girl you didn't know two days before—and whom you don't want to know two days later. Or, at boarding school or college, clinging to your roommate or to a girl you didn't care for at home. Or quickly identifying yourself with one group and excluding those not in the group. It is much better to give yourself—and everyone else—a chance to let that shiny veneer of newness wear off so the real girl can become visible.

Junior sisters Sometimes this system is a part of a school's plan to help the bewildered newcomers. Like everything else that involves people, the system is only as good as the people involved. It is possible that you and your junior sister won't get along: she may not work at her responsibility, and you may be a cheery, independent person who doesn't need sistering; she may be extremely shy or one of you just may not care for the other. Be civil, co-operative, and, if you think she's a dud, reluctant to discuss her "dudness" with anyone except your faculty adviser. (There is no point in running her down.

If you can't be idealistic about her, be kind—and realistic; she might have a stunning brother!)

Cliques They are just a part of life, whether they're called clubs, sororities, committees, groups or "our crowd." Everyone has the right to select her own friends—just as everyone has the right to be treated kindly and pleasantly by members of cliques she doesn't belong to. If you're group-minded—and not everyone is—look for one that fits in with your own ideals, standards, family rules and pocketbook. If you've rushed into a group you're not at ease in, try to drift gently into another group without making a great thing about it: be cordial as always, unavailable, preoccupied. (A marvelous way of avoiding unnecessary, useless showdowns is the very feminine art of appearing to be amiably confused and not quite with the situation.) If you find the group you've joined and love is changing its character—spending too much money, becoming more sophisticated than you care to be, concentrating on dissecting other groups instead of having fun—enlist a few close friends to help get the group back on its former even keel. If it can't be done and if it's a situation you can't live with, have the courage to give up the group—courage, because you may be lonely for a while and because this may be a showdown you have to face. ("I couldn't be sorrier, Joan, but I'm not coming to the meeting. I just can't afford those expensive lunches. It was fun when we went to the snack shop, but the whole thing is way over my financial head now.") It's often hard to come out with the real reason, but, when it's kinder, fairer and more honest, do your best to give it.

Sororities and Clubs Not every school has them, and at some schools they are less than important while at others they may dominate social and extracurricular activities and all the fun of school life. Talk to upperclassmen and recent graduates of the school you're going to so you'll know just how important sororities are there now. Find out how much you'll be giving up if you refuse to join a sorority. See if your present preconceived ideas are applicable to sororities at your school: perhaps being a sorority girl is no longer the all-important glamorous deal it was in your mother's day; perhaps joining one doesn't mean that you become a servile conformist, giving up all your cherished rights to be an individualist and an independent thinker; perhaps the rituals are as casual as a class meeting instead of the solemn, secret pomp you feel you can't go along with. You'll want to ask about the expense too—initiation fees, dues, extra charges for room and board if you live in the house, and any other expenses that will require a place in your budget. (You may decide that riding or music lessons can't be lopped from your heart or your budget but that belonging to a sorority can.)

Old rules for new girls

- If you're completely new in school, look for another new girl. Don't go off the deep end over this, of course; don't cultivate her *just because she's new*. But do try to find one who has similar tastes and interests, and then don't be shy about extending the first invitation. You don't need to wait for a boy to speak or smile first. Courtesy actually requires a girl to be the first to acknowledge a new acquaintance, you know.
- Whether it's a boy or girl you'd like to meet, remember that being in the same class or activity usually substitutes for an introduction.
- Every school has a few local customs all its own. Be alert to these. If you show adaptability to others' customs, your own very special personality will be more respected later on when you've "settled in."
- Be really careful of one thing: don't steal another girl's beau. No explanation of this rule is necessary. Just remember that such an act never will win a popularity contest.
- Volunteer for as many school activities as you think you can handle. Don't join just to join; if you're not really interested, you won't be at your social best. On the other hand, you might never know you have a flair for dramatics, reporting or ceramic design unless you give it a whirl. And the more things you're interested in, the more new and interesting people you're likely to meet.
- Shyness is not necessarily a handicap; being too forward can get you in as much trouble as being too withdrawn. On the contrary, shyness can draw people toward you, make them feel more comfortable with you, because at heart nearly everyone is shy about something—even those who appear talkative and animated. Also, remember that other people are not usually noticing your "shy" ways as much as you think. If you can muster the courage to start a conversation, you will probably discover that you are helping other people, and in your effort to make them feel at ease everything may well become easier for you.
- Sometimes a good way to make friends with others is to ask their help. Think of it this way: if an attractive girl or boy came up to ask your advice, wouldn't you be flattered? Especially if he or she didn't ask too much?
- Look around for situations where you might be able to help someone else, the reverse of the method above. This is often a gracious and efficient way to make friends. But again—don't offer too much or you might make the recipient feel uncomfortable.
- If you receive an invitation, accept or decline it promptly. It may be hard to do, but there are times when it is kinder in the long run to turn down an invitation you don't really welcome.

Reminders for the old girl

- Maybe summer was a turning point for you and you *know* you're now ready to join that attractive, more grown-up group at your school. It's up to you to prove it to them—and one way is to be cordial to new girls. Speak to this newcomer, that one; walk with them occasionally; introduce them to others. You not only show the manners of a lady but also get at least two bonuses—practice in poise that will brighten your path the rest of your life and more general popularity right now.
- Continue to see old friends. Dropping them for no good reason is such bad manners it might hurt you with new ones. As time goes on, of course, you may find yourself *drawing away* from some of your old friends—especially if your interests are changing—but this is quite different from dropping them.
- Be casual with those you hope to make your friends. Be gracious, of course, and be *there*—but don't be intense in your cultivation of them. Remember that you're definitely the "new girl" in this sphere, and if you're *too* eager you're apt to make them uneasy.
- Don't rush things. Although you might ask a girl you'd like to know better to have a soda or go to a movie with you on the spur of the moment, let her—or another of her friends—be the first to extend a really important invitation.
- Notice things. While you're in the process of not rushing matters, notice the way the other girls dress, speak, act. Not, please, with the idea of copying them slavishly! But if, for instance, you see that they dress more conservatively than you've been in the habit of doing—well, you certainly have nothing to lose with *anyone* by dressing a little more quietly yourself. It's better to lean to the casual, conservative side than to be the unhappy girl who's too dressed up.

  Or if a new group seems more mature in its actions than you—perhaps it's time for you also to behave in a more grown-up way.

ABOUT CLASS RINGS

Class ring customs vary so from school to school that we suspect some of them of growing from enthusiastic accident rather than the common-sense cornerstone of etiquette.

For boys, the first rule is that no ring is ever worn on the right hand. (Practical, because the friendship and pleasure symbolized by a firm, manly handshake must not be tempered by grinding pain!) The correct finger on the left hand is the third, or ring, finger. This stems from the old custom of reserving the little finger for the very personal seal ring (once a necessity in sealing letters). Since this is now outdated, the little finger of the left may eventually become the official class ring finger.

Girls have a wider choice. Although the little finger of the left hand is actually the correct one, either the third or fourth finger of the right hand is acceptable, too. (Girls evidently shake hands more gently!) But the engagement finger is taboo—for obvious reasons.

THE FACTS OF COLLEGE LIFE

Your college catalogue will describe the curriculum, the faculty, the campus, the costs, but some of the things it won't tell you include these first-year surprises:

Sharing a room, especially with a stranger. You may be amazed that anyone can be so untidy. You may discover that she has weird ways, like sleeping in her coat! (She may think you have odd ideas too!) If it's just a personal quirk of hers that bothers you, one that doesn't really affect the sharing of the room, better overlook it. When sleep or study or a reasonable right to enjoy the room is disturbed, talk it over honestly: explain your needs and feelings, try to see her point of view and work out a compromise. To share happily, you may have to agree to do your late-hours studying in the room of another night-owl friend and your roommate may have to concede to at least two inches of fresh air. Very likely you will be allowed to choose your own roommate the next year.

College is a chance to start fresh, to shed your old high-school tags. If, for instance, you were always regarded as a "grind," college may be your opportunity to develop into the belle you know you could be. Or perhaps you are a serious student and tried to hide it in high school because it seemed a social drawback. At college you may find it an asset! Lots of girls who weren't dated in high school are quite comfortably popular in college. It's in the wider world of the campus that they first meet boys they like and who like them—just as they are. Happy surprise!

If you come from a small, homogeneous world into a large, heterogeneous world on campus, you will almost certainly meet people who reject or scoff at ideas and beliefs that you have always held sacred . . . that you've accepted as surely as you accept night and day. In some classes, comparative and searching study may startle you by revealing ideologies completely strange to you. Your own beliefs may be shaken. Some students change dogmas with every new concept explored in their philosophy courses. Most students who find this broad exposure unsettling at first come to appreciate it as part of the learning and growing opportunity college offers. Usually—not always—they return eventually to their original beliefs, but with a more tolerant attitude toward the beliefs of others.

On the reverse side of the coin, some girls who grew up in a tolerant, accepting environment are shocked to find racial and religious prejudices in others. One girl said, "I had heard about prejudice but had never really seen it in practice or heard it expressed by people I knew." This kind of unpleasant enlightenment, too, may be part of your broadening world as a college freshman. It poses a new challenge: how will you react to the prejudice of others, whether directed against you or not?

Whether or not you want to drink or smoke is something best decided with your parents before you ever reach the campus. If your decision is no and you have your reasons well in mind, you won't be easily pressured into changing it. You don't have to drink to be popular! But watch that you don't take a "holier than thou" attitude: a simple "No, thank you" will suffice when a cocktail or cigarette is offered. If someone is insistent, you can lightly explain it's something you simply don't enjoy.

College seems wonderfully—and frighteningly—free after high school. Instead of enforced study periods, you have free periods between classes to use for play, sleep, study or a shopping spree. You must decide for yourself how much time to allot to dates, how much to schoolwork. Instead of having mandatory class attendance, your college may allow unlimited cuts, and if you don't appear, no one will even ask why.

But classes missed and work undone must be paid for—in frantic, all-night cramming; in lowered grades; in missing what you're really at college for: the opportunity to learn. Learn to budget your time. Study *every* night; don't save it all for the end of the week—or month! How to keep yourself away from the bridge game and glued to your desk? One solution that works for many students is to study in the library, where the atmosphere encourages serious attention to work, holds few distractions. Wherever you choose to study, you'll find it easier if you put yourself on a regular schedule: study from three to five, relax and eat dinner from five to eight, study from eight to eleven, go to bed at twelve . . . or whatever works for you. The main thing is to establish the habit of studying at certain hours and in a certain place; that way, you'll find it becomes easier and easier to stick to your schedule.

You may be surprised at the old, baggy clothes accepted for campus wear or you may find the reverse—that the girls have more expensive and elaborate wardrobes than you had imagined or than you can afford.

Clothes fads vary so much from campus to campus that it's impossible to outline a "sure-thing" wardrobe. One buying guide might be the advice of upperclassmen or recent graduates from your school. Another possibility is your favorite department store. Many stores offer the services of college advisers who are familiar with customs at various schools and will be happy to help you select your wardrobe. Do save part of your clothes allowance to spend at the shops right in your college town. They will cater to the taste and climate of your school. Don't despair because you see extravagant clothes coming out of the other girls' suitcases. Look some more: in even the most expensive colleges, a sizable percentage of the student body is managing on a shoestring, with scholarships and part-time work to help. There will be girls with less expensive clothes and less to spend than you, as well as girls with more.

Rules and regulations vary widely from campus to campus. In one school you may be perfectly free to stay up all night if you like; in another, "lights out" may be strictly enforced. Almost every campus college sets a curfew (when you must be in your dorm), and this is usually stricter for freshmen. Some schools now give seniors unrestricted privileges about hours (and we know one girls' school which does the same for freshmen, too!). Weekends away may be limited, and parents' permission may be necessary before you leave the college environs.

Other possible regulations you may be surprised by: no smoking in rooms or even in any part of the dorm (some schools limit smoking to a special recreation hall); required attendance either at a nondenominational chapel or at a place of worship you choose; required gym.

Why all the rules? Most colleges are concerned about your safety, health, physical being and spiritual self as well as your mind. Sometimes they may be even stricter than parents because they have to be "parent" to so many at one time.

Mastering the mechanics of higher education is essential. In note-taking, for instance, the first tendency is to write down *everything*. Later you will learn to listen first, then write down only the important points in a form that is meaningful to you. How to know what is important? One college freshman advises, "Do your co-ordinated reading assignment before the lecture. Pick out the major ideas presented and keep them in mind for the lecture period." The instructor himself will usually emphasize the significant areas—sometimes by saying directly that you will be expected to master the subject now under discussion, sometimes by the amount of time he devotes to a topic.

If you are a serious student, you may be disappointed to find that some fellow students are not. For not everyone is there to learn. Some go to expand their social life, some go because their parents want them to, some go just because "it's the thing to do." Their attitudes needn't have much effect on you unless you find yourself drawn into a "do-nothing" group. Then you might let your own work go, just not to seem a drudge or to spoil the fun. This is less likely to happen if you have your own goals clearly in mind.

If you react with too much disgust to the good-time crowd, you may shut yourself off unnecessarily from the fun of college life. With a little probing, you may be surprised to discover that some of the girls who seem to be quite giddy are actually good students. It pays to wait before you jump to judgments and unshakable conclusions.

It can be a rude shock to discover that your high-school status as student council president puts you not above but just about equal to everyone else. It's possible that every other girl on your floor was also either student council president, senior class president or editor of her high-school newspaper. Actually, it's not very surprising. Colleges are selective. Your high-school honors and offices helped you get admitted. Once there, the competition is keener. You may have to try harder than you did in high school to make a name for yourself. You may have to be satisfied with a second-rung place in the hierarchy.

You may find that the size of your college classes—particularly large freshman classes—prevents your being singled out, no matter how bright or nice you are. Even in small college classes, your star may seem a bit dimmed. But even if you can't be number one, the keener competition can spur you to develop the abilities you do have to a greater degree of excellence.

You will find that some professors are Dr., not Mr. or Miss or Mrs., and that male professors should be answered, "Yes, sir."

4. Nice To Be With: IN PUBLIC

You make or break a reputation for yourself, your school, your age group generally by the way you act in public. You can create an image of teens that is wonderful or awful, because adults react emotionally to disturbing public behavior. They reason in this summary if illogical fashion:

> *This* girl is noisy, rude, thoughtless.
> This is a *teen-ager.*
> *All teen-agers* are noisy, rude, thoughtless.

The key word in that corollary is probably *thoughtless.* If you thought about it, would you

- *take over* a crowded street by walking three or four abreast, like an advancing army platoon?
- *buck* the oncoming traffic by proceeding up the left side of the walk when you belong on the right?
- *barge* across the street against the traffic signals, causing considerable ravage to both cars and drivers as they screech and swerve to avoid you?
- *start* a conversation with strangers or be tricked into one—when it's so simple to move quietly away (or buy a paper to read or make a phone call)?
- *plant* yourself solidly in the front of the bus instead of making way for newcomers by moving to the back?
- *cut* a bruising path through any crowd (books, bags and all) without saying "Excuse me, excuse me" all the way?
- *smoke,* chew gum, or eat on the street?
- *remain* seated on a subway, train, bus or in a waiting room while any of the following stand—an older woman, a very old man, anyone holding a young child, any handicapped or overburdened person?
- *accept* a seat from someone else without a smile and a thank-you?
- *forget* to hold a door open till the person behind you can catch it?
- *rush* through a door ahead of an older person?
- *neglect* to say "You're welcome," when thanked for holding the door or whatever?
- *block* a doorway, any entrance or exit—especially when you're in a group?
- *get out of line* on any line—from the school cafeteria to the local movie—by crowding in out of turn or trying to make the line move faster by nudging the person ahead of you?
- *blast* the car horn insistently when you're snarled in a tie-up that blasting obviously won't resolve?

On the other hand, you could produce this sort of reaction:

> What a *nice young person—so thoughtful.*
> This is a *young person.*
> *All young persons* are nice, thoughtful.

At the snack shop—or the drugstore, a restaurant, the pizza parlor—you are welcome to the other customers as well as the owner because you brighten the day with talk and laughter . . . because you don't abuse your welcome by letting the gaiety become a disturbance to others. You leave the counter or booth in respectable condition. You leave before your welcome is up, instead of lingering for the afternoon.

In the park, at the beach, have fun—but you're careful not to plant your young party next to an older group if there's room for you a little farther on. Keep the hubbub of conversation (and radio!) down as well as the debris of your picnic confined to your own area. Like a good camper, leave without a trace of trash to indicate you were there. Put out a fire. You mind where you throw a beach ball or kick up sand. Save any demonstration of affection for your date until a more private moment.

In an apartment building remember not to stamp around, knowing that even moccasins can sound like ski boots. Reserve nerve-shattering forms of exercise (jumping, bouncing, leaping) for the gym. Apartments, old and new, may be poorly soundproofed, so while you enjoy the noise of a tuned-up record player you realize that the blurred din of your favorite music can be bedlam to neighbors—and you moderate the sound. If you're having a party, tell the next-door neighbors and the ones downstairs beforehand—and say honestly, mollifyingly, "We may be noisy, but the party will be over at midnight." Having had the warning—and knowing there's an end point in sight—neighbors will be more tolerant, possibly even indulgent.

Another nice thing about you: you never hold the self-service elevator (despite the buzzing protests from another floor) while Susie runs back into your apartment to find her books or answer the phone. When you're waiting, you control the impulse to whang on the door. If you've waited very long, you're late and becoming desperate—and you can hear the chitchat of those holding the elevator—tap the door firmly and call "Elevator, please" in a clear, polite voice.

In a suburban neighborhood with fenceless communal gardens, there is often the temptation for one's activities to overflow into the next back yard. You, thoughtfully, pretend there is a fence between you and the next garden and make sure your party doesn't spill across your lot line. Make sure not to impose by visiting with a neighbor just any time you see her in her yard; a smile and a good morning will mark your thoughtfulness.

This matter of concern for other people's comfort brings up *shopping,* which sometimes calls out all the hidden flaws in an otherwise admirable young lady —but not in you. You remember to say "please" and "thank you." Your voice retains its sweetness; your manner never becomes impatient, complaining or demanding. Be as careful with the store's merchandise as if it all belonged to you—never rummaging through white blouses with smudgy gloves (you take them off) or forgetting to pick up a dress that slides off the hanger when you're looking at it. Try not to interrupt a saleswoman who is busy with another customer; if she's the only one visible, you might say, "Excuse me, may I take these to the fitting room?" When you try on clothes, take them off the hangers with care, be gentle with zippers and hooks, put the things back on the hangers. If you're wearing lipstick or make-up that might smudge a dress, blouse or sweater when you pull it on, remember the model's trick of covering her whole head with a scarf. If the store is crowded, make your stay in the fitting room a brief one so other customers can have a turn.

At the hairdresser's you arrive a little ahead of time so you'll be prompt for your appointment; you understand that just one person arriving late can stack up the rest of the day's appointments and fray the patience of both customers and operators. If you have to wait, you wait calmly. If you have to wait frequently, you discuss it with whoever makes the appointments: "May I have the first appointment in the morning with Kirsten so I won't have to wait?" Should that fail, you might take work to do (required reading, letters to answer, knitting) or try another shop. When you are the late one, say you're sorry to be late and ask if Kirsten will be able to do your hair. Sometimes your own day is so closely scheduled that you can't wait until the hairdresser can take you; in that case, say quietly to whoever is at the reception desk, "Will you tell Kirsten that I had a four o'clock meeting and that I'm sorry I couldn't wait?" The receptionist may offer to make another appointment; if you're not sure you want one, say, "Perhaps I can call you?"

At some shops you may be shown to a dressing room and handed a smock or coverall. When the weather is warm or you will be there for several hours, say for a permanent, you may want to take off your dress and just wear the smock. (In fashionable hairdressing salons patrons always change into smocks for every service beyond a manicure.) The smock may or may not be used again by someone else, so you fold it up neatly just in case.

What you call the hairdresser and manicurist depends on the custom where you live. Usually when you're talking to them you say Michael and Kirsten; but if Michael or Kirsten is the head of a very large, handsome establishment and is quite famous, you would say to other employees of the shop, "Do you think Mr. Michael can comb out my hair now?" or "Can Miss Kirsten take me next Thursday at four?"

It helps the hairdresser and it helps you achieve what you want if you know how to describe the effect desired for your hair: "I'd like you to use number three rollers, please, so my hair will look quite straight." "Will you comb it out so it doesn't *look* as though it's been set?" Sometimes it helps to bring a photograph or a sketch from a newspaper or magazine. One of the surest means to a known end is to go to a hairdresser who has a customer whose hair is fixed just the way you want yours: "Could you do mine just the way you do Elsie Smith's, please?" Since hairdressers are artists at their craft, they may not always agree and you may find occasionally that you did not get the effect you asked for. Or your hair may not be responsive that particular day or may not be the kind of hair that can be styled like the photograph you brought along. Be polite about the result; if you are truly disappointed (through your fault, your hair's fault or the operator's), smile anyway and say, "Thank you so much, Kirsten." The next time you go to her, you might ask how she thinks your hair should be fixed. That doesn't mean you have to agree to have it trimmed drastically; you can say you'd like to think about having it cut and ask if she could set it to give the effect of the style she suggested.

When you are honestly hard pressed for time, tell the hairdresser that you have to be at school or wherever by a certain time (make it a quarter to half an hour earlier than the real time to allow for traffic delays, a broken heel or merely stopping for a sandwich). The shop may be a very busy one, so help by not delaying the operator with unimportant conversation. You can also help by asking how long you should stay under the dryer and watching the time yourself. When you crawl out from under it, say to the hairdresser, "I think I'm dry," and sit down near enough to be remembered but not near enough to disturb the customer he's with at the moment. In a small, informal shop—or even in a somewhat formidable one that you go to regularly—you can speed things up by taking out the clips and rollers yourself (not recommended procedure in a shop you don't know, though).

Hairdressers tell us that the customer they especially like to take care of is the one who doesn't leave her possessions strewn about, who takes only a few of the new magazines with her to the dryer and doesn't snip clippings from them, who is tidy about smoking, who doesn't chatter to a hairdresser or manicurist who's taking care of another customer, and who doesn't break appointments.

How much you tip and whom you tip are almost laws unto each shop. The surest procedure is to ask advice from one or two regular customers of the shop before your first appointment. Take the matter of the hairdresser who is either the owner or the chief stylist: usually you don't tip this man or woman, but the best thing to do is to ask at the desk whether or not to offer a tip.

In the average shop, a teen-ager is not expected to tip more than 20 per cent of the amount of her total bill, divided among all those who have served her.

The more beautiful and popular the shop, the more you'll spend in tips. Expect this, so your pleasure in the surroundings, the service and the workmanship (which may be every bit as good in the small shop) won't be marred either by resenting the system or by worrying that you've wrecked your budget.

In church Remember that participants in a religious service should be de-emphasized. You look your best, as a matter of respect, but low necklines, clanking jewelry, frivolous hats and conspicuous make-up, such as eye shadow, are put aside for gayer occasions. Speak a word or two to the usher, smile briefly to friends, and in some denominations you may even whisper to the person sitting next to you before the service begins. When you attend a service of another faith, you reserve any questions until after the service; if you're confused about when to stand, sit or kneel, hesitate before making a move until you see what the rest of the congregation does. (If kneeling to pray is not a part of your own religion, remain seated.)

Doing volunteer work The trouble with volunteer work is that so many volunteer and so few work. Schools and churches often encourage teens to give their help to a political party, a hospital, a settlement house or some charity—not just because extra hands are needed but because it helps a boy or girl to learn about people, life and the place he lives and also to discover hidden abilities in himself. (He can convince people of a cause; she's a whiz with babies; both can make old people happy.) Teens have a tremendous amount of talent, energy, kindness and simple directness to offer as volunteers, and it is distressing to have a few careless ones cast a shadow on the good work of so many teens. Some of the shadows cast include not showing up at the right time, not sending word that one can't come, arriving late, spending the time chattering with friends instead of doing the job, doing the job halfheartedly or grumpily (a patient may be much more interested in seeing a cheery face than in having a vacuum jar filled with fresh water). The point is that once having taken on a job, a volunteer worker should remember that others are depending on him to do something—however unimportant it may seem. No one has to keep on with a volunteer job he really wants to shed—but he should give notice just as he would for a paying job. And the worst shadow of all is the ex-volunteer who grouses about the organization he or she worked for. Constructive criticism? Certainly, but it should be given politely to the director of volunteers. No group doing a service for others should have to cope with gossips. Most services can be improved. If you have solutions for problems, your suggestions will be warmly welcomed.

Borrowing and lending Just about everyone knows it's better not to, but just about everyone borrows and lends.

if you borrow:

return the item in good condition at whatever time you promised to return it (right away, Sunday, in a week, *whenever*)

if you've harmed it, replace it or have it repaired (first telling the owner you're going to, since she might want a particular shop to fix it)

if you've lost the borrowed item—gloves you needed for a play—buy your friend a new pair that's as much like the old as possible (but don't give her money instead)

try not to borrow anything fragile, expensive or irreplaceable. If your friend shows the slightest hesitation, quickly and firmly stop the transaction

if you lend:

don't lend anything you'd be shattered to have damaged or lost

try to laugh off the damage or loss of anything you do lend

refuse chronic borrowers

pursue the nonreturning borrower doggedly but politely until that which was loaned is returned (but don't discuss the matter with others)

be sure you're not pressing loans on others to bolster your own self-esteem. Sometimes excessive lending or offering to do favors is a thinly disguised way of showing off or trying to gain friendship.

Extracurricular activities: The rules for joining and running a group These activities are fun and an important part of your young life—important, that is, if you don't try to join every club in the yearbook. You'll get more out of any group you join if you become a participating member—more friends, more information, a bigger point of view. Do work on committees, contribute ideas, and work to be the dynamic leader of the organization, if that's your heart's desire—so long as you keep a firm grip on the fact that you will probably be the Chief for only a little of the time and just a plain Indian for a lot of the time. It's all too human to be tempted to drop out of a group that fails to give one the hoped-for recognition or a group that is slow to give that same recognition. Take your time; look on the delay as a chance to know the organization, the purpose it serves and the people in it better: you'll do a better job if you do. And use the time to build the idea that you'd make a good chief by attending meetings or rehearsals faithfully, volunteering extra services, cementing friendships with other members, the coach and the faculty adviser. (Presidents, chiefs, chairmen, leaders of all sorts are *made;* they rarely just happen.)

If you are elected to office, it's a symbol of your popularity and your good building of the image of you as a leader; *much more than that,* accepting the office means that you are accepting a responsibility to serve well. If you feel you honestly can't handle the job, you can always regret and refuse—and people will like you all the better for your honesty. Give the honest reason: your schoolwork is slipping; you can't take on any more jobs than you're doing now, much as you'd like to; you find you can't afford the extra expenses you would face; your help is needed, unexpectedly, at home for whatever reason. Or admit what is often the plain fact: you realize with dismay that the job is simply a bigger one than you feel you can do.

If you accept the office, tackle your job enthusiastically and wholeheartedly —but smother any tendency to be a "loner" about it. Enlist the help and advice of other members, talk over problems with the faculty adviser, or with your family. And when the project is completed, give your helpers the credit and say how wonderful *they* were!

HANDLING A MEETING

Meetings can be a bore and a menace when they're not properly run, so perhaps the following skit will help you keep an indulgent but steady hand on any meetings you preside over:

THE SOCK-HOP SQUABBLE THAT NEVER GOT STARTED

The action takes place in a small assembly room, where the class president has called a meeting of home-room chairmen to discuss ways of adding funds to the nearly bankrupt class treasury. The class president—Amanda Baker—calls the meeting to order with a sharp rap of the gavel, but the buzz of conversation continues. She raps again for attention. . .

AMANDA — Will the meeting please come to order? Joe, Laurance . . . do you mind? We only have half an hour. . . .

LAURANCE — Sorry, Prexie. We'll be quiet.

AMANDA — Thank you. Will the secretary please read the minutes of the last meeting?

(*The minutes are read and the secretary sits down.*)

AMANDA — Thank you, Marian. Are there any corrections? If not, will someone please move that the minutes be approved?

JOE — I so move.

AMANDA — Second?

LAURANCE — I second the motion.

AMANDA — All in favor?
(*Loud chorus of ayes.*)
Opposed? (*Silence.*) The minutes are accepted. I think we can get right to the purpose of this meeting, then. It's nearly the end of February—three more months of school to go—and the treasury is down to its last few dollars. Mr. Blewer, our faculty adviser, suggested that the quickest and easiest way to get solvent would be to assess every class member a few dollars. I think this might not be so easy and I would like to ask for suggestions from the floor—suggestions for raising money in a way that would make our classmates part with it cheerfully. (*Laughter from the floor.*)

SALLY (*raising her hand and being recognized by a nod from the president*) — I think it would be great fun if we had a sock hop; they're always sure . . .

JOE (*interrupting and talking rapidly*) — No, no, a sock hop is no fun. What Laurance and I were talking about before the meeting started was a variety show. Now there's a great way to . . .

AMANDA — Excuse me, Joe—but Sally still has the floor. Please let her continue.

SALLY — Well, Sue was telling me about a sock hop she went to when she lived in Chicago, and it was the greatest party, so I thought maybe she could tell you about it better than I can. Is it all right for Sue to tell?

JOE — Hey, just a minute. I want a chance to talk up this variety show . . .

AMANDA — You'll have your chance, Joe, I promise. But let's finish with the sock hop. Sue?

SUE — Well, I'm new and of course I don't know whether a sock hop would be as successful here—but I'll tell you some of the things we planned for ours. First, though, about money. In a class of eighty, plus friends from other classes, we made a net profit of two hundred dollars . . .
(*She continues with her ideas.*)

AMANDA — Thanks, Sue. We'll definitely consider a sock hop.

JOE — Look here, Amanda—how can you say that so patly? You haven't given Laurance and me a square deal. We had this great idea—

AMANDA — Joe! Nothing is settled yet. Would you like to be recognized and tell us about your idea? We do have to keep this meeting running in order, you know.

JOE — Well, sure, I understand. It's just that we thought how can we get a little cash floating in instead of out, and we figured there's a lot of talent in this class, and if no one else will come to see it in action, we will and everyone's family is sure to come and . . .
(*And on talks Joe.*)

AMANDA — Excuse me, Joe, but we're really pressed for time. Your show sounds terribly interesting and we'll put it on the list too. . . . Now, are there any more suggestions to add to these two good ones?

LAURANCE — *Add* to them? Look, why any more? Why not just settle for the show?

JOE — Yeah, when you've got a sure-fire idea, why push your luck?

AMANDA — Are there any further suggestions?

MIKE — I just remembered that Bert Yorke plays the guitar and he'd be great in the variety show. Listen, Joe; do you want me to call him and . . .

AMANDA — Mike, I'm sorry, but you don't have the floor. Now we have two good suggestions and we've come to the end of the time we had. I'm going to ask Pam Jones, our class vice-president, and Johnny Drayton, president of last year's class, to meet with me and our faculty adviser to discuss the pros and cons of both these ideas. At next week's regular meeting we'll have some definite recommendations for you. Thank you all for coming. Will someone move that the meeting be adjourned? . . . Second? . . . All in favor. . . . Opposed? . . . The meeting is adjourned!

Without Amanda's firm but good-natured control and knowledge about the simple procedure for keeping a meeting in order, the sock-hop meeting might have ended in an uproar, no plan of action and a still-depleted treasury. You don't have to become a scholar of parliamentary procedure to run a good meeting. List the topics you want to cover, making the agenda for your meeting. Then keep these general rules in mind:

- The chairman introduces the subject to be discussed but takes no partisan part in the discussion unless he temporarily relinquishes the chair in order to do so.
- A member asks permission to speak. The chairman gives it. The member speaks without interruption from other members. If the member's point is controversial, the chairman can invite discussion of it then and there—or rule that individual suggestions will be discussed when all have been made. If there is to be immediate discussion, members still ask for permission to speak and the chairman must still give it to them, one at a time.
- If after full discussion a vote is needed, the chairman can take it by voice vote (all in favor say "aye"; those opposed say "no"), by a show of hands or by written ballot.
- Or the problem may be referred to a committee, which will be asked to report at a specific date. Since many a good idea dies in committee because the committee fails to work between meetings or is unable to make up its collective mind, a good chairman will check with the committee chairman before the deadline: if the committee can't come to an agreement, the chairman should suggest that the committee take a vote within itself—perhaps even present majority and minority reports. Then the problem can be presented to the membership for general discussion and a vote.
- After one question has been decided—by general assent or a vote—the chairman introduces the next topic.
- When all business before the meeting is finished, the chairman adjourns the meeting.
- Ideally, no member should leave the meeting before its close unless he has told the chairman beforehand and asked to be excused. This isn't always possible—for example, at a meeting that is unexpectedly long—so vanish,

if you must, as inconspicuously as you can, and explain your leaving to the chairman later.

This all sounds rather formal, but it's the best procedure—even for something as informal as a cheerleaders' meeting. You'll never decide what cheers to use at the game if your director doesn't keep things in order!

When an election for officers or directors is to be held, a nominating committee is frequently appointed at a meeting preceding the election. The nominating committee presents a slate of candidates at the election meeting; usually the committee asks the candidates if they will run before nominating them. The chairman asks if there are additional nominations from the floor and then a vote is taken. Sometimes the candidates leave the room during the balloting, especially for a voice vote or show of hands.

When there is no nominating committee, the chairman asks for nominations from the membership. Each nomination is seconded. The chairman then asks if there are any further nominations. If there are not, a member moves that the nominations be closed. This motion is seconded and the balloting takes place.

About writing minutes: the purpose of taking minutes at a meeting is to set down what has actually been decided; the side-line discussions can usually be omitted.

ATTENDING CONFERENCES

Going to a conference? Being chosen to represent your group is a great compliment; it means your friends think you will make an alert, observant, participating delegate, one who will soak up everything the conference offers and bring back a report that's vivid enough to make everyone feel he went to the conference too.

Be prepared—personally. Talk to seasoned conference-goers about travel manners, clothing to take, behavior in a big hotel, tipping. You'll need a carefully chosen wardrobe and a carefully packed suitcase to carry you through the conference. A twenty-one-inch bag will probably hold everything you need: toilet articles, two pairs of shoes, a change of lingerie, sweaters, blouses, skirts or a suit, a tailored or a dress-up dress, a hat or a veil (you may not wear it, but take it). Tag your bags, carry identification.

Be prepared—officially. Don't go to a conference empty-handed and empty-headed. When you have received the advance program, confer with your group and decide which meetings you will cover. Make sure you have all the necessary papers with you: your marked-up advance program, your conference registration, confirmation of your hotel reservation, transportation tickets. Put most of this material in a big envelope or zipper folder. Be definite about the handling of expenses; make sure you have the money you need.

Be businesslike during the conference, whatever your role. Attend as many sessions as you can—all, if possible. Be on time for the sessions and for any planned social events. Sit with different people at each session; do not huddle with a friend or the same group. If you are a delegate to a conference representing many different groups, delegates of all ages will undoubtedly be present. Here is a chance to make friends of every age. Take advantage of it instead of clustering in teen-age cliques. Adults like to talk to you but sometimes hesitate to intrude on self-sufficient groups of teen-agers.

Circulate through the conference exhibits and pick up the free materials that will interest your group at home. If you are on a panel, speak up clearly and intelligently. If you are in the audience, ask questions but don't monopolize the floor.

Prepare a good report for the group you represent. Jot down memos on high points of speeches, formal business, etc. If possible, bring back a copy of the printed program for each member of the group. If your organization has sent other representatives to the conference, get together with them to discuss what kind of report you will make. Make your report businesslike but not too brief. Give it at the first meeting after you return; don't wait for the official report to arrive.

Put your best foot forward: your organization will be judged by your behavior. If you are staying at a hotel, don't plan late get-togethers with other girls in your room. Don't take home hotel stationery or help yourself to towels—or ash trays. If you are staying with a private family, fit yourself into the family schedule and be sure to send a thank-you note on your return. If you are one of a group that is housed with a family, it's a nice gesture to send a group present to your hostess.

Have a good time. Enter into the fun of a conference—and there is so much fun! A co-operative, adaptable delegate can have a wonderful time. If the conference planners offer something special—a visit to the local produce market at dawn or a barbecue or tea—go along and make friends. If you are an only delegate, you'll soon find another "only" to team up with. You may also find that teaming up with adults is more fun than you expected. Adults who attend conferences are used to getting around, seeing sights and finding the best restaurants. Conferences are rewarding—for delegates who know the score.

5. Boys, Boys, Boys

Any girl can get a date, have a boy in love with her, become engaged and get married. Fix these facts in your mind *and believe in them* and you will be successful at getting along with boys. Everything is in your favor because most boys like most girls—whether the girls are smashing beauties, super-smart students, energetic leaders; whether they have brilliant talents, social position or parents who invented money. (If a real, pleasant girl has one or more of those plus values—fine.) This is your answer to "I wonder what he sees in *her*." What he sees in her is plain enough (and she may be very, very plain too): he sees a girl who's thoroughly confident about being a girl—a girl who likes people, who expects them to like her, who is fun to be with. But—first she has to meet the boy.

MEETING THEM

What is the approach; how does a girl meet boys, talk to them, get a date?

There are boys around; you see them, you don't know them and you haven't figured out a way to meet them. Why can't you just say hello? In some cases, you can: you can smile and say hello to a boy who lives in your neighborhood, to a boy who goes to your school or your church. You can speak to a boy who is a member of a club you or your family belong to. Just a quick hello, not a conversation—that's too much for a start; but if you keep recognizing he's alive, the opportunity to talk will soon come. The old rule was never speak to a stranger; the modern rule is you may say hello to strange boys in known places and to known boys in strange places (you're out with friends or with your father at his club, his college, his business). Of course, you may smile and speak to anyone there. But never speak to strangers in strange places.

There isn't a boy in sight; or, nearer the truth, maybe you haven't made yourself visible. Wishing to meet boys won't make it so.

Go places To parties, even if you don't have a date. Most young parties include unattached boys and girls. If it turns out to be a couple party, help your hostess organize the games, get the food ready, do the dishes (she may have a brother or cousin, or one of the male guests who doesn't have a permanent girl may notice and think what a good sport you are). Visit three or four friends every week, even if only to lend a record or borrow a book. Making friends of girls is one of the easiest ways to meet boys. Most girls enjoy bringing people together on the least excuse.

Go to every kind of school event at least once. (How do you *know* you don't like soccer? Boys do.) *

Go to exhibits at the library, local stores, the museum, the town hall, if the subject of the exhibit is one a boy might be interested in. Examples: boats, old cars, new cars, guns, Lincoln, fishing equipment, photographs showing the history of the town's fire department or softball games.

Local events that interest men: parades, sports exhibitions, pet shows, horse shows—or any kind of charity, garden or women's club "do," where mothers might commandeer their sons' help—to carry urns of hot coffee, flats of flowers, antique chairs; to take tickets, count money, keep the line moving.

Join something Any boy-girl group in your school, church, "Y." Any boy-girl group sponsored by a charity, a hospital, the Grange; a political, sports or social club your parents belong to or approve of; the Scouts or any all-girl group sponsored by one of the groups listed here. (Girls have brothers, girls know other boys, girls give parties.)

Do something Play tennis, learn to bowl, take skating lessons. Volunteer to help—raising funds for the new gym, serving the food at the church picnic, collecting clothes for the flood victims. Develop a hobby, such as photography or doing portrait sketches; when you're good at the hobby, offer to take the pictures for the yearbook or the school newspaper—or to do a dozen free portraits for the church fair—or to photograph old houses or old furniture for the town's centennial celebration. Learn to type rapidly and accurately; boys need theses typed. Get your parents to arrange for you to have lessons in driving, tennis, swimming, Spanish—an easy way to run into nice boys. Find a part-time job in a store where men shop: one that sells records, sports equipment, auto accessories, things like that.

Have an idea Give a party to raise funds (see pages 284-5, 290). Start a beginner sports group for young children in your neighborhood, in your church or in the younger grades at school: you have the idea and the plan; the teachers, the women's auxiliary at the church or the parents in your neighborhood find the men to help you.

---

* *Remember the object here is primary; for you to be seen everywhere and to make some boy want to ask, "Who is she?" by dressing nicely, behaving in a charming but inconspicuous manner, being attentive and interested. You don't want to be noticed because you laughed noisily, criticized the way the women looked, rattled a popcorn bag all through the speeches, walked on the tennis court with suicide-heel shoes.*

A boy at last You're both launched on a regular speaking schedule: you smile and say hello; he says hi and smiles. End of conversation. You're supposed to wait till he starts to talk, but it's not practical advice this decade. You're probably the only girl in the school who follows it, and the boy probably thinks you don't want to talk to him. But there are ways of letting your first conversation start naturally and casually. If you see an empty place at his table that obviously isn't being saved for someone else—or if there's a vacant spot next to him at the snack shop—you can smile and say, "May I sit next to you?" Then you can say something cheerful that requires an answer. Doesn't the field trip sound like fun, and what's he going to look for? You were devastated by the French exam; what would happen if the whole class failed the test? You read in the school paper that he's made the tennis team; what does he think is a good make of racket for your younger brother?

If you're both waiting to go into class, you can ask something about the assignment or if he's seen the science exhibit at the bank. You can ask his opinion about the vote coming up at the class meeting. You can volunteer the information that your family's so excited your brother's coming home tomorrow—and did he ever know your brother before he went off to school/college/the Army? (Mention where, because his brother might be in the Army or his father might have gone to the same college.)

If you're in luck and you have more time for your first talk—at a party, a half-hour bus trip, waiting in the dentist's office—you can promote a longer chat. Ask his opinion of the school's science program, the new football coach, the theme for the spring dance. Tell him you saw him at the track meet, adding, "Pole vaulting must be awfully difficult! How did you get interested in it?"

Sometimes you have to legislate a chance to talk. If the chairman of the dance asks whom you'd like to help you decorate the gym, say, "Oh, you know who'd be *wonderful*—that tall, redheaded boy who pole-vaults." Then when the chairman asks him, you get two credits with the boy—one for being a girl who is somebody in the class, another for proposing him. (Even if he doesn't really want to trim the gym, it's flattering to be asked.) You may even get a third credit if the chairman happens to say, "Elsie Adams thought you'd be a wonderful person on the dance committee. . . "

What you avoid Hankering after just one elusive male. Talk to *any* boy who looks moderately human: (1) it's practice; (2) he may introduce his brother, nearer the right age for you, who is delightful. Besides, the fellow with the sensitive, craglike face may be about as charming as a crag while that rather battered-looking boy with the crooked grin may be the nicest date a girl was ever blessed with. It's much better to be interested in boys than to yearn after one boy you don't—and may never—know.

What about a compliment from a boy you like? If he's really your beau—even your first beau—you know how to take the compliment—with a smile, a soft answer, an adoring look. If you're just advancing from the hello-and-hi stage, turn to him, say, "Aah—*thank* you, Tom," and smile straight at him. The effect is to say you like him too and you appreciate his liking you enough to pay you a compliment. (Southern girls have a marvelous answer—"Bless you for saying that!"—that's unbeatable for a sincere compliment and fairly unnerving as a retort for the obviously insincere compliment.) Just remember not to throw any compliment away with one of those unsure answers that include Oh-this-old-dress, I've-always-thought-I-was-a-terrible-dancer, No-one's-ever-said-I-was-pretty-before, I-know-you-don't-really-mean-it.

What about wolf whistles? They're much easier to appreciate if you have a boy of your own; you *know* you're worth whistling at! A whistle is a compliment, crude though it is; ignore it gently and walk on. The whistlers know you're a girl.

What about flirting? Yes and no. *Yes* if you flirt because you like the boy—or boys in general. *Yes* if you flirt to flatter the boy. *Yes* if you flirt lightly and naturally (girl talking to boy). *Yes* if girls are your friends too.
No if you flirt only to prove you can make the boy interested. *No* if you plan to drop him the moment he's interested. *No* if you flirt to take him away from a girl who really likes him. *No* if girls think you're bad news to have around.

GETTING TO KNOW THEM: *53 Tips for Successful Dating*

He asks you out! Accept or not (your privilege), but be happy he asked! Suppose you're in one of those binding situations where you are hoping—maybe pretty hopelessly—that Bill will call you for a date Saturday. Jerry asks you; your heart's set on a date with Bill.
Right: "Jerry, I'd love to." Then even if Bill calls later, you keep the date with Jerry.
Also right: "Jerry, I'd love to, but I have plans already." (Use this for flat turndowns too.) With this kindly answer, you take your chances. If Bill calls, you are free to go out with him. If he doesn't call, Jerry will never know you spent Saturday evening washing your hair. In either case, you spare Jerry's feelings.
Wrong: "Jerry, I'd love to, but may I let you know tomorrow?" Stalling Jerry and hoping that Bill will call is not nice. The only time you can honestly say "May I let you know?" is when you really don't know if you'll be free. Proceed to explain: you don't have your family's permission; you half-promised Mrs.

Allen to sit with her children; you're not sure you'll be over your cold. But if you find you're free, agree to go out with Jerry; *even* if Bill does call, Jerry asked you first.

Really wrong: "Jerry, I'd love to." Then Bill calls. You call Jerry and tell him you have a raging fever. You go out with Bill. If you run into Jerry in the course of the evening, he'll be hurt. Even if you and Bill stay at your house all evening watching TV, your peace of mind will be ruffled by the thought that you've been unkind to Jerry. Don't break dates. Keeping them is like telling the truth consistently: you never have to backtrack, wonder what you've said, cover your traces.

You may break a date for family reasons or when you're ill. But when you break it, sound as sorry as you are. Remember that one good honest excuse is more convincing than a lame half-truth. Show you're breaking the date fairly by asking him to a family cookout, to go to some event your family's going to, or just to come to your house for homemade pizza and listening to records.

When a boy asks you for a date, find out what time to be ready if he forgets to tell you. If you think his plans might include something other than standard Saturday-night fare (his class *is* having a dance that night), you may hint around the edges for information. For example, if you ask about what time you'll be home, he may say, "Oh, the band always quits at midnight, and we'll probably stop for a hamburger." If he says, "Maybe one o'clock," and offers no further facts, don't probe further. Take your chances and greet him looking ethereal in white tulle. If you're wrong, you can recognize bowling clothes when you see them and say, "Oops—*bowling;* what fun! Give me five minutes to change, please, Bill?" If he asks you to a private dance, ask him whether it's dress-up or not.

When you ask a boy out—to a school sorority dance—you tell him whether it's an informal or black-tie party, pay for the tickets ahead of time, and give them to him on the way to the dance. He may or may not give you flowers. If he doesn't have a car and if you know his chances of getting his family's car are slim, tentatively arrange to go with another couple who have transportation before you ask him. If he'd rather work out another plan, let him; thank your friend and tell her your date has a car, a friend he'd promised to go with, or whatever the story is.

You can always ask a boy you know to go to a picnic or a party—whether he's ever asked you out or not—if everyone knows the girls have been requested to issue the invitations for the event. Ask him simply, saying, "Tommy, the girls in my club are giving a swimming party at Mary Dee's house Sunday afternoon. Will you go to it with me? We're planning a Hawaiian supper, and it will be lots of fun." Don't be discouraged if he can't or won't come; keep asking till someone says yes.

Blind dates should be arranged by friends; making a date with a totally unknown boy is rather like playing Russian roulette. The reasons for agreeing to an arranged blind date are that you don't have a date that evening, you like the friend who planned the date, you want to go out and be seen out. Even if the evening turns out to be dreary, thank the friend who arranged the date; someday she might produce The Man.

The success of a blind date is partly up to you. The boy will probably turn out to be just average-nice and a far cry from what you have in mind. (Maybe you're not ready for the one you have in mind, either.) Even if he's hopeless in your eyes, be as nice to him as you'd want a terrific blind date to be to you.

Finding out some of this information will make talking to the boy easier.

- *What's he like?*

  A man's man? You can get him to talk about down-to-earth subjects like food or sports. Ask his opinion about who'll win the pennant, if tall basketball players are ruining the game, if Little League baseball should be banned. Seek his advice on learning to understand football plays, where you can find the best riding horses, whether practicing against the backboard helps or hurts your tennis game.

  Shy type? He will be happy, more relaxed, if you keep the conversation going with friendly, animated chatter. Make him think he's talking by slipping in such phrases as "What you said about cool jazz reminds me of an article I read . . ." or "You just reminded me that there *is* going to be a re-telecast of that marvelous show about . . ." Treat him as though he's quite a bit older than you and you really want his opinion: "You're the one who could really tell me what to do about my young brother (or pet). There must be a way I can get him to . . ."

  Very handsome? He may be fairly sick of being liked only for his looks. Find out what other interests he has; follow them up with enthusiasm, as though his only possible attraction for a girl was his clear-thinking and well-informed mind. If you find he adores being swooned over and his only interest is girls (and it sickens *you*), look on him as a research project in depth: find out what movie stars, television actresses, girls in school he thinks are attractive; ask what he likes about their looks, their types, the way they walk and talk; discuss whether men are more attracted by girls whose tastes are opposite or similar. You know what you think of boys who try to kiss you on the first date; ask him what he thinks of girls who will let him. Ask him if he thinks any less of a girl who says no—and how can she say it and still be friends. You may not like him any better at the end of the evening, but you will have gathered a lot of male point of view that will help you understand a boy you do like.

Great brain? If he's the positive, expounding type of boy, you can forget about flirting; he thinks it's silly. You can just be yourself and listen, argue, agree and expound on any subject you're a brain about.

Life of the party? He's probably basically a lonely soul who keeps up the gay patter because he's not very sure of himself or whether people will like him if he doesn't keep them laughing. Laugh at him, tell him he's funny if you can get a word in edgewise; if someone else slips in a joke or two, laugh a little less enthusiastically. Don't show much interest in other people. If he thinks that, for once, a girl is interested just in him, he'll probably relax a little and stop that mad pace. This kind of boy is usually too eager to be liked to tell a string of racy, dirty jokes; but if he does, you don't have to laugh. Just wait till he gets to the clean stories and say, "I like that kind of joke much better, Joe. That's *really* funny." He'll get the idea faster than if you stalk home to mother. (If you have a brother, you realize that all boys tell jokes girls don't much like and that presently they learn to save them for the boys.)

- *What will he like about you?*

You may already have your answer in the first question about what he's like. Your date-arranging friend may be able to supply some of the boy's known opinions: he likes girls who are good dancers, girls who are athletes, girls who can cook, blondes. He can't stand girls who try to be better at sports than men, smart girls who don't know how to act semidumb, girls who look made up, girls who boss all the arrangements, girls who won't consider another point of view.

- *What's the nicest thing about him?*

He has a wonderful disposition, he never makes cracks about his friends, he always helps beginners at whatever sport he excels in, he spends every Saturday morning helping children in the hospital's rehabilitation ward. This particular question may revamp your whole impression of a tall, skinny boy with glasses whose suit jackets are always too short in the sleeve.

- *Basics*

What school does he go to . . . what class . . . is he on the team . . . does he do something special, such as edit the paper? Has he ever dated much, was there any special girl, has he just broken up with a girl? Does he have a car, a job? Does he have very little cash?

Your date arrives. He looks better than ever and you want to be sure he asks you out again. Suddenly any number of nagging little questions pop into your mind and you realize you're not sure you know the right thing to do. If you act young and nice, he'll like you no matter if you do make a mistake or two. But you might have a better time if you are fortified with the right answers. Here you are:

Where do I meet him for our first date? At home. It's your obligation to introduce him to your parents, and he'll probably think it's queer if you don't.

Does he always have to come all the way out to my house to meet me? After dark, yes—unless your family is going downtown too and can take you, or you can stay at your aunt's house, or you are going to be at your father's office anyway.

I can't have a date meet me at my house because of a family problem. What can I do and how can I explain to him? Until you've had several dates, have a logical reason for meeting him somewhere else. You baby-sit for your aunt—or some sympathetic friend of the family's (perhaps your doctor's wife)—every evening from five till seven. Or you work in your dentist's office, filing the day's charts. Or you do your volunteer work at suppertime in the hospital. The point here is that you can't go this one alone; you need the support of some reliable older friend—aunt, minister's family, doctor, head volunteers at the hospital. Probably most of the girls and boys you know have some kind of family problem that isn't generally known. Your burden may be parents who are separated . . . a bitter mother who'd like to make you dislike all men . . . a father who drinks heavily or has an unpredictable, cross temper . . . an aging aunt who's been divorced three times and likes to flirt with your dates . . . an eccentric older relative who can be depended on to do something embarrassing. Bad as it may seem to you, you might prefer your particular problem to the ones some of your friends are trying to cope with.

You need to build friendship and recognition of your own good qualities before you explain why it's hard for you to ask the boy to meet your family. When you do explain, tell your story simply, with as much compassion as you can manage, without bitterness toward the person, without useless rebellion against the situation or pitiful sympathy for yourself. Say in effect that this is so and you have to live with it just now: "I wanted you to know it's not you I'm keeping from my family; I'm keeping my family from you." He may be too conventional, too young and untried to understand. But he may be one of those wonderful boys who is sympathetic and who can even manage to get along with both the problem and the problem person.

Oddly enough, he may like you all the more for the way you meet each day's tension, finding you just that much stronger and sweeter a person. Trouble can form a lasting bond between a boy and girl, underlining the boy's strength and the girl's dependence on his strength.

Do I always have to ask my date to come in? If your parents aren't home and there's no other grownup around, meet him at the door (you have to be *ready*). Most of the time your parents will stop and say hello when you ask him in; they're probably too busy for a long chat anyway. Sometimes you can be ready to leave as soon as he rings.

It's so awkward to have a date try to talk to my family; none of us can think of a thing to say, and then we all talk at once. You can always laugh when that happens! You're the slow one here, though. It's up to you to brief both your parents and your date on each other's interests and accomplishments. Suppose your mother is the sort who'd trill, "Janie says you're absolutely the *star* of the team!" You probably look extra pretty when you blush. Have some notes of mutual interest you can use to fill in the dead spots: his mother used to teach school, too, or is going to handle a booth at the bazaar, or his father is interested in sports-car rallies and has been looking at the same make of car your father has.

Won't I look too eager if I'm ready and waiting when my date arrives? You'll look organized, efficient, gracious and all that, but not too eager. There's no reason why you shouldn't be spending a few minutes with your family, and it's nice for him if you're the one who greets him at the door. Knowing that he won't have a long wait making conversation with your family will make him less self-conscious too.

What do I do if I'm dressed for the movies and my date says we're going to a picnic? Ask him if you have time to change. If he doesn't tell you till you're out of the house, be a good sport and make the best of it—and try to find out next time you date him what his plans include.

Suppose my date wants to go to a hockey game and I'd rather see that new movie? Go to the movie with a girl the next day.

Does it count as a date when the boy just wants to spend the evening at my house and not go anywhere? It's very flattering if he likes you and your house that much. (Maybe his own home isn't too friendly.) If he never takes you anywhere, try to arrange a bridge game at a friend's house or ask him to take you to some local event that doesn't cost money. If maneuvers like these don't work, and if you know he spends money generously on himself and all-male activities, better look for another boy.

May I drive my date to a party in my family's car? Yes. You may also drive him away from you too. If your father (or his insurance company) is strict about letting outsiders drive the car, let your date suggest transportation to the party even if it means walking. In bad weather you might tactfully arrange for a friend's beau to offer to pick you and your date up at your house.

Do I wait to let my date open the car door for me? Don't wait too long. It can hold up traffic. If he's one that does, appreciate him.

If I see a boy I like better than my date at a party, is it all right to talk to him? For a minute or two; but let him see what a nice date you are by being very nice to the boy who brought you.

How can I get a boy to ask me to a big party coming up? We're not going steady, but we didn't go out with anyone else last summer. Bring it up in a general way when you're talking to him. If he doesn't give any sign of planning to take you, you're free to make another date. You really can't ask him outright though, because if he's planning to take someone else, you'd both be embarrassed.

We double-date all the time with another couple, and the trouble is that the boys just don't talk to us any more. Maybe you use your dates' time in girl talk. Why not be quiet and look for ways to join the boys in their conversation—or bring up topics that will interest them? You might also try to find activities that will pair you off with your date (dancing instead of miniature golf).

May I ask my date to carry my glasses, lipstick and comb in his pocket? That's very hard on the hang of his jacket. Carry an adequate bag for your needs. Boys usually don't mind a single item, though.

If he looks really nice or has a new suit, should I mention it? He'll like it very much if you're brief and matter-of-fact about it.

Should I sit on the far side of the seat when he's driving? If you really like him, sit close enough so people won't think you're married, as the old quip goes. If you haven't made up your mind, sit halfway between him and the door so he won't think you're either a scared rabbit or icy.

Is it overdoing it to say something nice about his car? It's sort of a heap, but he's mad about it. No, and it's very nice of you.

Should I make suggestions when he asks what movie to see or where to go? You'd better, or he'll think all you want to do is neck.

Should I stand by his side when he buys the tickets? Amble on ahead.

Are there certain mannerisms that annoy boys? There are. Fiddling with rings, beads, locks of hair. Nibbling on fingernails, eyeglass flanges, a bobby pin (he'd rather see your face in repose than busy as a bunny's). Clawing away at your face, scratching your head, plucking bits of lint off his sleeve. (Stop fidgeting; you're making him nervous too.)

Do I have to say I liked the movie if he did and I didn't? If he chose it, you might comment about something in it you liked. You can almost always glow about the photography. If you picked the "lemony" show, speak out; maybe your date is just being polite about your taste.

I don't agree at all with some of my friend's ideas about books, politics, local and world affairs. Will I lose him if I argue with him? Not if you disagree pleasantly. Avoid name-calling and below-the-belt jibes and say, "Let's still be friends" when the discussion ends.

Is it proper to let a date know I like him? Tell him out of the blue what fun he is or how happy you are to be with him. No pretty speeches, though; they sound artificial.

What do I do if we're at the drive-in or a restaurant and I think he's low in funds? Say, "Jimmy, you order for me, will you?" Or, if you're too independent for that, ask what he's going to have and say that's what you'd like too.

Who gives the order when we're eating out? You tell the boy; he gives the order.

What do I order when I'm having dinner with a boy? Say, "What do you think, Harry . . ." And if you don't want the Salisbury steak, choose something else at about the same price. Just don't humiliate him by announcing right away that you'll have the cheapest thing on the menu (vegetable plate?). And don't cripple him financially by ordering steak unless he suggests it.

Who suggests that it's time to go home? You do, particularly if you have a time when you must be home. Sound regretful: "I can't bear to mention it,

Hal—I've had such a wonderful time—but I have to be in by eleven on school nights."

Suppose a boy just deliberately doesn't get a girl home on time? If he was stalling to get one more dance with you, that's a compliment. If he was just talking around with the boys while you burned, that's no compliment. Some families are explosive about a daughter's being even fifteen minutes late. In the first instance, tell him this ruefully when you accept another date with him. In the second instance, you might give him one more chance after you explain the curfew law in your house to him.

Am I supposed to give my date the key when we get to my door? It's a pretty gesture if you think he'll get the message. On your first date, hesitate a little as you take it out of your bag: a boy who expects to open the door for you will probably reach for the key and say, "Here, I'll open it for you" or "May I?"

Who thanks whom for a date? He thanks you; you say it's been a wonderful evening.

Is it all right to linger at the door for a minute? If you want to be kissed.

May a girl ever kiss a boy on a first date? Sweetly, quickly—if you're really smitten and you know he knows it.

Should I ask him in? Yes, if your parents are up and if it's agreeable to them and if you want to. (Maybe ask them ahead of time?)

Why doesn't he call? You had several dates; you liked each other and each other's friends; you had a wonderful time, no disagreements—and he just stopped calling. *Why?* you wail. What did you do wrong; how can you get him back?

Stop wailing for just a minute while we welcome you to the group; it's happened to us all. You probably did nothing wrong. And the only thing you can do is be your pleasant self so that when he gets around to calling you again, he won't be afraid to.

Here are seven reasons why a boy stops calling. After you've read them, you'll understand that it's no use pining for him.

1. Maybe he doesn't have enough money just now to take you—or any other girl—out on a date. But it's something he can't explain.
2. He may be saving up to buy a secondhand car and have taken a part-time job—leaving him neither time nor money for dating.

3. He may have met a girl he used to date before he met you and have been drawn back to her again. Maybe it will be only temporary.
4. Maybe he's playing hard to get and enjoys keeping you guessing.
5. Perhaps he doesn't want you to become too sure of him. When you least expect it, he'll probably call you.
6. He may be the kind who'd rather play the field—especially if he loves his independence and feels he is too attracted to you.
7. And he may have liked you a lot but decided you really weren't his type.

GOOD MANNERS IN LOVE

Keeping a beau (the one you like a little and the one you like a lot), the art of being kissable, of having good manners in love—all this can be managed successfully by girls who are wise about the rules along the road of romance.

Having caught the boy, you're not always sure you want him—or at least not as much as he wants you. You like going out with him, you want to stay friends, but you're not in love. The idea of kissing becomes increasingly important to him and you feel this would only make things worse. Should you pretend to be a little in love for the sake of having a steady escort?

Boys are much more matter-of-fact about kissing than girls. A boy likes a kiss, not necessarily from a *particular* girl; he can kiss any one of a roomful of attractive women and feel quite happy about it. A girl, for the most part, likes to feel that every beau is the first one she's really been in love with. It's probable that a boy you're not in love with is not pining with love for you; he likes you and likes to be with you, and a kiss is a sort of status symbol to him—but it seldom is a symbol of his undying love. A token kiss good night won't hurt you and won't lead him on. What will hurt you both is to pretend an emotion you don't feel, to let others think you're wild about the boy, to get involved in the routine of a couple in love—the long phone calls, the letters, the exchange of rings and sweaters, the necking. Stay friends with the boy, treat him as a casual beau and be honest with him: keep the lights turned up, the house full of friends he wants to see too; plan group parties (see page 271) and outings. Avoid the romantic situations, such as long drives to the country, moonlit walks on the beach, evenings in a firelit room with a thousand love songs on the record player. (Hide them! Leave the new jazz and the old twist records on the machine and move the ping-pong table nearby.) The boy may be glad you're not putting him through the oh-so-in-love paces. He has a lot of things to take more seriously than a girl: studies, college entrance, sports, saving money for a ski trip. If he's looking for love instead of friendship, he'll find another girl. And still like you. (And *you* will still like you.)

When you find the one you really like, how do you let him know? He tells you he loves you, but you can't seem to say the words. You daydream about a hundred perfect ways you will make this great announcement. None of them work out.

Don't worry about saying the words. You've probably told him many times: he knows by the way your face lights up when you see him, the happiness in your voice when he phones, your concern with his triumphs and woes, your interest in the sports and hobbies he likes, the way you build him up to his friends. The words will come. Meantime, if hearing the words becomes important to him, he'll ask you and you'll tell him indignantly, *"Of course I love you!"* (Which isn't the way you've planned it at all.)

You like him a lot; you want him to kiss you. You've gone out with him for weeks; you know he doesn't take anyone else out—but he hasn't tried to snatch one little kiss. Is it you? Is it he? Is it what?

Men are sensitive about being turned down; he needs to be sure you want him to kiss you. Men can be shy too, so if you stay shyly at the other side of the car he may never guess that you *would* like to be kissed. You don't have to be an aggressive snuggler—just available. In case. You can rest your head on his shoulder when you dance. You can slip your hand in his at the movies or when strolling. You can linger a bit at your doorway when he takes you home.

Or it might be that you haven't figured out what kind of boy he is. Perhaps he comes from a strict religious background; he's very much taken with you—and slightly thrown by your sophistication. He likes it but he's uneasy about it. He likes you because you're attractive but he's worried about whether it's all right for a girl to be so alluring. (His mother was probably the glamour girl of their crowd until his father married her, made her scrub her face and wear matching tweed coats and suits.) This is very disheartening to a girl who's longed for the day when she could look and act grown up. If you are serious about liking the boy, you'd best adjust your type. You can be chic, perfectly dressed, beautifully groomed—and look scrubbed, brushed, simple, enchantingly pretty. Many of the world's lovely, fashionable women make an art of doing *exactly* this.

Then of course you may break the spell just as he's almost ready to kiss you. As one young charmer said, "I find it hard to whisper sweet nothings to a creature who tastes like onion rings, Camembert cheese or postage stamps. Why would a girl want to be remembered as a jar of peanut butter?" Other spell-breakers include dialing the radio from station to station, bringing forth a choice bit of gossip, moaning about some problem he's facing, mentioning something he did that annoyed you, starting an argument, putting on more lipstick (at *this* time?).

Suggestions from the boys: Please remove your hat, the one with the big scratchy brim. Wear small jewelry that doesn't stab. Don't wear those chokers of pearls; it ruins the spell to have beads bursting all over the place like hailstones. Don't wear pleated organdy collars you don't want to have crushed. Don't break into screams of laughter if you see you've covered his face with lipstick (you should have blotted it).

Manners in love Other people rather enjoy seeing young lovers ("I've had a love of my own like yours," the song goes), but the radiance gets a little grimy if you don't place some limits on displays of affection. You don't have to kiss every time you're going to be parted for half an hour, hold hands in the school corridors, sit on his lap when the family and their friends are milling around the house. You don't have to drive out to the lake with another couple and neck in the back seat while they patiently discuss the best-seller list in the front seat. At a party or a moonlight picnic when you're not quite alone, hand-holding or a strong arm around your shoulder is on the approved list; kissing, however, loses its tender quality when it becomes a public matter. When he's driving, he needs both hands if you want to get where you're going safely. And occasional discreet hand-holding with a boy you date steadily, whom your family likes, is acceptable around parents, if they don't object.

You owe good manners to the one you love, too—not to discuss him, his secrets, any disagreements you may have. Everyone needs someone to confide in, but try to keep it to some *one* you know will be trustworthy. Your good manners in love tell you to be fair—not to flirt so it hurts him (good-natured flirting is just part of some girls' personalities), not to make a Saturday date with someone else if you have an agreement about that particular day, not to accept an important date (the big game, the spring dance, New Year's) without checking it out with him.

You also owe your beau understanding. If he's a senior and you're a sophomore and the rules are that only seniors go to the class dance—you'll have to understand and make sure he goes with someone else. Let your heart break quietly so he won't notice it and so he will be able to enjoy his only senior dance. If he has to study, practice, go out with his family on what you regard as your time, understand that he has no choice. If you sulk and complain, you just make it harder for him. (Eventually he may feel trapped by your narrowness.)

Having a steady beau—forsaking all others until a change of heart shall us part—is steadily discouraged by almost everyone whose opinions are supposed to carry weight with young people. It limits the chance to reach for a broader circle of friends, interests, activities; you don't get the needed practice in meeting and getting along with people not in your own small group; it's a monumental strain—however in love you think you are—to be tied to one person when there's no immediate prospect of marriage. You also lose the opportunity to be friends with many different types of boys. You stay green as May, not giving your own personality a chance to develop.

Why go steady, then? Some say it's because many young people need the security of a steady date, because they're afraid they'll be left home and miss all the fun. Some say it's a good thing because it puts the emphasis on a group of friends and their activities instead of a more romantic date with someone exciting and new. Young and old agree that the problems faced by the girl with a steady beau and the girl who plays the field are about as numerous—just different.

Suppose the boy's away at school and then away at a job or his family's place all summer. Or suppose he's home in the summer and *you* go away. He doesn't want you to go out with anyone else. You don't, because you promised —and also because someone would be sure to write and tell him. But you don't know whether he does or not, fifty or more miles away. This isn't any fun and it isn't very secure either.

Or he's at home winter and summer. But he doesn't have much time for you on weekends. Friday nights he helps with a boys' group at the church; he has a job Saturday mornings, and he devotes those afternoons to playing basketball or hockey. Sunday mornings you sing in the choir (but you can see him eleven pews away). Sunday and weekday evenings you each stay home. That leaves you Saturday evenings and a couple of hours Sundays to spend together—if he doesn't want to play some game with the boys. Lonely, isn't it? But you could always develop some outside interests of your own.

Or this is his first year away at college. You knew you'd miss him, but there was a bittersweet happiness in the thought of the letters that would come so faithfully—some funny, some serious, all with that special, tender last paragraph. Regrettably, although you have kept your promise to write every day, that space you cleared in your desk for his letters is now filled with clips of possible new hairdos. As far as you know, though, you have a steady beau.

Circumstances like these do sound like the sure road to spinsterhood. Must you go steady only because everyone else does? There's really only one way we know to break the system. *If* you can get four or five other girls to agree to play the field—thus liberating five or six boys—you all will have a chance to be asked out by a number of boys. You need to start a brisk social life, though, by planning girl-ask-boy parties in the beginning and by being such good fun that the boys are eager to come to your parties and to ask you out on your terms.

Sometimes a girl goes steady, no matter what the custom is where she lives, because she is completely entranced with one special boy. That's probably the best reason for saying no to all other dates.

The cost of loving can get fairly steep for a boy. A steady girl has first call on his time—to drive her where she wants to go, take her out, buy her presents. A thoughtful girl will try to keep expenses down; you don't have to go to a movie every week when watching television would help buy the tickets and flowers for the dance. (You don't always have to have flowers either; everyone knows you have a beau.) You can plan parties that you provide and pay for (see page 282) or give him tickets to a show for some minor anniversary or to celebrate passing his College Boards. Watch the papers for free events that would interest you both—sports, open meetings, lectures, exhibits. Perhaps you could get free tickets to radio and TV shows or to rehearsals of an orchestra or theater group. On a nice afternoon you could suggest a hobby outing—taking paintbox and easel or checkers to some nice outdoor spot. You might explore the world around you on long walks or attend openings of supermarkets, shopping centers, gas stations and banks, where all kinds of entertainment, door prizes and free gifts often abound.

Breaking up If you're the one to make the break, remember that there's no way you can do it without hurting the boy. True, some romances really do end by mutual consent, but the percentage is all on the side of someone's having a heartache. Be as kind as you can. It's hardest to give him the word face to face, but it's a courtesy you owe him. Telling him on the phone is a shabby way to escape an obligation, and the only time it's forgivable to write a Dear John letter is when the boy's away—at school, in the Army or just living far away. The most acceptable explanation is that you'd like to go out with other boys too; he may be willing to share you, but it's his decision and you'll have to go along with it. On the other hand, if you honestly can't stand the sight of him any more, don't say anything about continuing to date him—and if he calls, be pleasant, say you're sorry but you're busy. Over and over and over. If you're furious with him, have the courage to tell him you are *and why*. You may patch it up, you may not—but it's fairer to give him the whole story. The one thing you don't tell him (except if he asks you directly) is that there's someone else, because the hurt would be too deep. He'll find it out in time; he expects you will go out with other boys, and there's no kindness in aiming straight for the heart.

Things you owe an ex-beau: Any jewelry he gave you as a symbol of going steady or being engaged—fraternity pin, school ring, heirloom jewelry or an engagement ring. Pleasant manners when you see him. The kindest words when anyone talks to you about him. Silence—about his shortcomings, his confidences, his letters, his desirability as a friend or as a beau.

How do you get back into circulation? The word will get around fast enough, and that may be all that's necessary. If boys are scarce, try being where they are (see the beginning of this chapter). Giving a party is also one of the best ways to let boys know you're back in circulation.

One touchy little problem you may face is whether to date a boy who's just broken up with one of your good friends; she may, understandably, resent the idea. She'll resent it less if you tell her beforehand, to spare her the shock of suddenly seeing you two together. Be enough of a realist to know that if you get the boy, you may lose the girl as a friend—for a while, anyway.

If the boy you've been going with asks for his freedom, be as "golden rule" as you can about it. However much he wants it and for whatever reason, asking you is difficult for him and he's going to feel bad about it. Make the parting tolerable for him—no pleading, tears, groveling, threats, adoring notes or barrage of phone calls that will make him dislike you intensely and make you ashamed when you pull yourself together. Just about every girl has to face this situation at least once in her life, and what counts is how you face it. One thing you may learn is to recognize when a boy's interest is waning—and to win him back or make the break yourself. If he's interested in another girl, not just idly flirting, the only thing you can do is make the break. He'll be grateful to you, and the other girl may turn out to be dull indeed and you may get him back—if you still want him.

If there isn't another girl and you're just out of tune with each other, try to figure out what attracted him to you in the first place. Maybe you were sweeter to him, gladder when he called, sincerely interested in his likes and dislikes, his victories, worries and woes. The reason you're out of tune might be that you've just stopped noticing anything about him. No boy likes to be a commodity, and if you treat him like one, sooner or later he will discover another girl who is as interested in him as you were long ago.

6. The Art Of Saying No Nicely

By now you know how to say no to a romance you no longer care to continue. But there are many other situations involving boys, and girls as well, in which you'll want to say no. Even adults find it hard much of the time to locate the perfect phrase, create the right climate, in which to express their preferences without making enemies or seeming to be harsh or unpleasant.

But saying no nicely is as vital a part of your personality as doing the things that you are *sure* please people. When you express choices, you are giving others directional signals that help them to know The Real You, the person inside. What you value, what you dislike, what you want in your life and want to cast out of it—all are important things for your friends, or friends-to-be, to know.

So don't hesitate to say no; people will respect you for it, if you learn to say it honestly and nicely. And here are guides to some of the ways.

how to say no nicely The way you say it varies with what you're being asked, who's asking it and how. Most of the time you can say no lightly and change the subject. Then again there are times when directness is the kinder approach: like pulling off adhesive tape, it hurts less when you do it decisively.

There are many things you may want to refuse at one point or another in your life. Relatively easy things, such as a dance or a date. "Statusy" things, such as a drink, a cigarette, going some place you know is off limits. Entangling things, such as a loan or a favor—or going steady. Things that grate your conscience, such as being asked to do a friend's homework. Emotionally loaded things, such as petting or necking. Or just a kiss. Probably the most we can do is to give some examples, which you can adapt to your life. (There may be just one way to eat an artichoke, but there are a thousand ways to say no.)

how to refuse a date so he'll ask again You say you're sorry, you have a date, you're going out with the family, or whatever. *And you add,* "I wish I could—I would have loved it, Jack"—something that tells him you're not handing out a routine no.

when you want to turn him down Say, "I'm sorry; I just can't" without explanation (even if he asks for one). Thank him for asking you but don't lead him on so he'll ask again. To be too kind when you mean NO is to be cruel.

how to refuse a dance Say you promised the dance to someone else, you're waiting for your date, you can't Charleston, you'd love to have some punch. Just remember you can't refuse to dance with one boy and rush to the floor with someone else without explanation. Remember too that a boy who cuts in deserves a smiling welcome—even if he has just torn you from the arms of the only man you could ever love.

how to refuse a cigarette or a drink "No, thank you" is all you need to say, since this is a matter of very personal taste. No explanation. If you find you're involved with a pest, you can say, "Not just now" or "At the moment I'd really like a glass of water." If someone spikes your ginger ale, put the glass down and forget it; someone else will offer to get you something before long.

how to avoid a movie you don't want to see Try one of these:

"Oh, let's see .... instead."

"I thought that would be good too, but Joe and Linda saw it and loathed it." (You don't have to say why.)

"I understand it gets pretty dreary."

"Subtitles—*again?*" (Recommended for "adult" foreign movies.)

how not to lend money

"I'm absolutely stoney too. Sorry."

"I've just enough to last through Saturday."

"Can't manage; have to pay my library fine today."

how not to lend clothes

"It's at the cleaner's."

"I think I'm going to wear it myself that night."

"I'd love to let you have it, but it spots so easily I'm afraid to wear it myself."

how not to lend anything you value

"I just can't lend it to anyone. I'm very sorry."

to the girl—or, worse, boy—who wants to borrow your algebra homework

"Sorry, but I want to make college too."

"Forgive me; that's one of the rules I keep."

(You really never have to offer an excuse for refusing to do something you and the asker both know is wrong.)

how to fend off personal questions

Q. "What did you pay for that dress?"

A. "I really don't remember" or "It was a present" or "Too much, according to my father!"

Q. "Are your parents really separated?"

A. "I'm sorry; I never discuss my family."

how to refuse to go steady This is a tremendous compliment—like being proposed to—so build him up as you turn him down: "I think you're wonderful, Joe—but really, I think we're both too young to be tied down." Or "We'll both be away at school" or whatever.

how to refuse a kiss If it's a gay under-the-mistletoe or New Year's kiss, enjoy it and don't stir up a scene over nothing. If it's a determined, boy-has-plans kiss, humor or distraction is the best way to salvage the situation. If one or both of you starts laughing, or can be distracted, you can avoid the rather dull feminine defenses of scratching, screaming and kicking. Work up some sentences of your own along these lines:

"Joe! I've gotten you *covered* with lipstick. If you could just see how *funny* you look!" And keep laughing; it's very hard to kiss a laughing girl.

"Er, Joe—just a minute. Could you get me a glass of water?"

"Darling, are you asking me to marry you?"

"Look here . . . haven't you ever kissed a girl before? You're acting like an octopus."

The real kissing problem for every unattached female of any age is whether to kiss on the first date. Boys tell us they usually try for a kiss but don't really expect to get it. What does matter to them is how the girl says no. Something like "Jack, please—you're dear, but I just don't know you well enough to kiss you" is a highly acceptable turndown. A kiss should have some value. Still, if you and the boy obviously, decidedly like each other, it seems silly to refuse to kiss him as a matter of principle on your first date when you know you'll kiss him on the second or third.

But if you're mad about the boy and not too sure of his feelings, the principle is worth heeding: you won't know what you'll be missing and you will spare yourself the humiliating feeling of failure if he doesn't ask you out again. If he's very much taken with you and you're in doubt about him, you'd be fairer not to encourage him by kissing him.

It comes to this: boys are persistent; anyone who likes you will ask you out again whether or not you kiss him—and until you do!

know what you're going to say no to Settle on your own personal standards in some unimpassioned moment; you'll find they'll be easier to stick to when you need them. And then don't betray them—or appear to—by semisophisticated behavior. If you wriggle seductively as you push yourself out of an embrace, your no sounds a lot more like maybe or please. If you tell off-color stories or appear to enjoy listening to them, a boy may think you're fair game. (Just look blank or bored, not shocked or prudish.) Don't dress so you look like a fast girl—the too-pointed bra, the too-tight sweater, the too-short skirt, the lack of a girdle when one is obviously needed—or wear too much make-up or over-use the perfume spray.

If you don't want a good-night kiss, don't lean dreamily against your front door. Don't linger in the boy's car. If you go to a party that—with lights dimmed and parents away—turns into a make-out session, you can't expect your date to sit primly on the sofa and talk books while everyone else is necking. (He has his manly reputation to think of.) Take him out to the brightly lit kitchen and fix him a sandwich. Or suggest going home.

You'll avoid trouble as well as talk if you make these rules part of your standard behavior:

- don't ask a boy to your house unless a parent or an adult is there, will be there all the time
- don't give an evening party unless you have a chaperon; you might have a group over in the afternoon without adults present—but not in the evening
- don't go to a boy's house unless one of his parents or some other chaperon is on hand
- don't go solo to a boy's room at college
- don't give or encourage too-intimate presents (see page 170-171)
- don't encourage smutty stories; do avoid sexy movies
- don't imbibe any alcoholic beverages
- and finally—a smart girl avoids situations in which the "no" problem will come up.

7. Good Sports Go Places

GOOD SPORT It's the classic description of someone who's nice to have around—the good companion; the good opponent; the good-natured, easy, noncomplaining guest. Without sportsmanship the game's a bore. A good sport—girl or boy—is meticulous about obeying the rules. In general they are these:

- play your best; no matter how far behind you are, keep trying
- be a generous opponent—slow to take advantage of a technicality for yourself, quick to give another the benefit of the doubt
- take defeat gracefully: praise the victor's game instead of excusing your own (never *"I've been sick!"*)
- accept victory modestly: find something valid to say about your opponent's game—an unreturnable backhand, not one three-putt green
- never display "righteous" impatience about the game's being delayed, someone's talking during the play; no glares, sharp words, requests to play the point over
- accept criticism for breaking a rule with a quick apology
- call any infringement of the rules on yourself—particularly one not noticed by your opponent
- never criticize your partner
- adapt easily—and without complaint—to the house rules of the game when you are a guest

The rules sum up the good sport who's always asked to play, to sail, to join in whatever plans are being made.

Some sports have very specialized rules and customs—some for safety, some for protecting the golf course or the ski slope, some to add to the challenge of the game, some to give the participants every chance to play at the top of their abilities.

If you have fallen in love with a particular sport, look for magazines and books devoted to the sport; libraries and clubs usually have them. You'll enjoy the discussions of all the refinements of the game and ways to improve your playing. General rules for a few of the major sports follow here:

BOWLING

- be punctual: lanes are crowded these days, and you owe it to teammates and opponents to be on time, ready to start
- be ready to bowl when it's your turn—and *not* off buying peanuts or chatting
- when another bowler takes his stance, be attentive and quiet; say nothing, do nothing that will distract him

- never cross in front of a bowler ready to make his approach
- if the bowler on the next lane is ready to bowl at the same time you are, the player on the right should be given precedence
- a bowler never, never delivers his ball simultaneously with the bowler on either his left or his right
- when it's your turn to bowl, take your time (but not everybody else's!)
- using someone else's ball—without permission—is a major bowling offense
- be kind to the equipment: lofting the ball—dropping it hard on the lane instead of rolling it—not only damages the bed of the lane but also is bad for your game
- bowling shoes—your own or rented ones—are required to save the lanes and also to prevent your slipping on the glossy wood

BILLIARDS

- whether you call it billiards, pocket billiards or pool, it's a quiet game and you try not to distract other players by high-volume talking, whistling, humming, tapping
- stand to the side of rather than directly across from another player; this way you don't distract him or cast a shadow on the table that might distort his line of play
- take care not to scuff or rip the table-topping with your cue
- cues go back in the racks when your game is over
- wear comfortable clothes, the kind you'd wear bowling—many billiard rooms are connected with bowling lanes today—but don't wear anything too low-cut in front because of all that bending over the table

SWIMMING

- cardinal rule: never swim alone
- test the depth of pool or pond before diving
- ducking people, tossing the unwary into the water, other forms of potentially dangerous horseplay are to be avoided
- never swim beyond your depth if you're a beginner—and never out of reach of help if you're a strong swimmer (*Anyone* can get a cramp, get caught in an undertow or meet up with a blood-hungry fish in the ocean.)
- running around the edge of a pool is universally frowned on; one slip can break a bone and ruin your swimming for the rest of the summer
- most public- and private-pool owners want girls to wear swim caps—not just to keep the water clean but to protect the drainage system from clogging
- shower before swimming in a pool; slosh off grass or sand clinging to your feet

- and if Rover follows you everywhere, lamb-fashion, keep him from joining you in a fast paddle across the pool (tie him up, if necessary) and from drinking the water in the pool (not aesthetic, and the chemicals probably will do him no good)

TENNIS, BADMINTON

- wear sneakers—a must to protect the court, give you more secure footing
- on a busy day, play doubles rather than singles and vacate the court after one or two sets (or whatever the court or club rule is)
- on weekends and holidays, check schedules: adults usually take over
- change courts—usually on odd games—so the sun doesn't beat continually in the same eyes
- make sure your opponent is ready before you serve (you can always ask "ready?"). If it's the first game and you want to take a few practice serves, ask first if you may. If you're used to serving FBI (first ball in), ask your opponent if that's his practice too.
- if the third ball is lost, keep the game going with the two you have instead of holding up the game while you scuffle through the pachysandra
- the server is responsible for keeping and announcing the score
- always replay a doubtful point—*especially* if you think you've won it!
- if you hit someone with a ball, run into your partner, flub a crucial point, say distinctly, "I'm *awfully* sorry" but don't moan on and on about it
- many courts require a white tennis outfit, white sneakers

SKATING

- skate in the same direction others are going
- in most rinks, the center is reserved for figure skating; straight skaters have the path around the rink and *never* cut through the middle
- if you are practicing figures, wait till you can get a patch of your own rather than crowding in on someone else's patch. While you have the patch, work at your figures rather than idling with the girl near you—it's maddening to those waiting to see ice going to waste—and, if you see others waiting, surrender your patch after half an hour
- needless to say, no fast skating, racing, acrobatics or figure skating on the straight-skating path; beginners find that ice both hard and scary
- tag, hockey, crack-the-whip, locomotive and other ice games should be played when the rink is close to empty except for the gamesters. (Many crowded rinks forbid these at any time, as a matter of safety.)
- for everyone's safety, don't create hazards by gouging holes or ruts in the ice or by dropping scraps of paper, bobby pins, ice-pop sticks and such; and food, *drinks* never go on the ice

- if you fall, get up as quickly as you can to avoid pile-ups. Beginners should remember to roll as they fall—rather than land in a lump. Watch the football boys to get the idea.
- abbreviated fancy costumes are banned in more rinks than Boston's

The safety rules and general kindnesses to others listed above are as important at roller-skating rinks as they are on ice.

SKIING

- beginners should stick to the practice hill or "bunny" slope; once that's mastered, they can move on to the novice slopes and trails. It's folly—and a tremendous hazard to other skiers—to attempt expert or even intermediate terrain until ready and able.
- don't ski at a speed you can't control—especially in an unexpected emergency, such as a sudden turn or a possible collision with someone ahead of you who's taken a spill
- lessons are a good idea in any sport—but losing one's heart to the instructor is obvious as a *cliché*
- if you fall while skiing—and you will—get up immediately and smooth the snow over your *sitzmark* (just what it sounds like: the mark you made in the snow when you sat). (Skiing is so continental for the vocabulary.) If your ski binding has opened or you have gotten your gear tangled in the spill, move to the side of the slope or to the outside of the curve on a trail while you repair the damage. If you stay smack in the middle of the hill, you're a prime target for oncoming skiers.
- if you pass fairly close to another skier on your way downhill, call "track right" if you're passing on the right, "track left" if you're going to overtake him on the left
- always ski with runaway straps: these are leather strips (you could use shoelaces) which attach to your boot at one end and your ski binding at the other. Purpose: to keep the ski from flying off downhill if you should fall and break out of your binding. A ski on the wing by itself can gather enough force and momentum to shatter another skier's anklebone; it is actually as dangerous as a hurled spear. Skiing without straps is wickedly careless. If you're ever that careless and you do lose a ski, yell *"ski"* the minute you see it take off; hopefully, other skiers will be able to get out of its way.
- never walk on a slope or trail without skis; you'll break up the surface when you fall. Just remember that Sir Walter Raleigh did not ski—nor will your date haul you out of a snowbank—nor do skiers expect this kind of aid.

- when you're in line waiting for a lift, keep your place as you would in any line; and never trample on other skiers' skis.
- how not to be asked again: swing about on chair lifts, play look-Ma-no-hands on rope tows and indulge in other nursery-age tricks

SAILING, BOATING

- regardless of sex or age, the skipper is the absolute boss when afloat and is not to be argued with
- be shipshape and tidy; there's no extra room on a boat
- never crush out a cigarette or strike a match on a hull or deck; sailors are unrelenting on the subject of scratches
- sit down when you're told to and on the side you're told to
- on a sailboat, remember to duck the boom. And don't grab a line or do anything to help without orders—especially if you're a novice. You might be responsible for a number of friends *and* lunch bobbling around in the water—and for a lot of wet sail—and for a very angry skipper.
- never go aboard a boat or go ashore without being invited to do so by the skipper
- never wear shoes with leather soles or heels on a boat; they wreck the deck. Always wear rubber soles—or go barefoot
- never toss anything overboard to windward—especially cigarettes. If throw you must, pitch it to the leeward, sheltered side so the wind won't boomerang it back into the boat or someone's face.

GOLF

- wear sneakers, flat rubber-soled shoes, or regular golf shoes—never heels that stab holes in costly, hard-to-maintain greens
- walk on the greens as little as possible; circle around on the apron to reach your ball. If your approach shot has indented the surface of the green, use a tee to raise the dented turf gently to its former level
- never rest a golf bag or a club on the surface of the green
- silence is the rule when someone else is making a shot—no talking, rattling of clubs
- keep well away from the person making a shot and out of his line of vision. The best spot on the tee is facing the driver at a distance of four or five feet. This is not always possible on the fairway, where the important rules are not to move during the shot and not to stand where you might get hit.
- if your shot veers in the direction of another person, shout "*fore!*" as a warning

- the ball farthest from the hole is hit first
- if you have to play out of a trap, you are not permitted to rest your club on the sand when addressing the ball, but you are expected to smooth out footprints and the scuff your club made when you hit the ball
- taking a divot (a slice of the turf) is usually a sign of a good fairway shot; not replacing the divot and patting it back to grow again is a couldn't-care-less attitude.
- help anyone you're playing with to find a lost ball; keep up the search till he calls it off. If you're the lost one, don't keep the search up too long; it holds up your match and may jam up the progress of other matches.
- keep your score as accurately as you can. If a penalty stroke is incurred, etiquette demands that you call it on yourself. If you're not sure how to score the penalty, ask someone you're playing with.
- no temper on the links—not with your fellow players, not with yourself, and especially not with your caddie
- congratulate your opponent on his good shots; say *nothing*—particularly nothing sympathetic!—about his dub shots. Try to be Olympian about your own game—not elated by the good play and the good luck, not depressed by the poor play and the bad luck. A tall order, but it makes you much nicer to play with
- a twosome should wait to be invited to go through—but a foursome or any slow match is usually obligated to invite a faster match to play through. (Exception: some clubs do not permit twosomes on weekends or junior members to go through a grownup match.)
- never, *never* help someone else straighten out his game unless he asks your advice. The tension you create (he smothers his resentment and tries not to show how vexed he is) only makes his game worse than it was. This is vividly important if you are playing with a boy and if your game is at its brilliant best.
- if you use a golf cart, be fanatic about driving it only within the allowed limits and in the posted directions
- some clubs forbid shorts for both males and females—so ask before going to a club that's new to you. (*Short* shorts are unacceptable at any golf club.)

RIDING

- if you open a gate to ride through, be sure to latch it securely behind you (Remember all those movies with tragedies that were triggered by the carelessly closed gate?)
- never gallop by other riders; canter, if you will, but give others a wide berth: if you skim by inexperienced riders, their horses may shy and bolt

- and never move your horse in close to people on foot: even the most placid horse has his nerves-on-edge days and needs to be protected from unnecessary patting and poking
- don't pet or feed someone else's horse without permission
- when you're on foot, walk *in front* of the horse; those who circle in back of a steed often feel the force of a rear hoof
- straight from the horse's mouth: these beautiful beasts can only chomp and cannot nibble daintily like cats and dogs. When you offer tidbits—sugar lump, carrot, apple—hold your hand out flat as a plate with fingers and thumb close together and the tidbit resting on your palm. The horse can mumble it up with his lips, and you will retain all your fingers

WOODSMANSHIP

- be alert to fire hazards. If you light a match, break it in two to make *extra sure* it's safely out before throwing it away. If you've had a campfire, save plenty of water to drown it—and then stamp on it and disperse the remains.
- after cooking a meal at a camp site, replace any supplies you've used with others of your own (not necessarily the identical kind). Leave fresh firewood, neatly piled. And—whether or not you found the place spick and span—leave the site in good order
- if hunting, don't shoot unless you're certain everyone who's near you knows you're planning to. *Do* wear red and *don't* wear white
- if you're hiking, make sure branches and twigs you've pushed back don't snap in the face of whoever's directly in back of you; let him pass or clutch the branches as you release them

GOOD GUESTS remember that

- your host or hostess—never you—signs you in at any club
- you wait for your host to tell you where to change your shoes, leave your coat, take your tennis equipment and so on. You don't use property and equipment belonging to members unless your host indicates it's all right.
- you ask your host's permission for any special service, including use of the club's telephone
- you don't pay cash for food or drinks (unless there's a machine) at a private club. You don't sign a member's name to a check unless he has asked you to, and then you add "by Your-Own-Name" below his name
- in many private clubs you do pay cash for caddies, golf and tennis balls, swim caps and other equipment
- you don't tip—except with a smile and a thank-you—in private clubs except for a few specialized services: a locker-room attendant who helps get your bath or shower ready, shines your shoes, hangs up your dress or suit (ask

your host quietly if you should and also what sum). An attendant who parks your car is sometimes tipped when you leave (check with your host), and a caddie is tipped in addition to his fee. But no tips for the services of waiters, waitresses, the boy who minds the snack bar, instructors.

- leave the locker room, bathhouse, sunroom in apple-pie order—towels in the hamper, tissues in the wastebasket, no litter of clothes, bobby pins, powder to make members wish guests were not allowed
- and no litter on the beach, around the pool, tennis courts, golf course; paper, wrappers, used score cards, and pop bottles all should go in the designated containers
- reserve daredevil tricks (around the pool, driving a golf cart or whatever) for your own club; the parents of your host or hostess are responsible for your safety as well as your good time
- some clubs limit the number of times a guest may use the club. Before accepting repeated invitations to the same club, better ask your host the club rules.
- be sure you make a point of going up and speaking briefly and politely to your host's parents or grandparents and to other older members who have entertained you at the club
- a first visit to a new club will be more comfortable for all if you ask your host what the rules about dress are—whether shorts are permitted on the golf course and in the dining room, whether a boy must wear a tie and jacket in the dining room, whether two-piece swim suits are frowned on

CARD GAMES

- each card game has rules of fair play of its own which you'll want to learn to be a good card sport. In general, however, when you play cards remember to ask the group if there are any special conventions they observe in playing
- keep talk and interruptions at a minimum
- learn how to shuffle cards without damaging them
- and be pleasant about it whether you win or lose

spectator sports—baseball, football, basketball, hockey, track and swimming meets, golf and tennis tournaments—have a few requirements too . . .

dress comfortably so you can cope with heat or cold, rain or shine, walking or standing and sitting. In order to be competent and content, it makes sense to wear low-heeled shoes; you might have to park the car a long uphill hike from the stadium. It makes sense to wear a dress with a jacket or a suit or a blouse and sweater; when the sun goes down, the bleachers can be chilly in midsummer. It makes sense to wear a skirt that you can walk in, that won't get wrinkled or baggy sitting through the game. It makes sense to be prepared with sunglasses, pocket overshoes, a waterproof covering for your hair.

dress appropriately You can always ask your hostess or your host's mother what you should wear—or your older sister or a friend who's been to the matches or weekended at the college. Or you might ask your beau (lots of men aren't much help on this). At some colleges, girls wear wool shorts, knee socks, heavy sweaters and a raincoat to football games. At others, they arrive handsomely dressed for the parties that follow the game. At golf and tennis tournaments, any plain little dress with a matching sweater or a shirtwaist dress with plain skimmer flats will define you as one who truly knows. But for most spectator sporting events, find out what's worn by people whose tastes you respect and who belong to that community. Very important, that last thought: what is impeccable in your town may be considered impossible in a town only a hundred miles east or west. And the funny thing is that your beau—who only acted bewildered when you asked him what to wear—will very likely be anything but bewitched if you arrive in an outfit that's "all wrong" in the eyes of the group you'll be with.

If—horror—you find that you've chosen the wrong clothes, try *not* to be brave and apologetic about it. Tell some of the other girls how much you like the wool shorts and what a good, smart thing shorts are to wear to the game and to the picnic on Sunday (you may make a friend, and she may lend you an extra pair for the Sunday picnic). Be sociable to all, enthusiastic about the event to your date, delighted with him and his friends—so busy being nice and pleasant to others that the choice-of-clothes problem will disappear from your mind. If you have real problems—shoes that are torture to wear crossing a muddy, uneven field and up a rocky road to the gym, clothes that are too warm or not warm enough, clothes that don't keep out the wind, the snow and the rain—bear them in silence, since there is probably nothing you can do to better matters.

8. When You Go To Proms And Dances

Call it a dance, a prom, a cotillion, a ball—it's still one of the greatest occasions for fun, dressing up, seeing old friends and making new ones. The music, the flowers, the gaiety all inspire an evening of carefree happiness.

What will you wear? If it's your first school prom, you may be puzzled, and your beau, equally confused, may ask you what he should wear. The dance committee may think it has everything solved by announcing that the dance is "formal." At many high-school proms, a plain dark suit with a white shirt and dark bow tie is the accepted formal dress for boys. At others, the term indicates black tie and a dinner jacket. Ask an upperclassman or a teacher to set you straight.

Remember any dance is your beau's party even if it's your school and you've invited him to go with you. Give him the tickets when he calls for you and let him make arrangements to get you to the dance. (Don't chauffeur him in your father's car.) The same code holds for suggestions about what to do after the dance. Going with the crowd to so-and-so may not be in his budget plans. Carry this as far as not agreeing to plans proposed by a couple you've double-dated with for the dance until you've talked to your date; give the boy a chance to take the lead.

About flowers Is it all right to hint for flowers? Yes, if it's for a prom where every girl will wear them *and* if you know the boy can afford it. Don't ever hint for an orchid; carnations could be as pretty with your dress. Give your date some idea of the color of your dress beforehand so he'll know what to get.

Who pins on your flowers? The boy may do it, if he can do so adroitly (this depends on him) and modestly (this depends on your dress). It's usually easier, though, for you to thank him and pin it on yourself—or ask your mother's assistance. Large safety pins, incidentally, attached invisibly from inside your dress, provide better anchorage for flowers than do corsage pins. And they're less apt to spear your date during the dance.

❦ *How are flowers worn?* See pages 168-169 for all you need to know about this.

To get everyone in the mood for the prom, it's nice to have a pre-prom party. This can be anything from a buffet supper to a round of colas and cookies for you, your date, and another couple. Allow plenty of time to get to the prom after your party; somehow, the mechanics of a dance—such as fixing your hair, making sure your dress is perfect, etc.—always take longer than you think and your own party will, almost inevitably, start later than you planned. Added thought: if you're giving a buffet supper, wear your prettiest at-home pants or an unspottable date dress for the KP and change to your evening dress after dessert.

When you arrive at the dance, you check your coat, smooth your hair again, and perhaps pin on your flowers. Check your gloves, unless you plan to wear them while dancing. Keep your evening bag with you. Then join your date as swiftly as you can.

Greet the chaperons and go down the receiving line, if there is one, saying polite hellos as you go along. If you stop to chat, you'll hold up the line—and the dancing. Your date might dance with one of the chaperons after the line has broken up, especially if one of them is your mother or a friend of his family's.

Compliment the dance committee, especially those concerned with decorations. ("The gym looks beautiful. I just wouldn't recognize those old exercise bars!")

When you walk across a dance floor, be *somebody*—a mythical princess, a real live movie queen, anyone who would walk as though she owned a chunk of the world.

Look after your date (he should return the favor). If he's a stranger to most of your friends, be extra careful to introduce him around in any group you might join. If supper is served, be sure to eat it with him.

- This doesn't mean you shouldn't dance with other boys (you should; it will make the dance more fun), but it does mean you shouldn't flirt outrageously with them, chatter, wave, or indulge in sign-language conversation over your date's shoulder while you dance; or leave the floor too long with another boy; or settle down for a heart-to-heart with the other girls.

Duty dances If you've been to a pre-prom party or are invited to one after the dance, your date should leave you temporarily (with another boy or with a group) while he dances with your hostess. If there is a guest of honor at a pre- or post-prom party (a girl from out of town, for instance), he should dance with her too. If you've come to the dance with another couple, a double-cut is a must.

The stag line is vanishing fast in most towns. In pioneer days, such as the '20's, there simply weren't enough women to go around. Stag lines keep a party moving—but young stags rarely come out of the corners and dance.

Cutting in You're dancing with Mike. Bill walks over, taps Mike on the shoulder and asks, "May I cut in?" You say or smile your thanks to Mike and start dancing with Bill. Mike thanks you and stalks other quarry.
The rules here:

- Mike may not cut back in on Bill unless he sees that the two of you have been with each other so long you might feel trapped.
- Neither Mike nor Bill may cut in repeatedly on the other. The feeling of being closely followed around a dance floor could give a boy claustrophobia. (Exception to this rule: double cut, where couples exchange partners for one or two dances.)
- It's rude to refuse to dance with a boy who cuts in.
- If a boy asks you to dance while you're *not* dancing and you don't want to dance with him, you can refuse pleasantly: say, "I'm waiting for my date" or "Not just now, thanks" or "Won't you sit and talk with us instead?"

Getting stuck The custom of cutting in has its obvious advantages, as well as one obvious disadvantage: you may get stuck too long with one partner. (If it's a boy you don't especially like, your face may show it: you'll look unhappy and no one will want to cut in. *Look* happy.) Some solutions to the getting-stuck problem:

- "Let's go talk to Tom and Diana." You join a group off the floor. After a little conversation, Tom may ask you to dance and your former partner will dance with Diana. A boy may never abandon a girl in the middle of the floor, but he may leave her with a group of friends, particularly in a group in which there is an extra boy.
- "I'd love some punch; wouldn't you?" Another way of joining a new group.
- "Let's sit this one out and just talk." A new boy might come along or a new group might join you. Besides, your partner may be charming to talk to.
- "Will you excuse me?" Once you're off the floor, you can escape to the ladies' room for repairs. But never use it as a wallflowers' refuge. And never, if you're not having fun at a dance, join a group of girls. Talk to *any* boy. Few boys will have the courage to penetrate the mob and find you.

- If the boy wants to change partners (or is worried that you're feeling trapped), he can always thank you for the dance and walk you to a group. If he quietly disappears, don't be crushed; he may have a string of duty dances on his conscience.

An aside to the prom committee: If there have been vague rumblings of discontent in your area about the fact that "nobody dances with anyone but his date," here are ways to get couples to mix and like it:

- stage a mixer dance or two
- start double-cutting among yourselves
- invite a stag line at reduced rates
- plan some entertainment midway through the evening: as couples crowd close to hear a singer, they mingle

Do you talk to a boy while dancing? Of course.

Do you thank a boy for a dance? It's archaic not to. You smile and say, "That was fun, wasn't it?" If he thanks you first, you thank him in return.

What about the boy who can't dance well? Tell him he's great anyway. Some of the great dancers are nervous about dancing with new girls and seem hopeless. Some of the poor ones just need to be put at ease to dance fairly well.

Between dances you can stand and talk to your partner or walk off the floor with him. If he offers his arm, take it.

You can't dance a certain number? Admit you can't Charleston and ask if he'd rather sit this one out. If he wants to teach you, be an enthusiastic pupil —even if you're a clumsy one.

Gloves can be worn while dancing, and as a matter of fact, it's correct to wear gloves in public for anything except eating or serving refreshments (yes, you can even shake hands with gloves on—individually or en masse, in a reception line).

Evening bags can be left at the table while you are dancing if you have an assigned place to sit. Otherwise, if you're moving around, carry your bag with you. If it's a small clutch bag, hold it unobtrusively in your left hand while dancing so that it doesn't interfere with the hand your partner holds. If the bag has a handle, dangle it from your right wrist while you dance (it would bang against your partner's back if you held it with your left hand).

Some dance pests:

- the hummers and the ones who repeat "ONE-two-three, ONE-two-three" over and over to themselves
- the exhibitionists who dance well (and know it) and want to clear the floor (so everyone else will know it, too)
- the bulldozers who don't dance well but who attempt to clear the floor anyway. Their weapons are sharp elbows, outstretched arms. When backing up, they have no idea where they're going
- the lovers who act as if a dance floor were as private as a parked car in the moonlight
- the great stone faces, who take dancing so seriously they look as if they couldn't possibly be having any fun

Cheek-to-cheek dancing You can always say, "I can't follow you when we're dancing this close. And you're such a good dancer."

When you leave the dance, say good night to the chaperons.

After the ball is over, what? Nobody wants to go right home from a dance! Suggestions: a snack at someone's house. Pooled fun at the home of a friend with parents who tolerate the din is often more enjoyable and less expensive than going out on the town with your date alone.

9. 16 Point Plan For Making Good On College And Prep School Weekends

There are two sure signs you've been a success at a school or college weekend. First, you had a marvelous time: this puts you halfway up the ladder. Second, you're asked again: you may have to wait for this, but it's the definitive mark of success.

WANT TO HAVE A GOOD TIME?

1. When you accept, ask your beau where you will stay.

   Your parents might want to get in touch with you. If you will be billeted in a club or a fraternity house, or a dorm which has been cleared for the boys' dates, you won't need to pay for your room. Other arrangements may mean you'll need extra money to pay for your room; the answer to who pays varies in different parts of the country, so if you're not sure, ask the boy (on the day you leave) if you may pay for the room.

2. Ask what festivities have been planned; ask if he'll let you know any new plans.

   You'll have a better idea of what clothes to take if you know everyone in his house is going sailing, swimming, skiing or whatever on Sunday. You won't need a dance dress if the annual college show is held Saturday or if poetry, folk songs and coffee are the weekend special.

3. Buy a round-trip ticket or arrange for a ride home before you get to the campus.

   Transportation is your problem, your expense.

4. Talk to a girl who's weekended at the school recently—not your mother, not your aunt. Times change.

   Ask her what to wear, what the climate is like, how many parties are likely. Get her opinion of what the boys are like, what places to avoid, the best method of getting there and back—bus, car, train, plane.

5. Ask the same girl what the room-visiting rules are.

   At some colleges, parties after the game are standard but there is a curfew hour at which all rooms must be clear of girls. At others, room-visiting is forbidden. A sensible habit is not to visit unless another girl or couple is with you.

6. List special things you might need before you pack; the nearest drugstore may be miles away from where you're staying.

   Anti-allergy pills, oversize curlers, toothbrush and other staples? Repair tools, such as cellophane tape, safety pins, small sewing kit, travel iron, antiseptic cream and Band-Aids? Sunglasses, knee socks and scarf for the cold, rain hood, packable raincoat and rubbers for the rain, shoes for comfort? See about clothes for sports on pages 164 to 166.

7. Eat whatever you can, wherever you can during the weekend.

   After-game parties go on forever, so don't turn down even soggy potato chips and wilted carrot sticks. You'll be less than your best without ballast and with a hunger headache.

8. You don't need to drink to prove you're college material.

   Trying it, and not knowing how to handle it, could be disastrous and mark the end of your weekending at this school. Ask for a long ginger ale with a twist of lemon peel. Sip it slowly if you want to curb the next sport who's eager to fix you a drink. If some funny boy spikes your ginger ale, say nothing but manage quietly to leave it somewhere.

WANT TO BE ASKED AGAIN?

9. Don't be expensive.

   He probably has less money at school than he does at home. Asking for extras—food, flowers, souvenirs of the game, packs of cigarettes, mementos from the school store—can spoil the weekend for your date, even turn him into one of those canny college bachelors who boasts of never asking a girl for a weekend.

10. Don't get on the boy's nerves.

    He can't dance attendance on you every minute, even if it is the big weekend. He may still have an assignment to complete, tennis to practice, someone to interview for the paper. Go with him when he asks you, but let him go peacefully if he doesn't—and be glad to see him when he comes back. When you're together, let there be silence occasionally.

11. Be on his team.

    Like his friends; don't comment on the impossible ones (or his friends' impossible girls). For this weekend, his school is yours. No matter if your grandfather founded the rival school and your father is president of it, when you're with Joe at Old Ivy, you are for Old Ivy. Cheer when Siwash makes a point and you're risking both your life and your social future.

12. Enjoy the romantic lines his friends and enemies try to spellbind you with, but don't take them seriously.

    Don't let your date suspect you think there's anyone nicer than he around. It will humiliate him if you let yourself be taken over by some other man.

13. It's your move to end the evening's gaieties.

    If he says, "But there's a dawn breakfast at the club; you can't turn in now and miss it," you can always change your mind. But he may think you want to sit up all night listening to that guitar and hesitate to spoil your fun.

14. Help him keep love-making in bounds.

    Parking out in the far country, snuggling by the lake, necking with the lights turned low are part of young love. But it can be spoiled for you both if affection is replaced by straight sex. You have the greater control, so keep it . . . by suggesting sweetly that you'd love to walk around the campus in the moonlight with him before you turn in . . . or saying, "Darling, it's been such a great day. We both should be getting back before it's tomorrow." And there is always the magnificently acceptable distraction of lovely, lovely food.

15. Act as if you're having fun.

    Even if your date is only slightly better than impossible as a weekend host, let everyone think you're enjoying the weekend and are delighted to be there. It's kinder. There is the unexpected bonus, too: some nicer boy that you meet there may ask you to the next house party because you seem to be a great girl.

16. Thank the boy when you leave.

    Not just "thank you," but an enthusiastic recounting of how wonderful some of the weekend's highlights were. When you get home, tell him again—not in a long letter, just promptly and briefly.

10. When You Eat Or Entertain In Restaurants

a date for dinner What a wonderful way to spend the evening with someone you like—talking, laughing, perhaps dancing or listening to music . . . and—oh, yes—eating a very good dinner as well. You'll enjoy the evening even more if you aren't gnawed by constant little worries: "Which fork is which?" "What should I order?" "How can I find the ladies' room?" "What should I do when he pays the check?"

entering a restaurant When you walk in with your beau, let him open and hold the door for you. Unless a coat rack is provided, he will check his coat and probably ask if you would like to check yours. Don't, unless it's a soaking-wet raincoat. You wear your coat to the table, throw it back off your shoulders and sit on it, as you would at the theater. (The reason for this difference between the sexes: many restaurants, fearful of what could happen to fur coats crushed in a checkroom, refuse to handle any feminine coats—right down to the most durable tweed. A second reason: you spare your date the tiny, but additional, expense of having to redeem your coat when he redeems his.) You may check bulky packages, an umbrella, overshoes and anything else which might obstruct service at your table. If you're wearing a hat, leave it on—unless it's a rain hat, of course. Gloves? Wear them to the table, then take them off as soon as you sit down, lay them on your lap or put them in your bag. Never, never, never wear gloves at a table. That's a mannerism, not manners.

If a waiter or headwaiter leads you to your table, you follow him and your date follows you. The waiter pulls out your chair and hands you, then your date, a menu. If it's a more do-it-yourself sort of restaurant, your date leads you to the table, pulls out your chair and hands you a menu. The point to remember is that a man should always precede you to the table and to the door when you leave, to cut a path through the surging crowd, so to speak. However, if your date steps aside to let *you* precede *him,* don't be indecisive. Just go on ahead.

seating As a girl you get the choicest seat at the table, the one with the best view or farthest from the door. If the restaurant is one with banquettes (long, upholstered seats) running along the wall, the waiter pulls out the table, you slide into the banquette seat and your date sits in a chair on the opposite side of the table. Or you might be seated side by side on the banquette. Whatever the case, *you* are seated first. Don't try to clamber into the seat by yourself; hesitate long enough to give the waiter, or your date, the opportunity to help you. If you are dining with another couple, you are usually seated girl, boy, girl, boy, on the four sides of a table. Or, in a restaurant with banquettes, the girls are seated on the banquette, the boys on the chairs. In a booth, girls take the wall side.

Be considerate about your belongings; if you scatter them on chairs at the next table, you'll only have to move them when someone comes to sit there. Keep your handbag, if small, on your lap; if big, on the floor near your feet. You might leave a tiny evening purse and very clean gloves on your table, but if the purse is more than a hand-size clutch and the gloves have seen some wear, leave them in your lap.

Most boys will call for you at home, but you might be meeting after business hours in a downtown area where you both work or you might live in vastly separated suburbs, so that it is more convenient to meet in a central location. If you arrive first, ask the waiter to seat you. If you arrive after your date, ask the waiter to find him if you cannot see him from the door. (Suggestion: arrive a minute or two after you think he will. Not ten minutes—that's too long.)

ordering The usual large restaurant menu, with dozens of choices of food and drink, is more confusing than helpful. The easiest procedure is, if you are having dinner, to choose a main course; note its price (if you order the most expensive dish on the menu, you may weaken your date's wallet; with the least expensive, you'll surely weaken his pride) and relay the order to your date. Say, "George, I'd love pork chops." Some men are especially complimented if you say, "George, won't you choose for me?" You don't give the order to the waiter; whenever a boy and girl or man and woman are in a restaurant together, the male is always the one to talk with the waiter. One exception (you'll find a few others later in this chapter): you may ask a waiter to explain an unfamiliar dish ("Waiter, could you tell me what's in the Tomato Surprise?"). If, after he explains it, you think you would like the dish, you thank him, then say, *to George,* "That sounds good. I'd like it." Or, if you don't wish it, "I think I'd rather have the crab-meat salad."

It's part of the ritual of ordering for the waiter to ask what beverage you would like to drink, whether you wish an appetizer or soup, vegetables, salad, dessert. You relay these choices to George also.

There are two ways of ordering: *à la carte,* in which each item—meat, vegetable, beverage, etc.—is separately priced, and *table d'hôte,* in which a whole meal is offered at one inclusive price. A whole dinner of à la carte items often adds up to more than a table d'hôte dinner, so it is usually wiser, if you're hungry, to order the latter. But let your date suggest this. Don't blithely ask him for everything from soup to sundae; he may be planning to feed you no more than a sandwich and coffee. If in doubt about what to order, you can always ask your date what he plans to have. If he says a club sandwich, that gives you less latitude than if he says a steak. The waiter may offer suggestions, which you take or refuse. There's no reason for you to eat the specialty of the house if you don't happen to like it. Also no reason why you should eat more than you wish. If your date wants soup, salad and dessert as well as an entree, and you don't, you can offer to sit out those courses: "I really don't want any, thanks—but *you* go ahead." The thing not to do is bury your head in the menu and agonize over a choice while George and the waiter stare patiently off in space. Pick something (perhaps a dish you've had before and know you will like) and stick with it. You can change your mind if, for instance, you demurred on George's first offer of an appetizer because you doubted if he'd have one himself. If he does choose one, and you'd like to join him, you can say, "I believe I will have soup after all. Onion for me, please." But never make a waiter rewrite your entire order.

serving You should be served before your date. If your waiter appears with two separate dishes and has forgotten who ordered which, he will ask, "Who ordered the onion soup?" You can nod your head or tap your place once with your forefinger and say, "Here, please," and he will put the proper dish before you. Some restaurants, particularly those specializing in that marvelous Scandinavian mixture of dishes called smorgasbord, are set up like buffets. In these, you and your date find your table together, then go to the buffet. You serve yourself first; he follows. If you are having milk or coffee later, your date will get it. Ladies, old or young, don't get their own beverages when there is a man about to do it for them.

WHAT TO DO WHEN

- *Which fork to use?* There is such a bewildering amount of silverware on restaurant tables that one often does wonder which fork to use. Choose the pieces farthest to the left or right of your plate first, unless a dish is brought to you with a special implement. Examples: a shrimp cocktail, which comes with a cocktail fork, and snails, which come with both a cocktail fork and a little gadget that looks like an eyelash curler. (You use the curler to hold the snail and the fork to scoop out the meat. Fun.)

  Whichever piece you pick up, don't wipe it on your napkin. If it looks a bit dubious, ask George to give you another or just hand it silently to the waiter. He'll understand and get a substitute.
- *If you drop something*—a fork or a roll, for instance—don't dive under the table to retrieve it. If the waiter's seen your plight, he'll offer another piece of bread or silver. Or ask your date to mention it to the waiter.

- *If a friend stops by,* you may chat briefly. George should rise for any girl, you for a woman the age of your mother. Otherwise remain seated. Introductions? Maybe. Should a couple whom you know, but George doesn't, appear at the table, you do make quick introductions: "Helen Barnes, Bill MacDonald, this is George Dooley." But don't attempt to introduce your party of six to another of similar size; they'll never remember all the names anyway. If you enter a restaurant with a boy, you may stop to say hello to friends—but then move on. Never clog a restaurant aisle and never run back and forth in a restaurant visiting or "table-hopping."
- *If you smoke,* let George ask for an ash tray. Don't use the floor or a saucer.
- *If you don't like something,* be a lady about it. You can ask George to have your table changed if you're in a bad draft or to have something taken back to the kitchen if it's inedible. (You don't ask yourself, as you know by now.) But you—and George—should never complain, without serious reason, about the food, seating, or service. The customer who tries to look important by doing this impresses no one. If the waiter is surly and the service generally impossible, George should ask the waiter to send the headwaiter to your table. He or the captain will then appear solicitously at your table and attempt to right matters. Neither you nor George should rise to seek him out, however.
- *Shall we dance?* If you leave the table to dance, put your gloves and purse on your chair. Don't leave after two bites of steak, though. The waiter may think you have finished that course and clear the table. Better to dance only between courses!
- *Everything's so strange* That's part of the fun of dining out—experimenting with new foods, attempting to manipulate chopsticks or sipping tea from little hot porcelain bowls. Relax—much of it is probably new to George and to eighty per cent of the other customers in the restaurant! No one's watching *you.*
- *Having fun?* Fine—but keep the sound of it confined to your own table.
- *Toothpicks* In a moderately priced restaurant, they may be on the table or by the cash register. If you must use them, do so in utter privacy.
- *Make-up* At table you may touch up your lipstick or powder the tip of your nose, but don't comb your hair or give yourself a searching once-over in your compact mirror. The place for major reconstruction is the ladies' room.
- *Where IS the ladies' room?* Don't ask your date. Obviously, he's unfamiliar with it. There are two ways to find the ladies' room:

  1. Say to George, "Excuse me," then rise from the table and ask the nearest waiter; you won't embarrass him. Incidentally, you needn't manufacture

a telephone call as an excuse to leave George at the table. A simple "Will you excuse me for a minute, George?" without explanation is sufficient—and unembarrassing.

2. On entering the restaurant, look for the ladies'-room sign. If you find it and fix it in your memory, you won't have to ask *anyone*.

- *In the ladies' room* It's nice to leave a tip if there's a saucer waiting expectantly, but the washroom attendant will probably be content with a smile and a thank-you from a young girl. The amount ranges from a dime in a thruway restaurant or a rail-terminal women's room to a quarter in a more elegant restaurant or a hotel.
- *What to call the waiter* "Waiter." The headwaiter is "headwaiter" or "captain," the waitress "waitress" or "miss," and so on. None of them is "sir" or "ahem" or "psst."

time to go If your date has further plans for the evening, he will probably suggest them: "Let's go to a movie" or whatever. If not, and you've lingered too long over coffee, you should suggest leaving. (You sometimes suggest going home from a date, don't you?) If it's still early, you can offer the thought of a walk or another cup of coffee at your house—if your parents are in and expecting you. It's thoughtless to finish dinner with a what-do-we-do-now expression on your face, thus putting a boy in the position of having to suggest a movie or jazz-and-coffee when he obviously hasn't budgeted it into the evening. It's even more thoughtless to suggest further expensive entertainment.

the check George asks the waiter for "the check, please," and it arrives, usually face down, often on a little saucer or silver tray. (If on a saucer or tray, he puts the money to pay it on the saucer or tray and places the check, again face down, on top of the money.) Your date could and should examine the check to make sure it is correct and to figure the tip (usually fifteen per cent, with some exceptions; see tipping guide, page 156) in his head. What he or anyone else should not do is pull out paper and pencil and scratch away, turning a simple piece of arithmetic into a major exercise in calculus. Some unreliable restaurants do attempt to add to the total of the check deliberately. But very few. If there is a mistake, the waiter and/or headwaiter should be quietly called to the table and the mistake corrected. This is every customer's right.

To avoid sitting nervously while your date deals with the check, you could excuse yourself and head for the ladies' room. This will give George an opportunity to visit the men's room, which he may well wish to do himself.

If your check is to be paid to a cashier, you leave the table with your date, then stand aside while he pays, just as you would do while he paid for tickets at a movie box office.

leaving the restaurant When you wish to leave, your date should rise, walk around to your chair and pull it out for you—or signal the waiter to pull out the table if you are seated together on a banquette with the table in front of you, high-chair-fashion. Make sure you have your belongings with you before you leave.

in a restaurant with another girl—or several—there are a few pointers to observe:

- If you are meeting friends, wait for them near the door, unless the restaurant is so empty that the waiter or headwaiter offers to seat you. In a coffee shop you might walk through to see if your friends have arrived and are seated, but in the sort of restaurant which has a real or imaginary velvet rope barring the door you should ask the waiter to do your searching for you: "I'm meeting a redheaded girl about my age. Is she here, please?" It's unbecoming to cruise through a restaurant alone.
- Dividing a check with other girls can be a nightmare. When you are going Dutch with friends, ask for separate checks. It's no more trouble for the waiter, and you're spared a session of "You had the sundae with nuts but I had the whipped cream and another cup of coffee so I probably owe more than you . . ." You could split a check evenly, but that's not quite fair if you each had things of varying cost.
- If there is a guest of honor (three friends are taking a fourth out for a birthday lunch), she sits in the choicest seat at the table and should be spared as much of the check negotiations as possible. It takes the edge off a party to hear its cost caroled down a table: "Everyone but Marge owes $2.32."

  Do the dividing quietly or have one girl pay the bill, then tip, and settle with the others later.
- If you are in a restaurant with an older woman, let her have the best seat.

entertaining at a restaurant You might have a restaurant party as a special graduation treat. Arrive at the restaurant a little ahead of the hour for which you have invited your guests. Greet them at the door if there is some sort of lobby where a group will not obstruct traffic, or ask to be seated at your table and tell the waiter or headwaiter you are expecting friends so he will know where to direct them. You suggest ordering. If the group is small, you might transmit individual orders to the waiter, but if it is large, let each girl order for herself. You suggest leaving when the meal is finished. And in between you make sure your guests are happy, comfortable, fed—as you would at home.

You should call the restaurant beforehand to reserve a table. (It's hard to seat a party of six or eight instantaneously.)

The ordering and paying procedure can be handled two ways:

- Order the same lunch or dinner for everyone and pay the bill and tip in advance.
- Let each order her own meal (more fun). You could give your friends a clue as to what to order by stating your own wishes first. Ask, when ordering, to have the check given to you. Then tell your friends, when the party is over, that you will meet them outside the restaurant. Linger behind and settle bill and tip in private.

counter manners Crowded luncheonettes and coffee shops, which make their profit on a quick turnover of customers, are ill suited to dawdling. When such a restaurant is filled, particularly at lunch hour in a business district, you shouldn't inconvenience other customers by forcing them to wait unduly while you sip your coffee at leisure or finish a chapter in the book you brought along. Nor should you, when you're on the waiting end, hover impatiently over a diner's shoulder, barely waiting until she finishes the last mouthful of pie to pounce on her chair.

HOW TO TRANSLATE RESTAURANT AND BANQUET MENUS

The surest way is to ask the waiter, since chefs often like to create names for even the simplest dishes. However, you may feel more at home if you are acquainted with the accepted French terminology used in the menus in first-class hotels and restaurants.

If you see . . .	*It means . . .*
bisque	soup with shellfish base
consommé or bouillon	clear soup
crème	cream
potage	a soup, usually hearty
purée	strained or mashed
oeufs	eggs
entrée	a main dish
entremets	additional courses, often dessert
salade	salad
coquilles St. Jacques	scallops
escargots	snails
huîtres	oysters

If you see . . .	*It means . . .*
langouste or homard	lobster
maquereau	mackerel
moules	mussels
poisson	fish
saumon	salmon
truite	trout
agneau	lamb
boeuf	beef
cervelle	brains
foie	liver
jambon	ham
langue	tongue
mouton	mutton
porc	pork
queue de boeuf	oxtail
quiche Lorraine	cheese custard pie
ris de veau	sweetbreads
rognons	kidneys
saucisson	sausage
veau	veal
canard, caneton	duckling
coq au vin	chicken in wine sauce
dindon, dindonneau	turkey
faisan	pheasant
oie, oison	goose
poulet, poularde	chicken
volaille	poultry
à la king	served in a cream sauce
à la mode	with beef, means marinated and braised
à la mode	as dessert, means with ice cream
aspic, gelée	jellied
au gratin	browned with cheese or bread crumbs
au jus	with natural gravy
émincé, hachis	finely chopped; mincemeat; hash
fines herbes	flavored with herbs
jardinière	with diced vegetables
julienne	cut into strips
lyonnaise	with onions
noisette	small nutlike piece
pâté	a spread or paste; sometimes, a pie
chaud	hot
farci	stuffed
flambé	flaming
froid	cold

If you see . . .	*It means . . .*
glacé	iced
en brochette	broiled on a skewer
grillé	broiled
rôti	roasted
sauté or meunière	cooked quickly in butter
bifteck	steak
côtelettes	cutlets
côtes	chops or ribs
daube or ragoût	stew
gigot	leg, as of lamb or of mutton
pané	breaded
artichaut	artichoke
asperges	asparagus
aubergine	eggplant
champignons	mushrooms
chou	cabbage
choucroute	sauerkraut
choufleur	cauliflower
choux de Bruxelles	Brussels sprouts
concombre	cucumber
épinards	spinach
haricots verts	string beans
laitue	lettuce
navets	turnips
oignons	onions
pois	peas
salade vert	green salad
tomates	tomatoes
nouilles	noodles
pommes de terre	potatoes
riz	rice
ananas	pineapple
fraises	strawberries
pomme	apple
beignets	fritters
bombe	molded frozen dessert
crème anglaise	custard
crêpes	pancakes
flan	custard pie
fromage	cheese
gâteau	cake
glace	water ice or ice cream

If you see . . .	*It means . . .*
mousse	light dish of egg whites, whipped cream
pâtisserie	pastry
pots de crème	custards
sorbet	sherbet
tarte	pie
café au lait	coffee with hot milk
café noir	black coffee
filtre or espresso	French or Italian coffee

If you are in an Italian restaurant

and you see . . .	*it means . . .*
antipasto or antipasti	a plate of mixed appetizers—salami, tomatoes, black olives, anchovies, pimientos, etc.
zuppa	soup
minestrone	a thick, hearty vegetable soup with a meat base
cannelloni	noodles or pancakes, filled; with sauce
fettucine	a noodle dish featuring Parmesan cheese and butter
gnocchi	dumplings, often made from potato
lasagne	layers of pasta * and cheese baked in a meat-and-tomato sauce
linguine	skinny noodles
manicotti	pasta * stuffed with chicken, meat or cheese and served with sauce
pane	bread
pizza	a circle of crusty bread dough topped with chopped sausages and/or anchovies, etc.
ravioli	little pillows of pasta * stuffed with meat, cheese or spinach, and served with tomato sauce. (You sprinkle grated cheese on top.)
risotto	rice
spaghetti	known to us all, but you may be surprised to have it with a sauce of minced clams, shrimp, mushrooms, the familiar meat and tomatoes or just plain butter
frittata	omelet
gamberi	shrimp
pollo alla cacciatora	chicken browned in oil, simmered in a wine-and-tomato sauce
polpette	meat balls
saltim bocca	a dish with veal and ham

* Pasta refers to all or any noodles, macaroni, spaghetti, linguine, orzo.

If you are in an Italian restaurant

and you see . . .	*it means . . .*
scaloppine di vitello	veal cutlet pounded very thin, served many ways. *Limone,* with lemon sauce. *Marsala,* with wine sauce. *Parmigiano* or *Parmesan,* with cheese sauce.
spumoni	a rich ice cream with fruits and nuts; or tricolored ice cream of strawberry, chocolate and vanilla
tortoni (or biscuit tortoni)	rich vanilla ice cream with macaroon crumbs on top; comes in a little paper cup
zabaglione	a foamy custard, wine-flavored
espresso	strong, black coffee

If you are in a Japanese restaurant

and you see . . .	*it means . . .*
arare	crispy, salty rice crackers for dessert
chawan-mushi	"steam in a teacup," an egg and sea-food custard
gohan	steamed rice
lobster gusokuni	chopped whole lobster served in its shell with a special sauce
misoshiru	bean paste soup
nasu no shigiyake	eggplant, delicately fried, served with sauce
nori-aye	dried seaweed with special soy sauce
o-cha	green tea
o-shinko	pickled vegetables
o-shitashi	side dish of cooked green vegetables seasoned with flakes of dried bonito (like tuna)
sakanano teri-yaki	fish barbecued with soy sauce
sashimi	thin strips of raw fish served with soy sauce
shiwoyaki	pork, fish or chicken broiled with salt, served with lemon-soy sauce
sukiyaki	beef, pork or chicken sautéed with vegetables right at your table
sunomono	salad of vegetables and sea food
tatsuta-age	sliced beef, pork or chicken, with soy sauce, deep-fried
tempura	various sea foods and fresh vegetables deep-fried in vegetable oil
teri-yaki	strips of beef, pork or chicken marinated with soy sauce and broiled
tori-no-sashimi	thin-sliced raw breast of chicken, dipped for seconds in hot water to bring out the flavor; served with a spicy sauce

and you see . . .	*it means . . .*
yaki-nori	the paper-thin dried seaweed, a "must" for a Japanese dinner
yakko-dofu	cold bean cake served with soy sauce and assorted spices
yu-dofu	bean cake boiled in seaweed soup served as above

If you are in a Spanish or Mexican restaurant

and you see . . .	*it means . . .*
arroz con pollo	chicken and rice in sauce
biscochitos	little cakes or cookies
buñuelos or sopaipillas	sweet fritters
chile con carne	chopped meat in red chile sauce
con queso	with cheese
enchiladas	dish involving tortillas, cheese, sausage in a hot tomato sauce
frijoles refritos	refried beans
garbanzos	chick peas
gazpacho	cold soup containing tomatoes, cucumbers, green pepper, onion, seasonings and toast
guacamole	cold salad of mashed avocados, lemon juice, spices, ripe tomatoes, chile pepper and finely diced red onions
seviche	raw sea food "cooked" in lemon juice
tamales	corn husk spread with corn meal, wrapped around a savory meat filling
tortilla	corn meal pancake
tostadas	tortilla fried in oil until very crisp

If you are in a Chinese restaurant

and you see . . .	*it means . . .*
bird's nest soup	chicken and ham soup into which a noodle and egglike mixture has been stirred
chop suey	light stew of Chinese vegetables with chicken, pork, fish, beef or veal, served with boiled rice
chow mein	chicken or pork in thick sauce with bean sprouts and mushrooms, usually served with fried noodles
egg drop soup	clear meat soup into which beaten eggs are dropped
egg foo yong	basically an omelet, with bean sprouts, scallions, meat or fish and soy sauce

If you are in a Chinese restaurant

and you see . . .	*it means . . .*
egg rolls	crisp little pancakes, filled with chicken, shrimp or pork
fortune cookies	almond-flavored cookies folded over to contain a printed prediction
fried rice	rice boiled, then fried with cut-up pork, chicken, shrimp or lobster, bean sprouts and eggs
lobster Cantonese	it's sautéed with gingerroot, soy sauce and other exotic trifles
moo goo guy pan	main dish of chicken, mushrooms and vegetables
plum sauce	an almost jamlike sauce served with fried meats. At the same time a mustard-flavored sauce is served. You ladle a bit of each on your plate, dip pieces of meat first into one, then into the other.
sweet and pungent pork	pork with garlic, soy sauce, vinegar, pineapple
wonton	little pillows of dough stuffed with meat or fish and floated in soup: close kin to Italian ravioli and Jewish kreplach, but they have a different flavor

11. You're A Spectator: ATTENDING THEATRES, MOVIES, MUSEUMS AND SPORTS EVENTS

Performers need a good audience to inspire them to do their best. This is as true of sports as it is of theater and concert-hall performances. A baseball player needs the excited support of the fans to spur him on to break the home-run record. The school team needs the cheers of the crowd to get that last touchdown and victory. An actor can make his role bigger than life-size if the audience is with him. An artist can interpret a piano concerto so it glitters with excitement. Dancers can make ballet a shimmering experience instead of just a display of technical skill. For better or for worse, you and the performers are one for a few hours.

The point of entertainment is to enjoy the performance. Manners like these will make you a good member of the audience:

A boy asks you to a movie or show you've seen, and it's one you don't want to see again. Do you go anyway? No. You'll be poor audience material, restless and bored, and distress your date. He wants the evening to be a success, so say something like "I'd love to go with you, Bob, but I really ought to tell you I've seen that one. It just isn't a show you'd go to twice." If he doesn't suggest another show or idea for the evening, you can mention a movie you'd like to see or records at your house . . . but nothing that would cost more than the show.

A boy asks you to a movie you don't care to see or one your parents don't want you to see. Do you tell him the truth? Be frank and say, "I'd rather not see that movie. How about . . .?" If he asks why you're against the movie, tell him briefly: "I don't like horror pictures any more" or "I read the review and I don't think I'd enjoy that kind of movie" or "I'm sorry; my parents asked me not to see it." Don't launch into a crusade about it, though.

Be ready when your date calls, so you'll be on time for the performance. Most men like to see the teams warm up, like the excitement that precedes a game or a show. It's a courtesy to the performers and to the other members of the audience when you arrive in time to be seated and have your coat and bag disposed of before the event begins. If you're late at the theater, wait for seating until the end of the first scene; at a musical, wait until the burst of applause following a number. At the ballet or opera, the usher won't seat you during the first number or act unless you're sitting in a box. At a concert you will not be seated until the first number is concluded.

Ticket pointers intended to spare the boy embarrassment If there's a long line at the movies, you may stand with your date until he gets to the ticket window; then walk ahead until he joins you and you head for the ticket collector. You'd do the same at the box office for other theatrical and sports events. If you have the tickets to a play, give the boy the tickets when he calls for you. If you are going Dutch, find out the cost of the ticket and give him the money when he calls for you: "Here's my ticket money, Jim. I think balcony seats will be good, don't you?"

When buying tickets at the box office, everyone is entitled to check the theater seating chart hung next to the box-office window in order to be sure the seats will be satisfactory. Even if there's a crowd waiting to buy tickets or if you encounter one of those grumpy ticket-sellers, stand your ground; it is permissible to look at the location of the seats on the chart before you pay for them. Just say, "May I see where these are on the chart, please?" It is, however, a mark of courtesy to the others in line and may prevent many a scowl and grumble if the ticket-buyer familiarizes himself with the chart and the price range before going up to the ticket window.

When you head for your seats in the theater, know the right system
When there is no usher, your date goes first and you follow. When he comes to two seats, he may ask you if they will do. If you like to sit up closer, tell him you'd love to sit farther down if he thinks there are seats to be had. When there is an usher, the boy gives him the ticket stubs, you follow the usher and your date comes last. The usher will return the stubs to him and give him the programs.

Usher or no usher, you enter the row first. The boy helps you shrug off your coat, hands you a program. Going up the aisle when you leave, the girl goes first.

On double dates, one boy usually sits on the inner side of the block of seats, the other boy on the outer, with the girls seated between. This comes from a wonderfully unreasonable tradition that a lady should not be seated next to a stranger—

When you're with an older couple—say, a kindly aunt and uncle—the down-the-aisle procedure is this: aunt, you, date, uncle, since uncle is the host. (The host or hostess is always last down the aisle so he can retrieve the ticket stubs as well as let his guests go first.)

What about hats and headgear? If you wear a hat choose one that's small so that it won't block the view of those behind or endanger the sight of the person beside you. A sweep of feather or stiffened velvet can be enchanting across a table, but it is not so good in a crowded stadium or theater. Even those veiling cages can harass the people in back. If there's any question in your mind, take it off or at least ask the person in back of you if your hat will disturb him. If an apprehensive person asks you first, answer, "Oh, yes, of course," and quickly take the hat off—without bridling.

A boy tucks his hat and coat under the seat or else holds the coat neatly folded on his lap or checks it.

What about your coat?
Your escort should help you off and on with it. A young person always helps an elder, regardless of sex; a lady assists another lady in theaters and movies, and a gentleman always helps the lady or ladies he's with to shed wraps or coats. These rules apply for boots, overshoes, rubbers, when it's obviously easier to get them off gracefully with assistance.

Your seats are in the middle of the row and no one else makes a sign of going out at intermission. Can you keep clambering out? It's your privilege, so long as you say "Excuse me" while you thread your way and get back before the curtain is up. When you're the one staying put, help the climbers by picking up your bag and making yourself as small as possible—better yet, by standing up (a must, if the aisle is narrow and the climber is not).

Applause is the breath of life to all performers—especially at the right time. At the theater or the opera, applaud if you like whenever the rest of the audience does—or when an actor delivers a particularly good line, even if you're the only one who appreciates it. At the opera, a singer often moves the audience to vocal appreciation; if you join in, it's "Bravo!" for a man and "Brava!" for a woman as you applaud with enthusiasm. At a concert there is one taboo on applauding: that's between the movements of a symphony or other orchestral piece. Take your cue from the conductor: you applaud when he walks on stage and when he turns to face the audience after a selection is concluded—but not in between. The theory is that the conductor meant the piece to be heard as a whole; the pauses between movements are like paragraph breaks, not the ends of chapters. At many performances involving music—concerts, musicals, dance recitals—the conductor presents the orchestra to the audience for applause; the orchestra rises and bows to you and you clap hands.

Exceptions to the rigid rules about applause include jazz concerts, folksong festivals, and coffeehouse performances of the sung and spoken word. A certain amount of foot-stamping and soulful uttering of an occasional outcry is really expected of you.

At any kind of promenade or picnic concert, finish the potato chips before the first downbeat and sip your refreshments quietly. Sadly there are those who spoil the beauty of an event or exhibition by being a member of the "unforgivables," those noisy few who stampede their way into every and any place they can barge into or buy tickets for. To avoid inclusion in this group avoid their bad manners.

Museum and art exhibits are "performances" put on by those who create in the fields of fine and graphic arts. Dress conservatively when you visit these exhibitions. Shorts and blue jeans reflect upon your taste level, while high heels make a lot of noise and give you "museum feet." Many pieces of contemporary art—such as collages, 3-D oil paintings and sculpture—are tempting to touch. . . . *Don't.* Not only is much of it fragile, but touching could smudge, spoil or break a work of art. Guards at museums are there to protect the exhibitions; your good manners will make their jobs easier.

Word to the wise: You'll enjoy any of the performing arts more if you do a little research ahead of time—to find out who the composer was, what the play's about, something about the cast, the dancers, the costumes. Try your library for magazine and newspaper reviews or articles that will give you a preview of what is to come. At sports events, the boy you're with will enjoy the date more if you know something about the game and the players. It's equally wise to appear a little unknowing, so he can instruct you—but not utterly ignorant, by doing something like turning to him in the middle of the first quarter and saying, "What's a first down, Charlie?"

More about spectator sports on page 74.

These are the spectators who ruin an event . . .

- They run their own show during the performance—complete with dialogue, laughter, humming, whistling.
- They ruin the view as they cuddle, nuzzle, wrestle over a bag of popcorn.
- You know where the action is—at the movie they're "watching"—as they run back and forth to the soda machine, the candy counter, the water fountain or just to the next aisle for a noisy little visit with some friends.
- They crowd you at every turn . . . on the line waiting to buy tickets . . . waiting for a seat at the back of the theater. If they sit behind you, they prop knees or feet against the back of your seat and push . . . or they lean on the back of your seat, breathing heavily past your ear. If they sit in front of you, they throw their coats back in your lap. Seated beside you,

they take over your territory as legs, arms, bags, coats sprawl beyond the boundaries.

- Fighting the system is their joy: they applaud at the wrong time, giggle at serious moments, smoke in the nonsmoking areas, try to slip into better seats.
- They stand up, blocking the view at a game.
- They taunt the players, loudly accuse the other team of cheating.
- They take it with them wherever they go—their little radio, we mean—at the beach, at ball parks and stadia and drive-ins. What they forget is that if anyone else had wanted to take music or the broadcast of another game with him, he could have. What they should remember is to keep a radio tuned down to a pitch only the owner can hear. (This applies to car radios, too; about the only time one can indulge in a full-blast radio is on a country road or in a deserted area of the beach.)
- Don't be an unforgivable.

12. On The Move: PLANES, TRAINS, BUSSES; MOTELS, HOTELS AND SHIPS

The best travelers are

open-minded—they love new places, new friends, new experiences

self-reliant—they know at least roughly how to get where they are going; they cope tearlessly with little travel tragedies, such as late arrivals and misplaced luggage

organized—they can always find their tickets; they look neat, and so do their suitcases

considerate—they are quiet; they don't spread their belongings about on train seats which aren't theirs; they don't leave a trail of litter behind them

comfortably dressed—in wrinkle-resisting, easy-fitting clothes, in colors and patterns that don't show smudges readily. They have a sweater handy for extra warmth, a raincoat that doubles as a topcoat. They wear shoes intended to be *walked* in.

pleasing to the eye—on buses, planes and trains, they dress tastefully, conservatively. Girls forego shorts or slacks in favor of a skirt; they choose an easy, wrinkle-resistant skirt when a long ride on a plane or sit-up train is in prospect. Young travelers of both sexes are prepared for social emergencies: a boy has a tie, a girl has some form of head covering—a scarf, net bonnet, packable hat—for quick compliance with the custom of a restaurant, a concert, a church, an unexpected party.

Special advice

TRAVELING BY CAR

- Take your ordinary good driving manners along when you travel by car—and be especially careful about littering. (Travel trash seems to accumulate faster on a long trip than on a short one.) In national parks and at public camp and picnic grounds you should be really meticulous about cleaning up after yourself—and about extinguishing campfires, crushing out cigarettes and breaking up matches before throwing them away.
- With your family? If everyone is in a contented mood, the whole family will have a better time. You can help by being patient with parents when they reminisce or carry on about the history of sights you see. You can also take on some responsibilities in order to make the trip more of a vacation for them—writing the post cards to Grandma and the thank-you's to friends you visit along the way; emptying the litter bags; taking charge of the road maps, perhaps learning to read them. If younger brothers and sisters go

with you, take along a list of games you can amuse them with—ghosts, who can spot the most white horses or license plates from different states, etc.—and stories you can tell; the list helps because after days of travel, your mind may go blank. Get the children to amuse you in return with stories and drawings. Remember that everyone (including lifeguards and college boys working as summer waiters or forest rangers) loves to talk to little ones; if you're along, they'll talk to you too.

It won't help to feel sad because your beau is away and you long for a human hand to hold—or just a human boy to talk to. Take heart. Friends you visit along the way may have nice boys for you to meet. There may be a family complete with six-foot son spending several days at the same lake you plan to visit.

- With friends? A car trip can strain the friendship. What starts as a glorious adventure ends a little sourly because Janie was *always* late or Diana had that maddening habit of humming *sotto voce*. Be extra patient with your friends' faults when you are constantly exposed to them through the intimacy of travel. You probably have some faults of which you are unaware—and which your friends are attempting to bear in silence. If close harmony goes off key and there is a little quarrel en route, try to forget it quickly.
- No matter the length of the trip—a summer-long tour of the West or a few days' run to a friend's house at the lake—give your family an itinerary so they will know when and where you can be reached. Being foot-loose might be fun, but what if you and your family *must* get in touch with each other quickly?
- The money problem. Whenever and however you travel, take only a small amount of cash. Put the balance of your money in traveler's checks, which you can cash in banks, shops, motels or hotels and restaurants along the way. Buy your checks at a bank or travel agency. The cost is about 1 per cent of the amount of money you need in checks. Checks come in various denominations—$10, $20, etc. You sign each check when you buy it; when you want to cash it or make it out to someone's order, you sign it again, so that the casher of the check can compare the two signatures. Even though traveler's checks aren't as promptly spendable as cash, you shouldn't lose them in your wanderings; someone might forge your signature! So keep them in a safe place—and, in *another* safe place, keep the little slip you get when you buy the checks; use it to record the numbers of all the checks and where you cash them. If the checks are lost or stolen, let the bank or agency where you bought them know the numbers of the missing checks; it will stop payment on them.
- Visiting friends en route? Be a good guest, and do remember to write them a thank-you note. It could be no more than a post card sent from your next

stop. But if they've made notable efforts to entertain you during your stay, you should write a real letter.

TRAVELING BY TRAIN

- Buy your ticket ahead of time if you can. If you travel on a sleeper (Pullman or roomette), reserve your space in advance. If, however, you have to buy your ticket at the station, allow plenty of time.
- Keep your luggage to an organized minimum. In train travel you don't have the weight restrictions you have on a plane, but you may have other problems—such as a shortage of redcaps, or station porters. As train travel gives way in popularity to plane travel, railroad services are curtailed. Redcaps *are* on hand in large stations for trains with sleepers and sometimes for those with parlor cars. They rarely meet a coach anywhere, although a long-distance telephone call to the stationmaster at your destination—give your train number and time of arrival—will produce a redcap to meet you. In small and medium-size towns, redcaps don't exist—which means you will often have to wrestle with your luggage all by yourself. An overnight case will slide under your seat or, in a coach, can be put on the overhead rack—provided that it doesn't jut out perilously. A slightly larger bag might also slide under a seat; it should not be put on a rack, as it might fall off. A really huge bag will have to be left on the platform at the end of your car. If you are traveling with a closetful of clothes, you may be able to check your big bags through to where you are going. Ask if the railroad offers such service to your destination; if it does, present your bag, with your ticket, to the baggagemaster at your home station a day or so before you leave.
- In the station, find out the track number of your train and double-check your departure time. This information is usually posted at the track gate.
- Aboard the train, keep your ticket or ticket check with you at all times. It's an unhappy experience to be next for a table in the diner and have to leave to go back eight cars for your ticket.
- Strangers on a train (or bus or ship or plane) should be. Even if they're the friendliest souls in the world, you don't have to make them *your* friends; if you are traveling alone—or even with a friend or two your own age—you're wiser not to. The older man sitting next to you might be a brilliant architect with a string of international contracts. But he might be a crashing bore. Or he might be playing Wolf to your Little Red Riding Hood. You can't really know until you have talked to him awhile—but by then your problems may have begun. So just read your paperback or watch the scenery. You can discuss the weather or agree that "it's a shame they don't run trains to Maine any more"—but let it go at that.

On the other hand, the lad sharing your seat may be tall, blond, devastating. He says he is the captain of the Yale team (you think it may be true), and he wonders why you're reading Eliot (he just did a term paper on Eliot). He'd obviously like to talk with you. All right, talk. But on very general topics. Never let him (or any other train, plane or bus acquaintance, male or female) buy your dinner or even a cola in the club car. If he would like to let the acquaintance ripen into friendship, and you secretly agree this might be a lovely idea, you could invite him to visit you in your own home with your family on hand. If this seems like overdoing propriety, remember you don't know his friends or family, you don't know what he is really like. If you don't want to talk, say sweetly, "I'm really sorry, but please excuse me." Parry a conversational opening with "umm" and he'll get the point fast. If the talker persists and is annoying, you can usually change your seat. Do it subtly by heading for the ladies' room and taking a different seat on your return. Or even ask the conductor to change it for you.

Don't give a short-term traveling acquaintance your address, telephone number, the names or addresses of people you are visiting, or any of your travel plans. (Exception: the one whom you might meet again under carefully fenced circumstances.) If you are not being met at your destination, keep the fact out of your conversation. And certainly don't accept the offer of a ride from the station. Melodramatic as it may sound, you might not get where you wanted to go!

- The diner. Usually you wait for the head steward or stewardess to seat you and you order from a menu, as you would in a restaurant. But instead of telling your order to the waiter, you write it on a little check. Table-sharers in a dining car often talk through dinner with each other (it's hard to read while you're cutting a chop), but no one will be offended if you bring along a book to read. Tip the waiter 15 per cent or at least 25 cents.
- In a coach, occupy only the seat you've bought. You don't spread out your belongings or map across two seats if the second seat is wanted by another passenger. If you're traveling back to school with friends and staying up all night is part of the fun, do your talking in the dressing room. It's hard enough for people to sleep on a sit-up train without unnecessary noise.
- Pullman accommodations are more luxurious than coach travel. During the day the occupant of the lower berth in one section sits facing forward, the occupant of the upper berth faces the rear of the train. At some point the porter will ask when you would like your berth made up. (He'd like to get this done by ten at the latest so as not to disturb other passengers who wish to go to sleep early.) While you are still dressed, you wash and brush your teeth. Then, after the porter has made your berth, you undress in it. A feat! If you are in an upper berth, you are supposed to keep your suitcase in the berth with you. If you don't relish sleeping with an overnight bag across

your feet, you might take a small train case or zipper bag for your night clothes and a toothbrush: if small enough, this could be stashed in the hammock at the side of your berth. (If you have a lower berth, you might put your suitcase back under your seat after removing your night things.) Always use a ladder to climb into and out of an upper berth; the porter will bring one if you ring.

- "Dressing room" is a misnomer. You aren't supposed to dress or undress there unless you simply can't cope in your berth. You could put on bra, petticoat, underpants, slippers and bathrobe in your berth; then with your pin curls covered, you can take your dress, girdle and stockings and finish more comfortably in the dressing room. In either case, be neat and clean up after yourself.
- A roomette is a different matter. Here you dress and undress and brush your teeth *in* your space. Then you pull a ready-made bed down the length of the room, backing into the corridor as you do so. Before backing, you pull a curtain across the door to your roomette; once in bed, you slide the door itself shut. The whole procedure is fun, and a roomette, occupied by you and you alone, is a nice private way of traveling.
- When you leave the train after an overnight trip, tip the porter of your car: a dollar is usually right. The usual price for baggage-handling by a redcap is 25 cents per bag; anything beyond that is up to you.
- If you are not being met immediately, or you plan to sight-see in a downtown area before going on to meet a friend at her house, you can check your bags in a baggage room or a coin locker. These lockers are also provided in bus and plane terminals. Most won't hold baggage overnight; read the instructions posted on or near the locker to find out.

BUS TRAVEL

Bus travel isn't too different from journeying aboard the neighborhood bus that takes you to school every day. There are no sleeping accommodations; if you want a nap, you tip your seat back and stretch out. There is no diner. On many long-distance buses you can reserve a seat, there is a rest room, and a box lunch or supper is served by a uniformed stewardess. For short-distance bus rides the procedure is less formalized. At specified points the bus stops and the driver announces, "Rest stop—fifteen minutes" (or "half an hour"). If you eat a sandwich or visit the ladies' room at a rest stop, be sure to get back on the bus before your time runs out!

AIR TRAVEL

You check in for your flight by taking your ticket and bags to the agent at the ticket counter for the line you're traveling on. He'll tear a coupon off and write your flight number on the envelope. You show this envelope to the hostess when you board the plane. Most people fly in tourist sections of planes or on shuttle flights, where they are seated on a first-come-first-served basis. There are some flights where first-class passengers can select their seats from a chart before boarding the plane.

Sometimes the agent doesn't know what gate you'll use for boarding, and flying conditions sometimes change the departure time. As you wander around the airport, be alert to announcements made on the loud-speaker about your flight. There is also a blackboard near the ticket counter, where the time and gate number will be posted.

Your bags are tagged at the ticket counter and checked through to your destination. You claim them at the baggage-arrival area at the airport when you arrive; on overseas flights, you claim them at the international customs counter. The baggage allowance of 40 pounds on domestic flights (44 pounds for overseas flights if you're going economy class, 66 pounds for first-class flights) includes the weight of your suitcases themselves—so consider their heft as well as their appearance when you buy them. You're not limited to the weight allowed, but you will have to pay extra if your luggage is overweight. Not counted in the poundage: the flight bag you carry with you, your coat, handbag, umbrella, magazines and books, small camera. On the plane, read the instructions placed in the pocket in front of your seat; fasten your seat belt when you're asked to, and obey the "no smoking" announcements. The hostess may offer you chewing gum when you take off: chewing or yawning helps you adjust to changes in air pressure. Once you're in flight, you're free to walk around, get magazines and drinks of water, refresh make-up in one of the well-equipped washrooms. The hostess will bring you a blanket, a pillow, a writing kit, as well as whatever meals or snacks are served. If you want some cool fresh air, she'll show you how to adjust the air vent above your head. The captain or hostess may give you information from time to time about the scenery or place of interest below, the height you're flying at, the speed and probable time of arrival. But, no matter what services they perform for you, you never tip airline personnel. A gracious and sincere thanks is all that's expected of you. If you hear a sound like a giant buzzer during take-off and landing, it comes from the special motors that operate the wing flaps and the landing gear. On your first flight, you may wonder about the tone change on a four-engine plane: it's created when the pilot adjusts the propellers to take larger or smaller bites of air. If you're on a jet, that eerie whistle comes from exhaust gases being released from the jet engine. Sometimes at night the exhaust gases are vivid orange and red. Two reminders about air travel: *you don't* tip and *you do* confirm your reservation—72 hours ahead of flight time when you're abroad, 6 hours within the United States. Do this either at the ticket counter when you arrive or by telephone to the airline office.

You're a good air traveler if you

- keep a pair of socks in your flight bag, take off your shoes and wear the socks when you want to nap (very relaxing).
- check with the passenger behind you before lowering your seat; she might have a cup of hot tea or the baby's feeding dish on her lap board (terrible excitement can be caused).
- talk softly during evening flights so others can sleep
- tell the hostess if you're a bit anxious on your first flight (first jet flight, first overseas flight). She'll give you motion sickness pills if you need them.
- return magazines and newspapers promptly so other passengers can have them
- talk to other passengers (While you're aboard, a plane is a kind of club. If you're traveling alone, the same advice holds on planes as on trains; see page 104.)
- on landing, raise seat back to the upright position so people behind you can get out easily
- keep your place until the plane has come to a full stop—and then don't bolt to the door, because you'll just be crowding the aisle as you wait
- get out at intermediate stops, take a walk, look around—and listen for the announcement that tells you the plane will be leaving shortly
- leave the "occupied" sign on your seat when you're out of it (The sign is in the seat pocket in front of you.)

TOURS

The first general rule on tours, at home or abroad, is to stick with the tour when you're supposed to. Don't wander off and hold up the whole group.

Tour dating is often Dutch. Boys and girls in a group may go together to a restaurant or a concert, but the boys are under no obligation whatever to pay for the girls. The girls should assume they *will* pay their own way.

HOTELS AND MOTELS

- In big cities and busy resort areas, reserve your hotel or motel room weeks ahead—particularly if you plan to stay a few days. Otherwise you may not get the sort of room you wish or find that the place has no rooms available.

Here's how to reserve a room by letter:

12 Vail Road
Farmington, Connecticut
August 14, 1962

Manager
Silver Pines Motel
Vacation Lake, New Hampshire

Dear Sir:
Please reserve a twin-bedded room with bath for the nights of August 23 and 24. We plan to arrive about noon.
Would you confirm my reservation in writing and let me know the rate?
Thank you.

Sincerely,
Edna Struthers

And by wire:

Manager, Silver Pines Motel, Vacation Lake, New Hampshire
PLEASE RESERVE TWIN-BEDDED ROOM WITH BATH NIGHTS OF AUGUST 23 AND 24 PLEASE CONFIRM

Edna Struthers
12 Vail Road
Farmington, Connecticut

You might insert the name of your traveling companion, so that mail sent to her can be held until her arrival: "Please reserve a twin-bedded room with bath for Miss Myra Kurtz and myself for the nights of . . ." If you plan to arrive late in the evening of your arrival date, say so when you reserve the room. Otherwise the manager may think you are not coming after all and may rent your room to someone else.

❧ Arrival procedures vary. At a hotel you leave your bags on the sidewalk in the care of the doorman. He will have your car parked for you. Then you walk in to register at the desk. (Tip the doorman? Not usually—unless he has heaved a good many bags around himself. If so, tip 25 or 50 cents, depending on the number of bags and other items. The doorman comes in for tips at other times: if he summons a cab from a stand or hails one passing on the street, you give him 10 cents; if he has to go out in rain or sleet to get you a cab, a fair tip is 25 cents.) The manager takes the key to your room from its slot and calls "front," and a bellboy appears to carry your bags to your room. (One or two bags, 25 cents; more, 50 cents.) You accompany the bell boy. He unlocks your room; turns on the lights; tests radio, TV, radiator, air conditioner; opens and shuts windows; opens and shuts closet and bathroom doors. When he (and you) are sure everything is in good working order, you tip him. If you find you're short of towels or hangers, call the housekeeper.

- At a motel, you drive to the office, register, then pick up your key yourself and drive or walk to your room, handling your luggage yourself. In big-city motels where cars can't be parked in front of each room, there are now doormen and bellboys. They are tipped as they would be in a hotel.
- The management says it "hopes you enjoy your stay," and it means it. So if the heat or air conditioning refuses to respond to your coaxing, or your room turns out to be right next to a room occupied by four basso profundos training for the opera, you can ask to have it changed. Conversely, you shouldn't ask for out-of-line service or ring the manager if room service does not appear at your door promptly.
- The letter paper and matches are meant to be used, not to be taken home. Ash trays and towels also stay where you find them.
- Checking out. When you wish to leave a hotel, telephone the cashier and ask to have your bill made up. (In a motel, you customarily pay before taking your room; settle extra charges, such as telephone calls, when you leave.) If you need help with bags, call the front desk and ask for a bellboy. After he's come for the bags, you go to the front desk, pay your bill, arrange to have any mail which might arrive forwarded—and you're on your way again . . . but probably not without another tip or two. Tips vary with the lavishness and location of the hotel, just as room prices do. But whether you stay at the Waldorf or the Weeping Willow Arms, you'll find the staff expects only modest tips—and a smile and a thank you—from a young girl.

The following guide may be of help:

Doorman—25¢ or 50¢ if he takes care of your bags when you arrive; 10¢ for a cab (in grim weather, 25¢).

Bellboy—25¢ for one or two bags, 50¢ if there are more. If he delivers a telegram or a dress from the hotel valet, he should receive 10¢ or 25¢.

Room service—If a meal or a snack is brought to your room, you tip the standard 15% or at least 25¢. The 15% gauge is not always accurate, though, since room-service prices are on the high side. Keep this in mind when you figure your tip.

Chambermaid—You rarely see the chambermaid who tidies your room, but she, too, makes your stay in a hotel pleasant. For an overnight stop or a weekend, leave her 25¢ in a sealed envelope—addressed "Chambermaid" and marked with your room number—on your bureau. Because maintenance in motels is still sometimes tended to by the manager's family, it isn't customary to tip chambermaids in them.

- If you go to see someone in a hotel, ask for her room number at the front desk and either ask the desk clerk to announce you or announce yourself: you can use the house telephone to call. This is nicer than knocking on your friend's door unannounced. She might be taking a shower!

GOING ABROAD? If this dream-come-true is yours, put yourself in the hands of a travel agent, who will book your passage on trains, planes, ships and buses; reserve hotel rooms, arrange for guide service if you need it, and advise you on everything from passports to what's being worn in Madrid this spring. A good agent does not charge you for "booking passage" (the "carriers"—airlines, steamship companies, etc.—pay him a commission instead). He does charge for making room reservations abroad, though not usually for making them at hotels within the United States. Actually, it doesn't hurt to consult a travel agent when planning a trip through this country. He can interpret timetables and save you a good bit of running around.

- A travel agent, or the airline or steamship line with which you make foreign travel reservations, can tell you what documents (passport? visa? smallpox-vaccination certificate? other vaccination certificates?) are needed for travel to the countries you plan to visit and for re-entry into the United States. Whether or not you need a passport (and currently you don't for some countries: these include Canada, Mexico, some of the British islands off Florida), you do need proof of your U.S. citizenship. A photostat of your birth certificate takes care of this. Don't lose your passport; if you do, immediately notify the United States consul in the city you are visiting.
- When you make your packing list for a trip abroad, ask your travel agent what the weather will be like in the places you're going so you won't find you've taken things you don't need—and left things you do. You probably won't need the kind of dress you'd wear to a prom, unless you have some specific plans that require one. Cosmetics, cigarettes and film are available most places you go. You can rent sports equipment—skates, tennis rackets, golf clubs, skis—unless you're an expert with special requirements. Things you'll do well to include are an extra pair of glasses (if you wear them), sunglasses, a ball-point pen and extra cartridge, a small flashight, extra passport pictures, a travel alarm clock, a bottle opener, playing cards, a small plastic clothesline and clips. Take also such emergency items as a a sewing kit, cellophane tape to remove lint, adhesive tape, antiseptic cream, Band-Aids, scissors, lightweight rubbers and raincoat, and a rain hood and

a good supply of such scarce items as soap and cleansing and toilet tissues. You'll find more about what to wear on page 163.

- When you shop abroad, take along a pad and pencil: one picture is worth thousands of words in pidgin French. Safeguard your passport at all times: take it with you always, everywhere.
- Shop around before you buy; you'll get the best prices where the things are made.
- Consider how you'll get the things you buy home; the expense of shipping a heavy, bulky object—plus duty—may cancel out the bargain. Also, some shops in major foreign cities have mail-order departments and you can order things under $10 just as though the shop were in Chicago or New York.
- Remember not to buy from peddlers or street vendors—any more than you would at home (unless it's the custom of the country you are in).
- Before you set out on a shopping spree, find out what hours the shops are open. Most close during the middle of the day and on certain days.
- Keep your currency conversion table with you, pay for larger items with traveler's checks (you often get a discount that way), get a receipt for everything you buy (useful when you're clearing customs).
- If you're buying things for friends, know their sizes and how to convert them to foreign sizes. (Many airlines supply this information.)
- Don't bargain about a price unless you're sure it's the custom. (Certainly not in department stores or shops where prices are marked.)
- Presents of $10 or less in value can be sent without paying duty if the total value of presents received by one person on one day is not over that sum. No declaration to customs is required.
- Be sure antiques are over 100 years old if you expect them to be duty-free.
- Pack all your purchases separately so customs officials can examine them speedily.

ON BOARD SHIP

- If you have a trunk, you should check it and other "not wanted on the voyage" chattels a few days before you sail. (Ask the procedure when you buy your ticket.) On sailing day no one responsible will appear to have the vaguest idea where *your* precious trunk is. Hand baggage will be strewn from one end of the ship to the other and the prospect of each piece's being delivered to its rightful owner will seem terrifyingly remote. Relax. The bags and trunks always turn up shortly after you leave port. To be on the safe side, label each piece of luggage (including typewriter, tennis racket, guitar or anything else you might clutch yourself) with your name, home address, the ship's name, your cabin number, and your address in the foreign city which will be your first stop or which will serve as your headquarters while you are abroad.

- Get to the dock well before sailing. You'll have plenty to do before that thrilling moment when the ship ups anchor and the busy little tugs start nudging it away from its dock. You'll have to wait in line and have all manner of things stamped; you'll have to find your cabin; you'll make a stab at locating your luggage. And, if you get to your ship early enough, you and your "bon-voyaging" friends will have more time for festivities.
- On many ships you have a choice of first or second sitting for meals. (The first sitting is, obviously, the earlier shift.) There is no difference in price, as your meals are paid for when you buy your ticket, but the second sitting has two advantages: the crowd is often more fun; you can sleep later in the morning.
- You reserve your seat at a specified table when you indicate which sitting you prefer. The man to see is the dining-room steward, and the time to do it is before sailing (if things aren't wildly confused then) or shortly afterward. You can, at the same time, reserve a deck chair from the deck steward.
- Cabin living, particularly on a lower-priced student ship, can be cramped. Two, three or as many as four or five other girls will share a cabin with you. So be neat. Strew your belongings only on your own bunk.
- Shipboard tipping is really quite simple. There are two ways to determine how much to tip. One is to take 10 per cent of your passage fare and apportion that amount roughly like this: 30 per cent of the total amount to the cabin steward (add 10 per cent more if your room has a private bath), 30 per cent to the dining-room steward or waiter, 15 to 20 per cent to the deck steward, 10 per cent to the stewardess, 10 per cent to the bath steward if you have used his services (if not, this 10 per cent is added to the amount given to the cabin steward.) The second way to determine how much to tip is to allot a dollar a day to the cabin steward and dining-room steward, 50 cents a day to anyone else you expect to tip.

  Tip the cabin and dining-room stewards at the end of the trip if it's a week or less; if you're on a long cruise, tip every week, dividing up the total amount by the number of weeks.

CUSTOMS

When you enter a foreign country, and when you return to the United States, you will have to go through customs. Have your luggage in such order that the search won't embarrass you—tooth paste neatly capped, laundry in a plastic bag, and so on. When you are given a customs declaration (for listing all of your purchases abroad) to fill out, do it neatly and completely. You'll save yourself time, in the long run.

HOW TO PACK A SUITCASE

Whether you're packing for one night or one week, make a list. Plan on paper everything you'll need. Check off the list as you pack; then pack the list, too. You'll need it for the return trip.

Packing an unfitted case

Bottom layer: Here go all the odd-shaped and heaviest items. Include:

Shoes. Face them heel to toe, inside a plastic bag, and place at the back of the suitcase (the bottom when it stands up). Small objects may be stuffed in toes.

Cosmetics. If you're not taking a separate train or cosmetic case, put cosmetics and other spillables in a plastic bag. For plane travel, make sure no bottles are filled completely to the top, as pressure may cause leakage. As an extra precaution, wrap each bottle in aluminum foil or seal it with cellophane tape before putting it in the plastic bag. Don't let two glass objects touch.

Washcloth. Lay it flat inside a shower cap. When washcloth is wet, fold the cap in half to keep the wetness inside.

Big petticoat. If it's a permanently stiffened type, bag it in an old stocking to keep it in shape and save space. Cut the toe from the stocking. Reach your hand through the toe hole, pulling the stocking up onto your hand, and grasp the top of petticoat, folding the top edges together. With your other hand, pull the stocking down over the petticoat.

Sweaters. Roll them, as Navy men do, to prevent wrinkles. Use sweaters to fill in empty spaces and level off bottom layer. To roll: lay flat, fold sleeves across, roll from the top down.

Make this bottom layer level and snug before proceeding to the next.

Middle layers: Pack in many flat layers, using full dimensions of the case. For a trip when you will be living out of the suitcase, why not make dividers that will keep your suitcase neat and let you get to any item you need without disarranging everything else? Try this unique filing system: Cut sheets the length and width of your suitcase from Pellon or plastic (you can buy either one by the yard). These are your file "dividers." Cut handles for the ends of the dividers and stitch them on securely. Label the handles with names of clothing categories—"accessories," "sportswear," "date clothes," etc.

Pack each category of clothing on top of its correspondingly labeled sheet, folding everything as flat as possible and using the entire length and width of the sheet. Let the handles bend up at the sides.

When you want to get something from one of the lower layers, simply lift out each of the layers until you reach the one you want.

Top layer: This layer also goes on a divider when you pack by the filing system. In *any kind* of flat packing the top layer should hold the things you'll need first. (Chances are this will be your "nightwear-lingerie" category.)

Finally, secure the ties. Your suitcase should be full enough so nothing shifts about, since shifting causes wrinkles. If necessary, add tissue paper to fill. Overpacking, on the other hand, is just as bad. It may wrinkle your clothes and will certainly strain your luggage.

Here are rules for packing individual items. They apply to *any* flat packing, with or without a filing system.

Suits. Lay skirt flat (folded lengthwise if wider than suitcase) and let bottom extend over side from hipline down. Button jacket and place it face down on skirt with collar and shoulders at back of suitcase. Fold sleeves in, then fold skirt bottom in over jacket. Now flip jacket bottom up over skirt, into case, folding at waistline.

Dresses. For 21-inch case or smaller, lay dress face down (bust fullness is underneath, so there is less strain when you fold) with neck at back of suitcase. Fold sleeves in across back of dress, then fold dress back and forth, using up width of suitcase. Whenever possible, make folds where natural body creases will be. If skirt is full, gather it into its natural lengthwise folds before folding horizontally.

For a larger case, lay dress in suitcase lengthwise, face down, using the rules above.

Skirts. Fold straight skirts once lengthwise and once at hipline. Lay gathered skirts flat and ease into natural gathers, to fit suitcase; then fold at hipline. Fold wide skirts (ungathered) once at each side to fit suitcase width, then again at hipline.

Remember that each fold is a potential wrinkle. So tuck tissue paper (which you have accordion-pleated) in folds to round them out and prevent creases. Rolled up nylon lingerie or other knit items do the same job. Still another way is to let one garment keep the creases out of another: with two skirts, put the hem of one at the hipline fold of the other, and vice versa.

Stockings. Protect by tucking them inside gloves.

Jewelry. Cloth silverware cases are ideal jewelry files. The soupspoon case is the best because it has the widest pockets. Label each pocket with the category of jewelry it holds. Iron-on tape or adhesive makes good labels.

Nylon lingerie. Pack flat or roll to use as wrinkle preventives in folds of dresses and skirts.

Packing a wardrobe case

Pack the bottom half of your suitcase (the unfitted part) first, following rules for unfitted cases.

Unhook the curtain that covers the hanger section and fold it back over top of case. Release holding bars. Arrange dresses and blouses on hangers. Make sure each is neat and flat before hanging the next. Fold sleeves along side seams; do not cross in front. When all clothes are hung, secure the top folding bar.

Skirts may be pinned to hangers or placed over the lower folding bar so that hiplines coincide with bar. Bottoms of skirts extend out of suitcase. Jackets may be packed over the bar, on top of skirts, with waistlines at bar, jacket bottoms extending out of suitcase. When all the clothes are arranged, lift and secure the lower bar and pull down the curtain.

When you arrive at your destination, here's a trick that will help take out any wrinkles that may have sneaked in. Hang up your clothes on a shower-curtain rod and turn on the hot water in the tub full force until steam collects. Leave the room with the door closed for thirty minutes. The steam will help erase the wrinkles. Clothes will be ready to wear in another half hour.

Back to the definition of the good traveler on page one of this chapter. Now you know all about how to be self-reliant, organized and considerate; what about being open-minded? Every American girl who visits a foreign country can be a one-woman Peace Corps—or she can set a poor example. Foreigners often think that what's wrong with one person characterizes everyone from the same land.

The open-minded traveler is eager to find out *why* the people whose country she visits think, talk, act, react and even eat differently from those she's known all her life . . . and she's not eager to criticize them for doing so.

She doesn't make small-minded comparisons between life at home and life abroad. If slightly annoyed at the lack of plumbing in Paris, she reflects philosophically that, after all, there are no sidewalk cafés back home in Hartford. When in Rome . . . well, you know. She doesn't wear shorts downtown. She is extra careful about smoking, because "nice girls" in many European, South American and Asiatic families still don't smoke. She wears sleeved dresses and hats or scarves in churches she visits on sight-seeing trips. She pays attention to the boy-girl customs of each country and is particularly careful in Latin countries, where talking with a strange boy on the street could cause onlookers to wonder what sort of girl she is. She is extremely courteous to older people because, abroad, older people are given a great deal of respect.

She doesn't brag about her country. On the other hand, she doesn't apologize because it hasn't managed to solve the world's problems in its short career as a major power or because there are still slums in all our cities. She talks about school customs, dating, politics freely—but without rancor.

She reads about a country before she visits it. She learns its language, if she can. Even a poorly pronounced "*gracias*" makes a better impression than "thanks."

She smiles, makes friends and has a wonderful time!

13. Car Talk: THE RULES OF THE ROAD

A good (*safe, polite*) driver knows the rules of the road, especially those which apply in his state. These are usually available, in nonlegal language, in booklets obtainable from a state's Department of Motor Vehicles. You must know them to pass the written examination for your license; you should remember them as long as you drive. While this chapter isn't concerned with how to signal for a turn or how many feet to park from a hydrant, there are a few politeness pointers which relate to the rules. Rudeness on the road *may* not be strictly illegal, but it comes close and, because it's unexpected and irritating, it's often just as dangerous.

- *Constant lane-hopping,* even if you remember to signal before switching from one lane to another, is maddening to those in front and behind and could result in a collision.
- *Bumper-hugging* is just as annoying (as well as unsafe).
- So is *failing to dim your lights* for oncoming traffic or for a car you are following closely. (You blind other drivers with the glare of your headlights.)
- *Roaring ahead* at a stop light as soon as it changes can terrify drivers with slower reactions. On the other hand, dawdling is also bad mannered.
- *Turning abruptly* after a last-minute flash of a direction signal causes following drivers to jam on their brakes—or maybe to bump into you.
- *Refusing to let a car enter your lane* when it's pulling out of a driveway into a stream of traffic is pure selfishness—hardly worth the time it might save.
- *Double-parking* must be done sometimes (while you wait for your mother to emerge from the hairdresser, for instance). Keep the motor running so you can move out of the way if necessary.
- *Thoughtless parking:* blocking access to a friend's driveway or garage. Sometimes you can't help it when there's a jam of cars at a party or a meeting—but be prepared to move your car promptly and cheerily if another driver wants to leave before you do.
- *Illegal parking:* You'll probably get a ticket if you leave your car in a no-parking zone, too close to a hydrant or in front of a crosswalk. Did you know you can also get one for thoughtlessly blocking someone's driveway?

Less-than-good car manners:

- Leaving a trail of candy wrappers, banana peels and other debris along the highway (some cities and states fine those who litter). You can easily collect your trash in a paper bag and leave it in a trash can at a gas station, a roadside rest area—even at home. Equally thoughtless: strewing litter about any picnic area, beach, drive-in ice-cream stand or scenic lookout you may come across in your travels. There is nothing less inviting at a picnic spot than the remnants of someone else's picnic!

- Using your car as a closet. An assortment of tennis rackets and overdue library books inconveniences any passengers you may have, and raincoats or dresses on hangers in the back seat may block vision in the rearview mirror.
- Playing clown-car-at-the-circus by jamming a car so full of friends that you can hardly maneuver—or see out the rear window.
- Using the horn when it's not necessary—to hustle the cars ahead to move on the minute a light changes, to summon a friend from the house. (Boys, you are worse offenders here than girls.)
- Playing your car radio so loud it deafens those in other cars waiting at an intersection or wakes a neighborhood at night.
- Eating or drinking while driving. It's hard to handle both steering wheel and dripping ice-cream cone at the same time. It also is hard on the upholstery.
- Getting too affectionate (i.e., necking) in a moving car. All right, you're just ambling happily in the moonlight; but other, more sedate souls want to use the road.

"But, officer . . ." You break the law, hear the siren, pull over. Be mannerly with the policeman or trooper. (The nicest people sometimes feel they have to argue their way out of a ticket. Frank admission of their fault might net them a warning instead of a blemish on their nice new license.)

If you do have an accident or cause damage to another car, own up to it. Ethically, you should offer to pay for a fender you've dented.

Pedestrians require constant care. They can't move as fast as you. Besides, many of them have never driven a car and haven't the foggiest notion of how long it takes one to stop. So give them the right of way whenever possible (in many states it's legally theirs anyway). When you're on foot, avoid jaywalking, darting out from between parked cars. On country roads, walk facing the traffic so both you and oncoming drivers can see each other in time to avoid an accident.

Hitchhiking may be a low-cost way of seeing the country, but for girls it can be a pretty reckless one. Often it is illegal. On the other hand, there is no law that says *you* must pick up a hitchhiker, no matter how forlorn-looking. As a young girl, even with friends, *don't.* Remember that uniforms do not necessarily cover gentlemen.

Bike riders have their own rules. For the sake of courtesy, please don't

- ride more than two abreast
- ride on sidewalks
- play "Look, Ma, no hands" when there's danger of crashing into people, cars, other bicycles
- fling your bike down on someone's prized lawn (Instead, lean it against a tree or wall, if you can.)
- park your bike in a driveway so that it prevents cars from using the same driveway

How to be a passenger A passenger can help a driver drive by checking maps, watching for route numbers and providing keep-awake conversation on dreary stretches of turnpike. A passenger can be a menace by chattering when traffic or weather conditions demand the driver's complete attention; fiddling repeatedly with the radio dial; lighting unshielded matches or turning on the inside light at night and, so, blinding the driver; climbing from front seat to back seat while the car is moving; being a back-seat driver—at any time. If you're a passenger, Do Not Disturb the Motorman. If you're the driver, try to make your passengers behave. If you ask nicely enough, they'll remain companionable—unless they are children. The hotter the day, the longer the trip, the more cranky and restless most children become. If you're ferrying small brothers or baby-sitting charges about, try to get them "played out" before you start a trip of any length. Hopefully, they'll sleep the trip away.

Boys and cars If a boy has his own car, he's probably madly in love with it. If he thinks it's beautiful, it's shrewd for you to agree, no matter what you may actually think of it. Admire all the gadgets—if it's a new car—or the clever way he painted the dented fender—if it's an old one (even more important if it's a new one). Never, never advise a boy on driving, car maintenance or how to change a tire. That way lies spinsterhood.

Opening the car door This is one of those agonizing customs. The car stops; your date turns off the motor, climbs out of his side of the car, shuts his door, walks around the car, opens your door, sticks out his hand to help you out—which you accept as gracefully as you can, battling the obstacles of tight skirt, high heels, large purse, low-slung car, high curb. It's good manners for him to open the car door for you, just as he would open the door of a house for you, so it's good manners for you to wait until he can get around the car to do it. You can fill the endless interval by gathering up gloves, purse, books or pretending to rummage about in your purse for something. Don't just stare. If, however, he gets out of his door and then just waits for you to join him, hop out by yourself. On returning to the car, wait a second to see if he wants to open the door for you. If he does, let him. If not, open it quietly yourself. In either case, try not to embarrass *him.*

Where you sit in a car with a boy Not so close that you interfere with his driving; but not over by the door. The first posture will confuse him; the second will make him feel like Jack the Ripper.

Who gets in first when there are two girls, one boy? If you'd rather have the boy between you, let one girl get in, then the boy, then the second girl.

When there's a grownup? For a long time it was thought polite to let an older person (a woman your mother's age or a man your grandfather's) enter a car ahead of you. However, it is almost impossible for a not-so-nimble person to reach the far corner of the back seat of a low-slung modern car with ease—especially if the car has only two doors. If this is the case, it's sometimes more considerate to say, "Would you like me to climb in the back?"—that is, if you won't be needed to help the older person *out.*

Special taxi manners The boy gives the directions to the taxi driver. If he pays the driver before getting out, the girl unobtrusively stays in her seat until he has finished. A boy never allows a girl to sit on one of the jump seats in a taxi unless she *wants* to.

When you are paying the fare, have your money ready before the cab stops. Figure the tip swiftly (usually 15 per cent; see the tipping guide on page 157) and leave the cab as soon as you can without holding up more traffic than necessary. When sharing the fare with a group of friends, do your arithmetic before the cab stops, if you have an idea of what the fare will be, or after you are on the sidewalk. There is no reason the cabbie should wait while you do long division! ("Does everyone owe a quarter or twenty-seven cents?") You don't have to talk to a cabdriver, no matter how conversational he may want to be. If he can't be stopped from pouring out his soul, you can ride to your destination in comparative peace by throwing in an occasional "mmmn" or "you don't say" or "oh, really?" whenever it seems appropriate. Never try to persuade a cabdriver to carry more passengers than the law allows. He could have his license suspended. Remember that a cab is a public place—not the spot for arguments. For affection? Yes, if it's *discreet.*

Who gets the car? The family car belongs to the whole family—but, more particularly, to your parents. They own it, pay for its upkeep, and, in many states, must pay extra insurance because you, as a teen-ager, are driving it. With a brand-new license in your hand, you may feel covetous about it. But your mother needs the car for shopping, club meetings or taking a younger sister to the dentist. Your father needs it for business or a golf tournament. They both need it—just for themselves—for the fun of it sometimes. So be considerate in your requests. If you wheedle constantly, they may make sacrifices they needn't, just for the sake of family harmony. If you let them know a few days ahead of time that you would like to borrow the car ("please") for Thursday night's play rehearsal, they're apt to be understanding and accommodating. If you're consistently thoughtful about asking for the car, they'll acquiesce to spur-of-the-moment requests as well. Combine the fun of driving with a favor. Offer to pick up groceries or run other errands when you use the car. Occasionally you should replenish the gas tank or wash the car. And leave the car—always—as neat as or neater than you found it; empty the ash trays, sweep out the sand.

If you don't drive (either because you're under age for a license in your state or because your parents, for reasons of their own, will not yet let you apply for a license), you can run into awkward transportation situations—particularly if you're with a date and he can't drive either. Solutions:

- Your parents (or his) can drive the two of you to a party and call for you later. If you don't want them to pull up at the door of the party, they can let you out a block ahead.
- He can call for you with his parents, who will then drive both of you on to the house of an older friend (who *can* drive). Older friend and date can double-date with you and *your* date.
- He can call for you with older friend.
- You can take the bus. (In many large cities, the postcollege group usually goes to parties, plays and movies by bus or subway. Private transportation is too expensive, and both sides know it.)
- You can walk. (Good for the figure, puts roses in the cheeks.)

HOW TO REFUSE A RIDE If a boy you like pulls up to the curb and offers you a ride, accept it. If a boy you don't like—or don't even know at all—offers, you can turn him down gracefully with "Thanks, but not now" or "I'm just going a little way." Say this, then smile and walk on without a backward glance. It's not rude to refuse a ride, just as it's not rude to refuse a date. The politeness or impoliteness is all in how you do it.

A CAR OF YOUR OWN If you reach the dizzy heights of owning your own car, remember that a car is just what the ads (and your own lunch-period conversations) imply—a status symbol. A shiny convertible must be *kept* shiny and in constant repair or it will look tawdry—and so, by implication, will you. A jalopy, on the other hand, may single you out as the class individualist; but if the brakes won't work, you may find yourself billed as the class fool as well. The happy-medium compact (second-hand or third-hand, inspected) is probably somewhere in between.

Keep your car in good running condition. If you have any doubt about the brakes holding, take the car for a checkup. Occasionally ask a friend to watch while you test the lights and directional signals. For everyone's sake, and the car's health too, both brakes and lights should work perfectly. Keep at least a quarter of the gas tank filled all the time so you won't risk being stalled on the road. Have the oil and water checked regularly, and be sure that tires are kept at the correct poundage. The windshield, rear window, side-view and rearview mirrors should be kept clean and clear. Acquire a working knowledge of car parts—a big help in an emergency when no mechanic is on hand.

Learn to change a tire! (Father, brother, beau and the fellows at the garage and gas station willingly instruct a girl who wants to learn about cars.)

Nice compliment to pay your father: once in a while, ask him to drive your car and tell you if he thinks it's in good shape.

14. When You Speak

The way you talk gives listeners a word picture of you that's as revealing as a candid camera. It tells whether you're sensitive, cultured, kind, cheerful. It describes your family, your friends, your schooling and your interests. Your manner of speech is one of the most important parts of your personality, as basic as the color of your eyes—yet a part of you easily improved.

Do you know how you sound? A simple method of finding out is to cut a record of your voice at a fair, an amusement park or a recording studio—or to make a tape recording if you know someone with a machine. The two things that surprise many people the most are the pitch—much higher than you expect—and the marked regional accent. (Like the darling Southern girl we know who said, "Now how'd he guess Ah'm fum the South?") The high pitch is something to correct, because nearly everyone would sound more attractive with more bass and less treble—particularly girls whose voices can quickly spin from soprano into a squeak, a shriek or a whine. The marked regional accent is another matter. It's a very nice facet of your personality to be able to convey by the sound of your voice the information that your family comes from Savannah or Boston or Dallas: it makes you somebody right away. If you want a standard to rate your speech against, make it this: do you sound like the nicest people in your home town?

Lack of exercise is a prime reason for a voice's sounding less than perfect. Singers, as well as actors, have fine speaking voices, because daily vocal exercises keep their jaws from becoming stiff, their tongues sleepy and their lips lazy. Singing a little every day will help keep your vocal apparatus in better condition. (Sing in the shower, if your family is unappreciative.) Another excellent exercise is to read or talk aloud in front of a mirror: you watch, you listen, and your speech improves magically in a few weeks. Here are five sentences you might read aloud slowly, giving every sound its proper value:

1. For distinct enunciation, every word, every syllable, every sound must be given its proper form and value.
2. Think of the mouth chamber as a mold in which the correct form must be given to every sound.
3. Move your lips noticeably.
4. Your teeth should never be kept closed while you are talking.
5. As your voice is the most direct expression of your innermost self, you should be careful to do yourself full justice with it.

Perhaps you've noticed the way people from other countries—friends, maybe, or actors in foreign movies—love the sound of their language. The French, Italians and English are especially devoted language lovers, vocally caressing each word they speak. On the other hand, lots of Americans slur and blur words so that sentences come out sounding like this: "We lissenda program Saddy—sumpinon Amurcan govuhment." It's all the fault of that lazy mouth. Thus, doing your vocal exercises will correct the slur and blur. You'll also find, as you practice in front of your mirror, that you look much prettier talking with a mobile mouth.

Knowing the way a word should be pronounced helps, of course, and a good dictionary is your best authority. Usually the first pronunciation given is the one to choose—*unless* the second one given is used in your region. (Classic example of such regional variations: the New Englander's to-mah-to as against the Westerner's to-may-to.) And knowing a lot of words not only makes you more interesting to listen to but also gives your vocal apparatus more varied exercise. *Marvelous, great, swell, cool* and *neat* are much more effective if they're not the only adjectives you use. Think of others you could alternate with—as a starter, *superb, rare, splendid, exciting, masterful, flawless, pleasant*. Instead of *O.K.*, try *fine, certainly, surely, decidedly, positively, my pleasure, yes, indeed*. Having a more versatile batch of words at your command will also prevent you from vexing little vocal fidgetings, such as "The book was . . . er . . . ah . . . well, it was neat" or "she . . . uh . . . she was . . . uh . . . O.K." Colloquial speech also loses its punch if you use it relentlessly, whether it's jazz slang, teen talk or regional.

By a wider vocabulary we don't mean a fancy one, richly larded with foreign words (even if you pronounce them perfectly). You'll be teased to the point of torture if you start talking in elaborate synonyms—like a crossword puzzle. There are plenty of natural words to choose from. That doesn't mean that, to make a point, you wouldn't say lady instead of woman—or that, to paint a vivid word picture or to be amusing or incongruous, you wouldn't choose an offbeat word. Words that you shy away from in speaking are also often just the ones you find useful when writing a school paper or a composition.

But when you're talking, be natural. Here's a suggested guide list:

avoid these	*use these—they're simple, natural*
affair	party
apparel	clothing, clothes
arise	get up
ascertain	find out
attend	go to
boy friend	friend, date, beau
condolence	sympathy
contact	see, telephone, write

avoid these	*use these—they're simple, natural*
converse	talk
couch	sofa
cultivated, well-bred	nice, civilized, cultured
davenport	sofa
dentifrice	tooth paste or powder
drapes	curtains, draperies
endeavor	try
evince	show
evening meal	dinner or supper
expecting	pregnant or having a baby
finalize	finish
folks	family
formal	evening dress, dinner dress, dance dress
foyer	hall or entrance hall
garment	dress, slip or whatever it is
gorgeous	stunning, beautiful
gown	evening dress, etc. (or nightgown!)
hosiery, hose	stockings, socks
lounge (as a noun)	sofa—or living room, sitting room, waiting room
luncheon	lunch
outfit, finery	costume, clothes
pardon me	excuse me or I'm sorry
permit me	may I, let me
prior engagement	have a date or an appointment
position	job
purchase	buy—or bought something
residence	house
resides	lives
saleslady	saleswoman
sufficient	enough
suite of furniture	furniture, set of furniture
suite of rooms	several rooms, apartment
tender	give
transpire	happen
tux	dinner jacket or coat
undergarment	underclothes
vanity	dressing table
wire	telegram

Last word on the spoken word: do suit your speaking manners, like your other manners, to your audience. The goal is to be nice to talk to, to be understood and to have the conversation remembered pleasantly. As an example, you use slang with your contemporaries if you wish—but never with your employer, your parents, your teachers, or members of the clergy or medical profession.

15. When You Telephone

Talk with a stranger on the telephone and you conjure up a quick picture of the caller. If a voice sounds dull, mean, cross, overbearing—or friendly—you imagine a personality to match it. Your voice sketches your portrait, and the one humming over the wires will surely be a pretty one if you use this trick: as you talk, pretend there's a mirror propped up in front of you. Are you smiling?

Do make certain that people can understand what you're saying—basic advice—and if friends often ask you to repeat what you've just said, check your voice and diction (see how on page 124). Or one of these foibles might be blighting your telephone personality:

- *mumbling* Speak up!
- *bellowing* Those miles of wire between you and the other person will do the amplifying. If you have a bad connection, make the call again or, if it's long distance, ask the operator if she can clear the line. Sometimes all you need to do is turn down the radio.
- *yatatayating* at supersonic speed—or drawling.
- *not talking into the mouthpiece* The telephone company has designed the instrument for perfect reception—and to what avail if you wave it off in space or hold it so close you deafen the listener?
- *drumming* absent-mindedly on the base of the instrument: it blurs what you're saying.
- *eating, drinking, cracking gum* while talking.

THE PHONE'S RINGING

Answer at home with a happy-sounding *hel-LO!* (*Smile* as you say that!) It's enough to make a boy stop calling if you mutter a dispirited, toneless *h'llo*. In a business office, you answer the phone with "Jones and Company; Miss Baker speaking" or "Mr. Giannini's office."

Suppose the caller asks for you.

Caller:	"May I please speak to Jane?"
You:	"Speaking." (rude, abrupt)
	"You're speaking to her." (even ruder)
	"Who's calling?" (*impossible*)
	"This is she." (sounds stiff)
	"This is Jane." (right)

If the call arrives in the midst of dinner, you're dressing for a date, or there's some reason you can't chat long, explain and ask, "May I call you back?" Your caller will either come quickly to the point of the call or say, "I'm sorry, Jane; will you call me?" If you don't know the number, ask for it and jot it down to save time later. Then be sure to call back as soon as you said you would!

WHEN YOU MAKE A CALL

Start right by dialing the correct number. Don't trust your memory if it's a bit woolly on the subject. Look it up in the directory or your own telephone list. It's a shame to bother Information for numbers you can and should find yourself in the directory. When you must ask Information for a number, write it down so you won't have to ask for the same number twice (if the line is busy or if you need it another time).

Allow enough time for an answer. The friend you call may be in the cellar, the attic or the tub.

Identify yourself. If you call a friend who knows your voice by heart, there's no need for this if she answers the phone. Just say, "Hello, Sue," the minute you hear her voice. But if she's not likely to recognize you immediately, be clear about saying "Hello, Sue; this is Jane" or "Hello, Sue; this is Jane Thomas." Don't ever play that ancient game of "Guess who *this* is?" If someone other than Sue answers the telephone, say, "Hello. This is Jane Thomas. May I please speak to Sue?" Don't make Sue's family shudder with a curt "Sue there?" or "I wannatalkta Sue." (It's obviously nicer to say "*May I please* speak to . . ." rather than "*I want* to speak to . . .") If the answering voice sounds like that of Sue's mother, say, "Hello, Mrs. Henderson. This is Jane Thomas. May I please speak to Sue?" Adults think better of you if you use your last as well as your first name. There may be several Janes among their children's friends.

Should you leave a message? If Sue isn't home, take your choice: ask that she call you, say you'll call back, or, in business parlance, cancel the call.

You ask that she call back	"Could Sue call me when she comes in? My number is . . . (in case it's unfamiliar to Sue). I'd like her to come swimming with us tomorrow." (You may leave a brief, uncomplicated message like this one.)
You offer to call back	"When will she be home, please? May I call then?"
You cancel the call	"Thank you. I'll wait to see her at school tomorrow."

Whatever the case, don't greet the news that Sue is out with a mere "oh." At least say your thanks before hanging up. It's always proper, always considerate, to leave your name. ("Would you tell her Jane called? Thank you.")

You have a captive audience when you make a phone call. Before launching into a discussion, down to the last earring, of what everyone wore at the prom, ask your friend if she has time to talk or if it would be better to call her back later. Don't filibuster, so that she has to interrupt: "I'm washing my hair. Let me call you back." That's embarrassing to both of you.

A word about monopolizing the phone. The telephone is a wonderful instrument for the promotion of friendship, romance, etc., but your family (and your friends' families) would like to use it too. Avoid scenes by being considerate. Further consideration: If you talk to Sue for an hour every night, Bob may give up trying to call *you*. An egg timer kept by the phone is one way to cut the length of your calls; you can say quite a lot in three minutes too. Even if, lucky girl, you have a telephone of your own, you shouldn't abuse the privilege—any more than you should make a series of unbidden collect calls from boarding school or use your father's telephone charge card number without permission.

Think of this: Six hours of baby-sitting a month times 75 cents an hour would pay for your own phone.

About public telephones. It's harrowing for a line of busy people with urgent messages—"I missed the 5:07. Can you meet the 5:34?" . . . "They haven't any butter pecan. Will peppermint do?"—to have to wait helplessly while a chattering magpie gossips on. That's more typical of middle-aged women than the young, and it's a habit to avoid acquiring.

The walls and woodwork of public phones aren't meant to be oversized scratch-pads. If you have to write down a number, use the scratch-paper in the rack of paper in the booth or near the directories. Or use the back of an envelope.

WHO HANGS UP FIRST? The caller. Supposedly the girl ends the conversation when a boy calls her, but sometimes he makes the first move anyway. You have to play this by ear. Certainly it's not tactful to cut him short in mid-paragraph, but if he makes a date, chats a while longer and then says, "Good; I'll see you Saturday, eight o'clock," you take the cue with "Wonderful, Jack! See you Saturday. 'By." Then he can say good-by and hang up. If you feel he's floundering for an exit line, you can say something like "My mother's making noises about my homework. I guess I'd better finish it . . ." The ending of the chat may spur him to ask you for a date, if that's really why he called—or if he's been building up his courage to ask.

Lulls in a talk with a boy are nice—like holding hands over the phone. So don't feel driven to fill every minute of a telephone visit with bright conversation, any more than you would in a face-to-face talk.

Much as the phone is a part of your life, there are times when you want to end a call quickly and get back to what you were involved in when the phone jingled. Polite white-lie excuses like these will spare your caller's feelings:

"Have to go now, Jill. My father's waiting for a long-distance call."

"Mother just told me she'd like to use the phone. I'll see you later."

"I have some cookies in the oven. I think they're *burning*. Meet you at five." The final word: when you say you're signing off, sign off. Little can be worse than to say, "I have to hang up now" and then talk another ten minutes.

WHEN A BOY CALLS, sound pleased, whether you really want to talk to him or not; listen interestedly to what he has to say. It's polite of you.

If he asks you for a date, and you refuse, do it briefly: "Oh, I'm sorry, but I'm going to be busy that night." Not, "My aunt is coming to visit, and we're going to a concert while she's here, and I might have to baby-sit, and . . ." This sort of response is so vague and confused he'll know it's not true. The rudest phone trick you can play on a boy is to let him ask you for a date, pretend there are complicating circumstances, and ask him to call back later when you know for sure—translated: "When I've thought it over and if no one better has called in the meantime." If there *are* such circumstances, explain them briefly.

What about accepting last-minute dates? Depends on you, the boy, the circumstances. If it's a good spur-of-the-moment idea, why not? If the boy is a constant late-dater, you might occasionally refuse. If his only plan is to raid your icebox, you have to weigh lad against larder and decide which you value more highly. There are some couch-warmers who never take a girl out, preferring to sit on her sofa and eat her popcorn. You needn't say yes to these.

The boy who asks, "What are you doing Saturday night?" This vexing type causes all kinds of misery. Answer "nothing" and you commit yourself automatically to his plans for the evening or brand yourself a social outcast. Answer "I have a date" and you lose the chance to see him. (But you still have your pride.) The safest answer is, "I don't really know yet." That's vague, but so was his question. The way to ask for a date is, "Would you like to go to the movies with me Friday night?"

The boy who calls while you're entertaining a date? It's not good to talk and talk with second boy when another is visiting you. It's better to tell second boy that you have a guest. If you fail to tell him, he may settle down for a long visit and—when you suddenly remember first boy—be mystified when you break off the conversation. You are not required to spell out the fact that your g-u-e-s-t is a b-o-y.

The same principle holds if a girl calls when another girl is visiting you, unless you're all good friends and you can turn the call into a three-way conversation.

If a boy calls when a girl is visiting you—others girls understand; it's accepted procedure to go ahead and talk.

When does a girl call a boy? Any time there's a change of plans, any time she has important news, any time she wants to ask him to a party. But not just *any time.* A boy you see a great deal may ask you to call him now and then, but be wary: if you call often, young brothers and sisters may tease him about it; parents, possibly taught that girls *never* call boys, may be sharp-tongued about your excessive interest in their son. If this keeps up, girl may lose boy. You can also call a boy when he's phoned and left a message for you to return his call. (That doesn't happen often.)

Telephone invitations, acceptances and regrets Usually when you ask a friend to a party, you need say only, "Im having a record party this Saturday at eight. Can you come and bring a date?" But suppose you've arranged for certain boys to call for certain girls, or you want everyone to bring his tennis racket, or it's a surprise birthday party. Then give all the details. Tell your guest the date and hour of the party (and when it's to end, if it's other than the usual evening-long sort); whether to bring a date; whether special clothes are in order. If the party involves a meal, be sure to say so or you will have guests for your clambake arriving fresh from their own supper tables. Name the date of the month if the party is more than three or four days off: "Saturday, the twenty-third." People get confused between "next Saturday" and "a week from Saturday."

In accepting an invitation made by telephone, say, "I'd love to come!" It's wise to repeat the date and time: "This Saturday at eight."

It's perfectly proper to telephone an answer to most written invitations. (Exceptions: *formal* invitations to weddings or other ceremonies.) If you're responding to a written invitation from a boy, you may feel shy about calling him, although this is another case of When a Girl May Call a Boy. Write him a note:

Dear Charlie,

Thanks so much for asking me to your party Saturday. I'd love to come and will bring a date.

Best,
Jane

You may already have a date for the evening of the party to which you're asked, but you'd like to go anyway. If you're not sure of the boy's plans, or lack of same, you should not accept the party invitation instantly. Could be your escort has bought tickets to a tent theater or has made plans involving another couple. In such a case, tell your hostess you must ask your date first and you'll call her back as soon as you have. Then ask him: it's his privilege to suggest the evening's activities. In declining an invitation, say you're sorry you can't come and give the reason briefly: "I'll be away that weekend; we're going to the shore." Or even "I'm sorry, but I've made other plans already."

If you must decline an invitation after accepting it—and you may do this only for a good reason, such as illness or a change in family plans—do it by phone if you can't do it in person. It's courteous to let a hostess know of a change in your plans almost as soon as you do.

May I use your phone? At a friend's house you may ask to use the phone if it is necessary, but not for a spate of social calls. If you make a toll or long-distance call, you should pay for it, no matter how trifling a charge it may seem. A weekend guest can do this quite simply: she asks the operator for charges on each call; at the end of her visit she itemizes these on a slip of paper and leaves the paper, with the correct amount of money, on her dresser. It's best not to call from a busy doctor's or dentist's office, but if you must, offer to pay for the call. Your offer will probably be refused, but it should be made.

When the telephone rings for a friend you are visiting, it's polite to busy yourself with a book or magazine, or leave the room unobtrusively, rather than listen in stony silence. If there are others there, you can talk quietly among yourselves until she's finished.

Handling the phone for someone else The telephone rings. You answer it; it's a friend calling your mother. Ideally, you say, "Oh, yes, Mrs. Goode. I'll tell her you're calling." Then you lay the receiver down gently. You do *not* bang it down and yell "Mo-ther!" If you must raise your voice to call someone to the phone, cup your hand over the receiver. If there will be some delay in your mother's getting to the phone, explain it and ask if the caller can wait. Don't just drop the receiver while your mother's friend waits, murmuring plaintive hellos into a silent instrument. If your mother is not at home or cannot come to the telephone, offer to take a message. And write it down. (Well-organized households always have a pencil and a pad of paper by every telephone. The sort that clip on or are held to the phone by magnets are most apt to stay put.) Repeat the caller's name and number, for clarity. Then remember to give the message to your mother as soon as you can. It's polite to ask the caller if she would like your mother to call back. This is somehow nicer than requiring the caller to try again.

Extensions and party lines About extensions: It's as wrong to listen in without being asked as it is to read another's mail or diary.

Party lines, with several families sharing one wire, are still fairly common. They should be used politely. Keep your conversations shorter than you might if you had a line of your own; allow at least three minutes between calls so that others on the line will have an opportunity to make or receive calls.

If another party-line user interrupts your conversation for an emergency or simply because you have been talking a long time and she needs to use the phone, give up the line gracefully. Of course, eavesdropping on a neighbor's party-line conversation (no matter how deliciously filled with local gossip) is as evil as any other kind of eavesdropping.

Sorry, wrong number If the number you get is obviously wrong, ask, "Is this MAin 1-2345?" (Not "What number *is* this?") And you apologize before hanging up. If you're on the receiving end of a wrong-number call, don't hang up silently as soon as you hear the strange voice. Tell the caller nicely, "I'm afraid you have the wrong number." There would be fewer of these if callers made sure of the number before dialing, and if they dialed carefully and slowly.

Crank calls It may seem like the funniest thing in the world to phone a friend and just breathe heavily into the mouthpiece . . . or to get a boy to call a girl you know (and he doesn't) and flirt with her . . . or to leave a strange message . . . or to give false new instructions about a party. Just as you don't mail a letter you'd be ashamed of, you don't make phone calls you'd rather not remember.

If you get crank calls, handle them briefly and firmly; it's humiliating to string along with an unknown Romeo and have the conversation end with howls of laughter from the friends (the what?) at the other end of the phone.

Just say, "I'm sorry. I have to hang up." And do it. If the teaser calls back and you recognize the voice, quietly disconnect the call by depressing the connection on the instrument.

Sometimes a series of crank calls can be alarming. If the unknown voice at the other end tries to get you to meet him somewhere, don't go—even with another friend for so-called protection. If the unknown has the voice with a leer instead of a smile, doesn't try to meet you but calls often or at queer hours —or if the unknown makes some kind of threat—inform your family so they can ask the telephone company to monitor the calls and arrange to have the annoyer and the annoyance stopped.

Smile at the voice with a smile There's little point in losing your temper with a telephone operator. If "all the circuits are busy, Miss," they're busy, and no amount of annoyance will free them. Most telephone operators are noted for being helpful and courteous, so be the same to them.

If you wish to signal an operator, push the little plunger on your set slowly. This will light a little bulb on the switchboard and let the operator know something's amiss. Jiggle the plunger too fast and the light won't work; all the operator will hear is a senseless clicking.

The telephone at work When you have a job, you will use the telephone as your employer directs—to intercept calls for him, take orders, or whatever. Refinements vary from office to office, but these pointers will help you get off to the right start. They are instructions which your employer expects *not* to have to give you:

- Keep personal calls, incoming and outgoing, to the barest possible minimum. (Many employers forbid them entirely, except in cases of emergency.) Before calling a friend at her office, find out whether she is permitted to receive calls.
- Take messages clearly and completely and deliver them promptly. Write down the caller's name and number (and, if the name is unfamiliar, ask for his company affiliation); the date and time of the call; whether the caller wishes his call returned or will call back himself; and any brief message he asks to leave. Like this:

  > 9/12—11 A.M.
  > Mr. Lucas of Jones Brothers called. Will the shipment be ready by the first? Please call him—MAin 1-2345

  Don't feel shy about asking how to spell a complicated or unfamiliar name. People with complicated names have long since learned to take this in their stride and would prefer to spell the name out for you than have you garble it.

- If the caller must wait for your boss to answer, reassure him from time to time: "Mr. Jones is on the other extension. Would you mind waiting a minute? . . ." "Mr. Jones will be with you in a minute." Don't leave the caller hanging on a dead phone.
- Be helpful—never curt. Don't say, to a caller who asks for Mr. Jones, "He's not here." Instead, say something like "I'm sorry. Mr. Jones is out of the office. I expect him back in about an hour. May I take a message?"
- Thank the caller: in a business office, "thank you" is a much better sign-off phrase for a very junior staff member than "good-by."

As you come to the end of a call you've received, it's very pleasant manners to say, "Thank you for calling"—whether the call is business, social or the department store trying to sell you moth crystals. Volunteer workers who call to ask you to make brownies for the church cake sale, to sell you Christmas cards for a charity or to ask for your help at the hospital especially deserve this kind of courteous treatment; even if you can't help them, they deserve appreciation for what they're doing.

16. Good Guestmanship

One of the nicest compliments is to be a guest: someone thinks enough of you to want to entertain you. Being a dinner guest or a house guest involves more formality than lunches, teas and parties with your friends—because grown members of a family are present.

HOW TO BE A DINNER GUEST

Suppose a boy asks you to dinner—on a Sunday, perhaps—to meet his family. You're delighted, of course, and possibly a bit edgy, because in a sense you will be on display. You want very much to be at ease and to be the kind of girl his mother expects her son to like. This guide will help you:

wear a simple, pretty dress; pumps; gloves—the same kind of clothes you'd wear to church on Sunday. Leave gloves, coat, hat, if you're wearing one, wherever you're told, but keep your bag with you if you like.

ask if you can help when your hostess heads for the kitchen after you've all talked awhile. "Could I do something, Mrs. Clark—carry in plates, perhaps? I'm used to helping my mother . . ." She may take you up on the offer or say, "Why don't you stay with Jack? He wants to show you his record collection." Do whatever she suggests. If she has no maid, offer some positive help during dinner: "Would you like me to take the dishes out, Mrs. Clark?" Some hostesses adore the friendliness of guests' helping; it makes others nervous.

before dinner some families serve sherry or cocktails, and often tomato or fruit juice will be passed too. "No, thank you" is the only answer you have to give if you don't care for anything.

when you go in to dinner wait till your hostess sits down before you take your place (which very likely will be on your host's right, unless there is another older woman present). If your hostess says to sit down and not wait for her, wait just long enough to give your beau or his father a chance to seat you.

a blessing is often asked, especially on Sunday, by the host or one of the younger children. Wait before starting to chat, until you're sure it won't be. Bow your head, if it is, and you may murmur "amen" at the end. Quaker families say grace with all around the table joining hands, and some families belonging to other faiths have adopted this charming custom. Some families say grace after meals too.

if your host is carving the Sunday roast, have a positive opinion when he asks how you like your beef or whether you prefer the dark or the light meat of the turkey. "Rare, please" or "Dark meat would be fine, thank you" is much more appealing to the carver than "Oh, just anything."

if you're not sure your hostess has placed the silver in the order you'll use it, wait to see which implement she uses (good reason for waiting till she begins to eat)—or casually note which one your host, who'll be nearer to you, is using. After all, he knows her system.

if food is "portioned"—tomato juice at your place when you walk in to dinner or cups of jellied consommé served by a maid—don't refuse it. Accept and go through the motions of taking a little.

if wine is served, the way to refuse it is to say "No, thank you" to whoever is pouring. You don't cup your hand over the whole top of the glass or turn the glass upside down.

taking seconds is a cheery sight to a hostess, so you're wise not to help yourself too bountifully the first time. Wait till you're asked, though. But you may ask for another glass of water or for rolls or jelly, which is passed around the table. Eat every last bite on your plate if you want to; it's a great compliment.

you may refuse, quietly, any food which either makes you sick or conflicts with principles of your faith—such as ham or shellfish for an Orthodox Jew or meat on Friday for a Roman Catholic. Eat vegetables and rolls and don't ask for substitutes. Some devout people feel a guest should eat whatever is served, but this is a decision you should work out with a clergyman.

during the meal try to talk first with the person on one side of you, then with the one on the other—so the table will "turn" and so you won't neglect either. At a small dinner, of course, much of the chatter may be general or even crisscross.

if you help clear the table for dessert, it's usual to take away almost everything. Remove salt dishes and pepper pots, butter plates—all but dessert fork and spoon, if they're on the table (see page 268). You'd leave nut and candy dishes, ash trays and cigarettes—and, of course, the centerpiece.

you serve and remove everything from the left—except for water, coffee and other drinks, all of which are served from the right, where they'll be used.

don't be apprehensive about making a mistake at the table or when you're helping clear or serve. People with nice manners aren't critical of guests.

leave the table when your hostess gives the signal by getting up herself. And, again, be ready to help.

if you help with K.P., do things the way your hostess (more likely his mother) wishes. If Mrs. Clark wants you to use a dishpan and you're used to washing dishes under running water, use the dishpan. It's her kitchen.

stay no longer than an hour or so after dinner unless you've been especially asked to beforehand.

say good-by to everyone visible, with a special thank-you to your hostess and some mention of how good the dinner was.

tell your beau you think his family is great and you've never had a better time.

HOW TO BE A HOUSE GUEST

This is a little like being a dinner guest for several days, with some added hurdles—which, like all challenges, become easy when you've met them once or twice.

a written invitation calls for a written answer. If it comes from a boy asking you to visit his home, his mother should also write and ask you. Sometimes she means to and doesn't quite get around to it. See page 141 for what to do about this. If the invitation had few details in it, you might ask if you'll need anything special—for parties, sports, a hat for church. Give the exact time and place (railroad depot, bus terminal) of arrival.

if fetching you might pose a problem, let your hostess know you can manage your own transportation; stations, depots, terminals have taxi service.

pack cannily, including the things you'll need—your tennis racket, extra stockings, a little sewing kit, your own book to read. But don't alarm your hostess by arriving with enough luggage to stay the summer!

take something for your hostess. There are always books and candy to choose from—or seed packets or bulbs for the garden; tennis balls, if that's the family sport; a record; a new game you think everybody might enjoy playing; a tenpenny item for each little brother and sister.

if you visit the family often you needn't bring a gift every time—but you must write a thank-you.

Here's a description of the perfect house guest:

- She was kind to the house—didn't leave her own things strewn around the living room or the terrace, made her bed (even when there's a maid, she should offer), kept her room as pretty as it was when she walked in, left the bathroom as neat as a pin.
- She observed the customs of the house. If everyone got up for breakfast, she did too—and she asked first if shorts were acceptable for breakfast and lunch. If the family dog was meant to stay outside, she didn't play with it in the living room.
- She made a point of being agreeable—to prearranged blind dates, younger brothers, all family friends. She stayed out of any family fracas, took no sides in any disagreement, but went along with whatever decision was made.
- She joined in all the fun: she played the games, went to the pony show, tried to learn the new dance.
- She didn't have to be amused every minute—she had a book to read, socks to knit when everyone else was busy—and she didn't feel left out or slighted.
- She didn't raid the refrigerator or the cookie jar unbidden.
- She didn't at any time, during her visit or after, reveal her hostess's family secrets, discuss family tiffs or in general discuss her hostess or the family unpleasantly.
- She didn't call up local friends (whom her hostess or beau didn't know) and chat away. She didn't ask any friend to visit her unless her hostess suggested it. And she didn't make plans to visit one of the friends—with or without her hostess—until she'd asked if her hostess would like to meet the friend.
- She kept a list of any toll calls and the charges (see page 133) and left both list and money for her hostess.
- She didn't accept any outside invitations—unless they included the boy or girl she was visiting. And then she checked with him or her before saying yes.
- The day she left, she rounded up all her possessions so no one would have to wrap and mail her book or sweater. She asked whether she should strip her bed before making it. She left her room looking fresh and neat.
- She thanked the maid or the cook, if such there were, when she left. She gave the maid (and any other servant who had helped her—the cook perhaps, but not a child's nurse or a gardener) a modest tip. (One dollar is usual for a weekend.) If she had felt shy about handing the money to the

maid, she would have left it on her bureau in an envelope with "Thank you, Hannah"—the maid's name—and her own name signed below.

- She left when she said she would—unless sincerely urged, for a special reason, to stay a day or so longer.
- She said good-by to all the family and thanked them.
- A day or so after she got home, she thanked her hostess and the boy or girl who was her junior host—and anyone else who had entertained her with a party or some special treat. (Good chance to keep in touch with boys one meets—assuming you were visiting a girl.)

Break anything? A house guest should apologize (not over and over) and offer to replace it if it's something she can afford—for example, a plate from a standard pattern. But no teen can replace or repair a marred tabletop or ketchup-splattered porch sofa—and no hospitable family will accept an offer to pay the furniture-repair or dry-cleaning bill. (So don't make the offer.) Do avoid trouble—by not leaving wet glasses on tabletops, tipping back in straight chairs, and all those other tricks that bring on trouble.

ABOUT VISITING A BOY'S FAMILY

Is it proper for a girl to visit a boy and his family for overnight or longer? Yes, provided you know his parents expect you and will be on hand to chaperon you. They might go to an afternoon or early-evening party and leave the two of you to your own devices, but they should be at home in the evening (if you are), and certainly *they* shouldn't take this opportunity to make an overnight visit of their own.

You needn't submit the boy to a Victorian cross-examination on these points before your visit, but if you know him well enough to have him invite you to visit him, you either *know* his family will be around or you can ask him subtly—perhaps even by saying, "I'd love to come—and I do want to see your family again (or meet them)." If your family and his haven't met, you ask him, "Will your mother write mine, so I can come?"

If you are left at the house a long, long time, just the two of you together, you might suggest a walk or drive—particularly if it's after dark. It isn't so much a question of what you might do; one can do what one wants just about anywhere. It's a matter of conventions—which are intended to safeguard you and your good name (and also your hostess's).

Pay for your own transportation to and from your host's, unless you are driven both ways. It's always a good idea to buy a round-trip ticket and save the embarrassment of a good-by interrupted with a mad dash to the ticket window. (You can cash in the return ticket later, should your beau offer to drive you home.)

Don't flirt freely with, or date, other boys you might meet during your visit. Should you ask him to visit you? It's nice, if your parents are willing.

Visiting a club? You'll find details on page 73-74.

Guest on an outing? Suppose Jane's family asks you to go out to dinner with them or to the beach or the theater. You act as you would if you were visiting them at home, with this important extra: *You are exactly on time when they call for you.*

When you're the hostess The happy guest is the cared-for guest—but not the one who's goaded into activity, constantly fussed over or—at the other extreme—left to find her own amusement.

The perfect hostess

- welcomes a guest at the door, introduces him to others present—but never struggles to make a complete circuit of a crowded room
- sees a guest to the door at the end of the party, makes sure he has transportation home: finds another guest with a car, if first guest is going more than walkable distance and bus or subway transportation isn't available, or calls a cab for the guest (If girl guest is going home alone at night, the hostess asks a boy to take her—or at least to wait with her for the bus.)
- is definite about plans for entertaining a house guest: lets guest know, in invitation, whether to bring skates, if there will be a dance Saturday night; is specific about length of visit so guest can keep his family informed
- gives house guest a good bed with clean sheets and pillow cases. (If this puts the hostess on the folding cot, she takes the cot.)
- makes other provisions for guest's comfort—towels and washcloth and a place to hang them, either in the bathroom or on the back of a closet door. (Good idea: give guest towels in different color from ones used by members of the family.) Put out enough blankets, clear some drawer space, and make sure lining paper is fresh. See that there are enough hangers, including skirt or trouser hangers—and enough hanger space. Make sure there are ash trays and matches, a drinking glass, facial tissues, a few books, a readable alarm clock.
- tells guest what time breakfast is, when and where lunch will be, other plans
- remembers her guest if asked to stop by at a friend's house: says, "I'd love to, but I have a house guest . . . " (Gives name.) Usually both will be asked to come unless hostess was being asked as a fourth for bridge.
- doesn't go to a party without her house guest. If guest is a boy, no problem. If a girl, hostess may not be able to scrounge up one more boy, so don't feel

sorry for yourself if you miss the party. If you have a beau, he may be able to arrange a double date.

Two unwanted guests to avoid, to avoid being:

1. The unbidden soul who shows up just before mealtime and almost *has* to be asked to stay for dinner.
2. The overnighter, usually a country dweller, who takes over a city friend's spare bed every time she has a dentist's appointment or a date in town. It's not good to use a friend's apartment as a hotel.

   If a long-time friend offers come-and-go-as-you-please hospitality—and you know she means it and won't be inconvenienced—make a point of seeing her at breakfast, saving enough time for a real visit, doing something special for her or her apartment, bringing her a special present. But don't just check in and out.

WHEN TO ARRIVE AT AND LEAVE A PARTY

Lunch—Brunch Arrive on time or up to 15 minutes late. Leave half an hour to an hour after meal is finished, unless afternoon activities are planned by hostess.

Dinner Arrive on time or up to 15 minutes late. Leave about an hour or an hour and a half after meal is finished, unless evening activities (charades, dancing, etc.) are planned by hostess or you sense "come to dinner" means "come for the evening."

Tea Stay half an hour at a big tea at any time during the hours of the party (four to six). (At sorority rush teas you often stay even less time, particularly if you have several sorority houses to visit.)

Open house Come and go any time during the hours of the party. Don't arrive at the start and stay till all other guests have left! Minimum stay: one-half hour to one hour.

Evening party (records, etc.) Come 15 minutes to one-half hour after stated opening hour; leave when invitation says to, or at approach of your curfew hour—or when hostess or her family start making go-home noises.

Dance (prom or any formal dance) Come half hour to one hour after opening hour—no later! Leave before the band does—or at least *when* it does. Don't linger longer than that.

Dessert and coffee Come on time, though up to 10 minutes late is permissible. Leave no sooner than an hour after food is eaten.

Morning coffee Come on time or 10 minutes late at the latest. Stay about an hour or an hour and a half.

Shower Come on time. Leave about half hour to an hour after presents have been opened and refreshments eaten.

Wedding Get to church or other place where ceremony is to be held at least 15 minutes ahead of time. Don't leave reception until bride and groom have cut cake (if there is one to cut). Be sure to leave immediately after bride and groom have left.

Other ceremonies Be there on time, *always.*

If you are guest of honor at a party, come on time or when hostess tells you to. Stay until all other guests have left, if possible. If party is dying and other guests are waiting for you to leave, however, take the initiative and leave.

Never leave a party until refreshments have been served. If you must leave early, tell your hostess beforehand or on arrival. Otherwise she is apt to feel hurt.

If you are unavoidably late for a meal, phone your hostess and urge her to go ahead without you. (This doesn't hold in the case of teas.) And she should go ahead: there is no point in penalizing guests who have come on time.

If you are giving a party and one or two guests are very late, go ahead and serve dinner or lunch. When the late-comer finally arrives, just smile and say, "I'm sure you wouldn't have wanted us to wait." If you've had a soup course or appetizer, don't bother to give the late-comer that, but do feed her a main course, even if other guests are eating dessert. Then let her skip dessert or bring hers into the living room.

17. Table Manners That Take You Anywhere

Any meal is a sociable occasion, and good table manners add to the sociability. The one magnificent reason for having them is so everyone can enjoy the food that's served. *Relaxed but thoughtful* is probably the key phrase that describes the kind of person you like to eat with. Most of the rules have been dinned at you since you were bib age, but constant repetition may have dulled some of the points, so perhaps a review is in order:

- Wait till a few others have been served before starting. When you're a guest, take your cue from your hostess; some families say grace before a meal. Mind her, though, if she says go ahead and don't wait for her.
- A *napkin* goes on your lap unless you tuck it under your chin at a spaghetti or lobster feast. When you leave the table, deposit it at the left side of your plate; the only time you fold it is when you're given a napkin ring.
- You sit up straight, with the chair pulled in to the table. You'll look better and the food won't dribble on your clothes or the floor.
- *Elbows* are fine on the table—occasionally—except when you have food or eating implements in hand.
- *Fidgeting* spoils the appetite (the other fellow's). Stop it if you find you're carving patterns on the tablecloth with a fork, fiddling with the silver or running a finger idly around the rim of your glass.
- If you're not sure *which fork* to use, eye your hostess. Most tables have the silver set from the outside in, toward the plate, in the order in which it will be needed. Many restaurants put every piece of silver they can find at each place; that's when you have to take your chances. Most people will just think you're absent-minded if you take the wrong implement.
- Food stays pretty much at plate level until you're ready to put it in your mouth. Hold bread close to the butter plate when you break and butter it.
- *Elbows* stay at table level even if the meat is tough to cut.
- You *don't reach* across anyone else's place. "May I have the salt, please?" is the way to get it.
- *If you drop* an implement, leave it on the floor until the meal is over. If you're in a restaurant, you don't pick it up at all.
- *Any glass* with a stem is held by the bowl for better balance. Otherwise it might wobble and spill.
- It's a nice idea to pat your mouth with a tissue before drinking out of a glass: it avoids unaesthetic smudges.

- *The long spoon* served with iced tea, a soda or a milk shake goes in the saucer when you're not using it. No saucer? Leave the spoon in the glass and brace it with your forefinger when you drink so you won't jab your eye.
- *Mouths are zipped up when chewing.* Soup is not slurped. Teeth are not clicked noisily with spoons. Only puppies are cute smacking their food.
- Follow pattern of host or hostess before you pick up drumstick or chop bone. Some people do. Some people don't.
- Learn to answer a question neatly when your mouth is full.
- But not too full! Food should be cut to manageable size—one piece at a time. A plate of "minced-up" food looks right at a toddler's place, not at a teen's.
- Butter and jelly are never spread on a whole slice of *bread* or *toast*. Break, butter and eat is the order. For *rolls,* too. But you'd probably break and butter all the pieces of a hot popover so the butter would melt nicely.
- When you need a *pusher* to help corral stray morsels on your plate, use a crust of bread.
- If there's no spoon for the *salt dish,* use the blade of a clean knife.
- Be matter-of-fact about *removing the uneatable* from your mouth. Slide prune pits out of your mouth onto your spoon and then to the plate. Olive pits, fishbones and slivers of bird and chop bones should be chewed reasonably clean before you remove them with your fingers. A piece of meat you can't chew is slid onto the fork and put on the rim of your plate. (Don't retire behind your napkin for any of these maneuvers.)
- Choking a little? Take a sip of water—or leave the table till you've recovered.
- When a platter or dish is *served to you,* use the serving fork to steady the food and the serving spoon to lift the food to your plate. Then replace the fork and spoon, side by side, so handles stay clear of food. Take small portions; you're almost sure to get a second chance. When a serving dish is *passed around* the table, hold or steady it for the next person.
- Hand a *pitcher* with the handle pointing toward the receiver.
- Put *sandwiches* and other finger foods on your plate before eating them.
- Implements you have used never go in dishes others will share—your spoon in the sugar bowl, as an example.
- If you see an implement in a dish, use it instead of fingers—a pickle or lemon fork, sugar or ice tongs, nut spoon.
- Never leave a spoon in the coffee, egg or soup cup or in the dessert dish. Rest it on the saucer or plate beneath.
- When you pass your plate for seconds, or *when you've finished,* place the knife and fork, the spoon or fork, or the dessert spoon and fork side by side on the plate—so the handles rest on the rim and the tips are in the well of the plate. That keeps the silver from bouncing off.

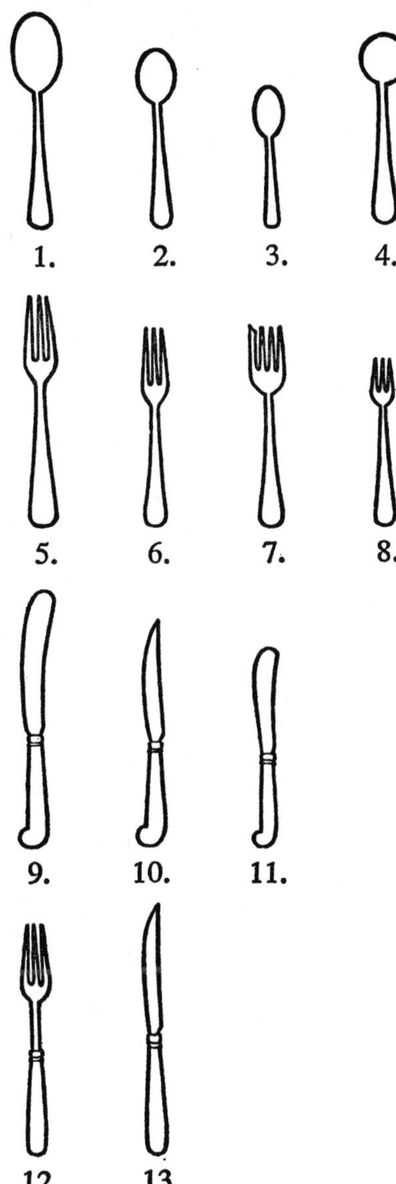

1. Dessert or cereal spoon; also used for soup, unless it is served in a soup cup. (Use #4, round-bowl soupspoon, or #2, teaspoon for soup cup.)
2. Teaspoon; used for tea, large cups of coffee and desserts (custard, mousse, *pot de crème*) served in baking cups or glass dishes, where it would be cumbersome to use #1, dessertspoon.
3. After-dinner coffee spoon.
4. Round-bowl soupspoon.
5. Dinner fork.
6. Smaller fork; used for lunch, salad, dessert.
7. Salad or dessert fork, with broader first tine for cutting.
8. Oyster fork; also used for lobster, shrimp, crab meat.
9. Dinner knife.
10. Steak knife with short, razor-sharp blade—often serrated—and long handle.
11. Butter knife or spreader with flat blade; useful for serving cheese and dips.
12. Fruit fork, usually with three tines.
13. Fruit knife with sharp steel blade.

- When finished with main course knife and fork are placed neatly side by side, blade-side turned toward center of plate.
- Don't push the plate away from you when you've finished.
- When a *finger bowl* is served it usually rests on a doily (paper, linen or lace). Pick up the dessert fork and spoon that rest on either side of the bowl and put them on either side of the plate. Then lift the finger bowl and doily and place them about where the butter plate was—in front and left of your plate. When you've had your dessert, dip the fingers of one hand in the water and dry them on your napkin; then do the other hand. Brush wet finger tips across your mouth too, if you like. Finger bowls also may appear when lobster, steamed clams and other "exuberant" foods are served.
- When *soup* is served in a cup, you sip it from a spoon or directly from the cup: that's the reason for the handles. Soup served in a plate or bowl must be sipped from the spoon. For either kind, move the soupspoon away from you to fill it, to prevent stray splashes on your clothes. Drink the soup from either the side or the tip of the spoon. To get the last mouthful, tip the soup dish away from you.
- Eat *steamed clams* with your fingers. Hold the clam by the neck, dip it in the melted butter and pop the whole thing in your mouth.
- *Oysters* and *clams* on the half shell are eaten with an oyster fork. Spear, dip in sauce and eat whole. These can't be cut. (Order littleneck clams if cherry stones and oysters are oversize for you.)
- *Shrimp, lobster* and *crab-meat cocktails* are eaten with an oyster fork. Eat the shrimp whole. If oversized, they should be cut in half with fork.
- *Japanese butterfly shrimp, French fried shrimp, and Italian scampi* are eaten with the fingers: lift the shrimp by the tail, dip it in the sauce or eat it plain.
- You crack the claws of *lobster* and hard-shelled *crab* with a nutcracker. (They're usually partially cracked when served.) Use an oyster fork to extract the meat from the shell. Use the fork to spear the claw meat and dip it in the sauce. Eat the delicious meat and green roe in the lobster's middle as well as the white meat.
- *Trout, bluefish* and the like can be boned in one flourish, after first trimming off the head. Steady the fish with your fork and gently slit it from head to tail with your knife. Using both fork and knife, open the fish out flat. Insert the tip of the knife under one end of the backbone, ease it up so that little bones won't break off, and put the skeleton aside. The waiter usually does this for you in a restaurant. A few bones may remain, however skillful you are, so use caution in eating.
- Birds—*chicken, duck, turkey, pheasant* and *other game birds*—are eaten with a knife and fork unless you're among friends—and the meal is exceptionally casual. Chop bones and crisp bacon obey the same house rules.

- *Baked potatoes* need lots of butter. Use your fork to work the butter into the potato and to mash it through, prongs up. Use the same procedure if you butter the skin: you'll need your knife to cut it and eat it, piece by piece.
- *French fried potatoes* are eaten with a fork; you cut them in half with a fork if they are bigger than bite-size. (Eat them with your fingers at a picnic or drive-in.)
- *Spaghetti* is slippery. Eat it peasant-style for pleasure, winding it around a fork held against a large spoon.
- *Corn on the cob* is neater when you butter, salt and eat only a few rows at a time. Hold the ear in both hands if you want to.
- Hot and cold *artichokes* are eaten leaf by leaf until you get to the heart. Dip the plump edible part of the leaf in sauce and glide it between your teeth to get the meat; scraped leaves are placed in a neat circle on your plate. When you come to the thistly part, scrape it away with your knife; eat the heart with a fork, dipping each bite into the sauce.
- Eat *asparagus* with your fingers. You may eat the tips with a fork if the spears are too long to manage.
- Use a spoon for avocado (alligator pear) when it's served in its shell and filled with French dressing or some kind of sea food. Use a fork, of course, when it's removed from the shell and sliced.
- Cut a club *sandwich* in smaller wedges if it's hard to handle. You may use a fork for a gooey sandwich, and you need both knife and fork for hot sandwiches.
- *Pizza?* Just bend it so you can get it in the mouth.
- *Condiments*—jelly, mustard, ketchup, relishes—go on your plate first instead of directly on the food. Bring the cranberry jelly to the turkey rather than dunking the bits of turkey in the jelly. Use your knife to transfer the relish or the ketchup from your plate to the hamburger.
- Put *celery, olives* and *pickles* on your butter plate. Use your fingers to transfer all three unless there's a pickle fork for the pickles.
- *Honey* is less likely to drip if you twirl the spoon quickly just before carrying it from the jar to your plate.
- *Grapefruit* is easier to eat if the segments have been separated with a curved grapefruit knife—or if you have narrow-pointed grapefruit spoons (some of which have saw-toothed tips).
- When fresh *strawberries* are served with their hulls on—in a ring around a little heap of sugar or with tiny bowls of brown sugar and sour cream—grasp the hull, dip the berry in the sugar and/or sour cream. Don't let the hull out of your finger tips until you've placed it back on the plate.
- *Fruit cocktail* is eaten with a spoon.

- *Cherries and grapes* are eaten whole; your cupped hand catches the pits and puts them on the plate. Incidentally, break off a small bunch of grapes from the stalk rather than plucking one grape at a time from the centerpiece.
- *Apricots and plums* are eaten whole or in several bites. Remove the pits from your mouth with your finger tips.
- When *apples, peaches and pears* are eaten at the table, they should be quartered and cored with a fruit knife—peeled, too, if you like. Eat the pieces with your fingers or with a knife and fork, as the Europeans do.
- If you're served a *parfait* for dessert, eat it as it comes, without attempting to scoop up the ice cream and sauce at the bottom until you have eaten the whipped cream and cherry on the top.
- *Fruit cake and poundcake, angel cake,* and tiny, iced, bite-size tidbits (called *petits fours* by caterers) are eaten with the fingers. *Sticky cakes, éclairs and napoleons* are eaten with a fork—better yet, with a fork and spoon. *Any complicated dessert* is managed more easily with a dessert fork and spoon. Cake à la mode is a well-known example: you may eat it with a fork; if you have both fork and spoon, you can steady it with the fork in one hand, cut and eat both ice cream and cake with the spoon in the other. (The prongs of the fork are held down, with the front of the fork turned your way.)
- Eat *pie* with the dessert fork; a *fruit tart* may need both implements.
- When *candy* is passed to you—whether it's still in the box or more attractively placed in a dish—pick it up with its paper frill. Don't agonize over the selection, and always take the piece of candy you touch. (Eat the candy, put the frill aside.)
- *Say something nice* about the food—to your mother or your hostess. Anyone who cooks or plans a meal has tried to please, deserves your appreciation.
- *Smoking* at the dinner table bothers some hostesses. Better not to, if you're among elders. Moreover, it dulls your taste and cuts down your own enjoyment of the meal.

18. For Men Only

Men are nice to have around—and if you're not absolutely certain of this, just watch the girls' faces light up when an attractive boy joins the group. An attractive boy can be tall and thin, short and thin, tall and husky, short and husky. It isn't a way of looking that makes him attractive—it's because his manners are those of a gentleman. You can tell because he

- stands up promptly when a girl, a grown woman or an older man comes into the room or crosses it to talk with him
- opens doors for such people and steps back to let them through first
- is the last to get in a car and the first to get out
- carries parcels for ladies of any age (not packages that look too feminine or a handbag; besides, no sensible girl would let him)
- says "sir" to older men
- gives up his seat on the bus or subway to someone who needs it (not necessarily to a pretty girl who is perfectly able to stand—unless she is holding a baby, looks as though she will be shortly or is carrying a large rubber plant)
- never uses a small courtesy—picking up a package or a glove—as a wedge for starting a conversation with a girl in public places, such as the subway and the movies
- helps a lady remove her coat in a restaurant, movie, theater, church—and hangs it up or checks it, if necessary
- leads a girl to a restaurant table and pulls back her chair—or, in a more formal restaurant, lets the girl follow the captain, who will pull out her chair
- gives the order to the waiter or waitress (or captain) after asking the lady what she would like: he gives her choices first for each course, and this makes serving the meal smoother for all. (More about restaurant behavior on page 85.)

Attractive men know all the complimentary customs, the little extras that make a girl feel attractive, too. (Actually this being attractive is as "catching" as the common cold—now referred to as a virus—and it certainly raises the happiness level.) The attractive boy knows how to say hello; he smiles, shakes hands firmly, doesn't fuss about taking off his glove if the delay would make matters awkward. When he passes a girl he knows on the street, he touches his hat in a sort of half-salute. If he stops to talk, he takes it off (not by the brim but by pinching the crown and lifting the hat off). The hat also comes off in an apartment-house elevator, when he's introduced, or talking to any older person. The hat stays on in office elevators, lobbies and halls, such public buildings as post offices, terminals, stores.

A proper bow is an extra courtesy when greeting girls or women, especially on the street, and when acknowledging introductions—"proper" meaning a low nod with a little shoulder action added, but not the dancing-class bow complete with flapping forelock.

When he walks down the street with a female of any age, the attractive boy automatically walks on the curb side—but if the pair is crisscrossing streets, he doesn't scurry to the curb side every time. He helps a girl across the street (curbs, broken paving, traffic provide an opportunity to protect the little lady). He doesn't cuddle arm in arm when strolling (well, not *always*), but he does offer a girl his arm. He may grab her hand as they walk but never clutch her elbow and use it as a rudder to steer her along. He does take her elbow firmly when he's helping her board a bus or train; if they're both getting off a bus or train, he goes first so he can hand her down.

If he smokes, he offers the girl or woman he's with a cigarette every time he takes one—unless she's said, "Thank you, but I don't smoke." He asks, "Mind if I smoke?"—before lighting up—if no one else is smoking. When a woman takes a cigarette, he lights it for her.

And speaking of asking permission, he doesn't take off his jacket when he's with older people or visiting a girl's home unless he asks first. (Same thing holds for rearranging furniture at someone else's house, playing the phonograph or television, putting the sofa cushions on the floor or the feet on a coffee table.)

Getting along with girls (a free translation of dating problems) Girls like the boy who calls well ahead of time for a date; spontaneous dates are fun, but if he always calls on Friday, a girl isn't sure whether *he's* not so great and everyone else had turned him down—or whether *she's* not so great because she's near the end of his list. A boy who asks "Would you like to go to the movies with me Saturday?" or "Would you like to go with me to the prom?" is much less likely to get the busy signal than the one who asks, "What are you doing Saturday?" or "Do you have a date for the prom?"

Popular boys plan the evening's entertainment—even if it's as modest as a walk and a frozen custard—instead of arriving at the girl's doorstep and hanging around until she suggests the movies or whatever. (Most girls hesitate to make suggestions because they too have known the embarrassment of being short of funds.) A girl's family likes the idea of a boy's spending the evening at her house occasionally—but not date after date after date. (Boys who are poor but smart find out what can be fun without funds—a concert in the park, a rehearsal of the local pipe and drum corps, a special exhibit at the museum, a dress rehearsal of an orchestra or a show, even if it's a local-talent production.) And there are always other short-of-cash friends who can play bridge, games, dance—at the *other* girl's house.

Girls also like the boy who arrives on time for a date, even if he knows she won't be ready. Since he doesn't sit out in the car, honking impatiently, the time he spends waiting with Mr. and Mrs. Brown can be put to very good character-building. Such conversational topics as "I've been helping with the Sea Scouts, Mr. Brown, and at the meeting yesterday . . ." or "What time would you like me to bring Melissa home, Mrs. Brown? I realize next week is exam week. . . ." mark Melissa's beau as a very good young citizen.

Out on the town the boy hails a cab, if it's needed. He pays the fare, settles the bills, buys the tickets smoothly and matter-of-factly. If the tariff on a group date has gotten out of hand and he finds he's short of cash, he quietly floats a loan from another boy—but doesn't borrow from his date. If he wants to bring a girl flowers to wear, he can surprise her with a white camellia or a gardenia—always safe. Or he can ask her what she's wearing and talk the matter over with his friendly florist (it helps if he can give the florist a capsule description of the girl: she's tall and casual . . . she's little and likes oriental clothes . . . she always pins flowers to her bag).

At a party he brings friends to talk to his date and brings her into the conversation. If the girl is a duty date (his mother's best friend's daughter) or—worse luck—an unattractive blind date, he's as nice to her as he would be to a girl he really liked.

At a dance he dances with his date, his hostess and the guest of honor at a pre- or post-dance party. He makes sure his date has someone to dance or talk with while he's making the rounds of duty dances—never leaves her stranded. He waits at a prearranged spot while she goes to the ladies' room.

Things he never does include standing a girl up, breaking a date except for a very good reason, talking lightly of a girl's morals or describing his conquests, making his date feel conspicuous in public by talking too noisily, arguing (especially with waiters), or being too affectionate.

Speaking of affection, a boy is expected to take the lead and also to understand that *no* often means *no*. Most girls feel that a good-night kiss on the first date is less than flattering.

Unless it's really in fun, a boy should never trick a girl into kissing him. He shouldn't attempt to brainwash her or force her into necking with him. Girls aren't too happy about having to make a scene or to discourage a determined boy: it's humiliating to have a date get out of control.

Be honest about it, men. You will chase the girl till she catches you. If she doesn't know how to catch you now, she'll find the way in chapter 5—and make you enjoy the chase!

LOOKING THE PART

When you go out—whether it is on a date or to school or a job—how you look can help to make or break the impression you create.

Styles in the men's department don't change as fast as girls' fashions do, but the same standards of good taste, individuality and wearing the right thing hold true. Fads often dictate boys' taste in clothes, particularly the ones they wear at school: one year they're all in chinos and sweaters, the next in shorts, button-down oxford shirts and a straw fedora. Year in and year out, though, the pattern of dressing is pretty much like this:

Slacks, a sports shirt and a jacket for casual dates—the movies, bowling, going for a drive. Boys who live in cities, especially eastern ones, wear a shirt and a tie instead of a sports shirt on a date or at an informal party. All of them do so when they're going to a restaurant.

A dark suit, a white shirt and a tie for bigger dates—dinner with a girl's family, parties, church services and weddings.

A dark or light suit; a plain, colored or striped shirt; and a tie for business. Many large corporations forbid slacks and a sports jacket and permit only suits.

Black tie and a dinner coat (or a summer dinner coat) for most dances, any dinner party where the hostess asks you to dress. Black tie can also mean whatever the current fashion is: Paisley silk bow ties and cummerbunds, madras cotton and authentic wool tartan bow ties and cummerbunds, as well as maroon ones, have had, have, or will have their times of favor. A white tie is worn only with a tail coat when full evening dress is in order—an evening wedding, a coming-out party, an elaborate ball. Summer dinner coats can be just lightweight versions of winter ones, in black or that midnight navy, but they might also be madras cotton, Paisley silk or cotton, natural-colored linen or synthetic, white, or some strong, masculine-looking, bright color—yellow, light blue, a hunting pink (red as red). Lately some men have been wearing black-satin-faced tartan dinner coats in the winter. (Brilliant tartan trews (trousers) have been worn with a dress coat in Scotland for generations.)

Fitting—and proper when it does fit. This is very important to remember when you're buying a suit. Mothers aren't often alert to fitting details, and not many fathers have time to help sons buy suits—so here are the four ways to tell whether the fitter is doing a good job on your new suit:

1. The collar of the jacket should be low enough to show about half an inch of your shirt collar.
2. The sleeve of the jacket should show about half an inch of your shirt sleeve when your arm is down (a little more, of course, when it's bent).
3. The jacket shouldn't buckle at the point where the sleeves join the rest of the jacket.
4. The jacket shouldn't wrinkle across your back.
5. The jacket should button easily without dragging at the buttons as though the suit had shrunk.
6. The trousers should hang straight from the hips and just escape the tops of your shoes.
7. The trousers should fit trimly but comfortably—no baggy-pants-comedian effect.

What color shoes? Brown by day, unless you're heading for a wedding, a funeral. Older men often wear black shoes with a blue or gray suit in the daytime. *What cut?* Conservative laced oxfords or bluchers when you're not wearing moccasins or sneakers.

Good clothes care is "in" for men too. Well-shaped hangers for jackets and trouser hangers that keep seams plumb-straight are investments that will save both your suits and your pressing bills. Learn how to remove spots, even if you can get your mother or sister to fix them most of the time. Use shoe trees in the shoes you keep so slickly polished, and have new heels put on just before they are really needed.

And since families are the frankest, ask your father or your sister if your clothes look all right. Occasionally, we mean. They'll be pleased—even to the degree where your sister dedicates the next pair of Argyle socks to you.

19. Tips About Tipping

There's only one rule to learn about tipping—and that's to ask someone who knows the community and its customs. Your parents when you're at home, your hostess when you're visiting, a well-informed friend who's lived a number of years in a place that's new to you. Not only the amount you tip but also *whom* you tip may differ from town to town and from shop to shop in the same town.

Why tip? For three reasons, at least—as a mark of appreciation of good service, because the tip is an expected part of a service employee's weekly earnings, and to make sure you will continue to get good service. Knowing how to tip makes you more a part of the grown-up world. Since you are young, no one will expect you to tip as generously as an older person; your nice smile and polite thank-you will make the amount you tip acceptable.

Here is a check list of situations where you may be expected to tip and probable amounts. Do check the tipping customs where you are to make the suggestions accurate for you.

DELIVERY SERVICE

supermarket	No tip. You pay a fixed amount for delivery when you pay your tab, but you tip a boy if he carries large bags of items to your car.
laundry	No tip
department store	No tip. Unless a parcel is delivered as a special service—perhaps in bad weather—by an employee not hired to deliver packages

CHECKROOM SERVICE

	10¢ to 25¢, depending on the quality of the place. At a hotel or top restaurant, 25¢. At a skating rink, 10¢—unless you are checking many bundles, an umbrella and schoolbooks in addition to your coat; if so, 25¢

FOOD-AND-DRINK SERVICE

curb service	15% of bill but not less than 15–20¢
counter service	No tip. Unless you've received extra service or you are a frequent customer; 15¢ for the former, an occasional 15–25¢ for the latter
restaurant	
waiter or waitress	15% of the bill
captain or headwaiter or headwaitress maître (short for maître d'hotel *or the boss, he should never be referred to as the "maiter dee")*	$1 for helping you with a large group or special party, or for getting you a table at a crowded hour. Or if you are a frequent visitor to the restaurant—then tip $1 every ten visits or so; $1 for a special service—like getting you a better table, some out-of-the-ordinary dish, helping with a party, straightening out a mistake in the bill or returning some culinary mistake to the chef and getting you something else
bus boy or girl who brings rolls, water	No tip

TAXI SERVICE

	No tip in most suburban and country cabs who have a fixed price. In most cities, 10¢ for when the meter reads 40¢ or less; 15¢ if its under $1.; 20¢ up to $2. If you've had the driver wait while you picked up a package or a friend, 25¢

HOTEL SERVICE

doorman	No tip, unless he's gone to some visible trouble like minding your dog or parking your car.
bellboy	25¢ for one bag, 50¢ for several pieces, 25¢ for bringing ice, newspapers, clothes from the valet.
chambermaid	$1 a week; 50¢ for 2 or 3 days. Leave the money in an envelope on the dresser, marked "For the chambermaid, with thanks"
as a houseguest (after first asking your hostess if you may)	For a weekend, $1 to the cook and $1 to a maid who's unpacked for you, pressed your clothes. If the family's staff of one is both housekeeper and nurse, tip her $1. For a week's stay, double the amount. Most important is to find Anna, or whatever her name, to say, "Thank you, Anna, for making my visit so pleasant" and to give her a good-by handshake—with the money discreetly palmed from your hand to hers. Nine times out of ten, she will say, "Oh, miss, you didn't need to do *that.*" Smile and say you hope to see her again soon.

For suggestions about tipping hairdressers, see page 37.
For suggestions about tipping when traveling, see pages 109, 110, 113.

20. The Ins And Outs Of Fashion

Fashion—the art of personal appearance, the knack of having style or clothes sense, of knowing how to dress—is a skill some are blessed with; others have to study and practice to achieve it. It's easier to understand fashion if you think of it as being remarkably like understanding boys: both are unpredictable, positive, changeable, charming, indispensable—with a lot of rock-solid strength underneath the surface. As your taste and judgment become surer, you realize that the kinds of clothes you like fall into a pattern that suits your particular life.

You don't like every boy, you don't like every style—just the one that suits you. When you discover the strength underneath the whims of fashion, you can be decisive about what is best for you.

What makes for a strong fashion sense?

- *having a sense of style,* a willingness to accept the current and the new *within the limits* of what's becoming to you. Example: a full-swinging coat that foreshortens arms and legs, if you are small—so you get a flared coat that gives the effect of the full coat within your dimensions.
- *recognizing what is in good taste* and pleases the eye, whether the wearer is standing, sitting or moving. Examples: you like a sweater that fits easily instead of one you bulge in. The dress or skirt you buy has a gentle swing; it doesn't cling to your thighs, ride up or wrinkle when you walk or sit.
- *being individual,* catering to your own special likes. Example: you wear a pale-blue belt with a navy dress instead of the obvious red one. You team a sherbet-colored sweater—orange, lemon or lime—with a beige dress instead of the expected red, white or blue.
- *learning to dress for yourself* instead of just for special occasions or special people. As a young teen-ager, I had a crush on a sophisticated older woman who was a friend of my family's. I admired her very much and was embarrassed one day to discover she had come to lunch—and there I was, looking very scraggly and badly put together. I mumbled something about being sorry to look so awful when she was there, and she said gently, "You should always be well groomed *for yourself.*" Her words made a great impression on me, and I have learned that dressing for myself, trying always to look my best—whether I'm at work, going to a dance or digging in the garden—adds immeasurably to the self-confidence and inner serenity that make for happy living.
- *wearing the right thing* at the right time. Example: you take a small bag on a date and save the larger one for your trip on the jet. You never wear

socks for town, business or dress occasions. You look pretty in a dress when you go to a tea, not careless in a sweater and skirt (*right* for school).

It figures that fashion varies with where you live and what the local customs are. Still, you needn't follow the herd over the cliff—if that's what following it would mean to the way you look. Suppose everyone in your group wears shorts for casual summer dates and you know you look terrible in them; you wear a tennis dress (one of the most ravishing of sports outfits) or a knee-capper skirt or culottes. As hemlines wander, you consider your own figure. Thin legs? You wear your skirts a bit shorter than average. Heavy legs? You wear yours a bit longer than average.

Suppose you live in a decidedly conservative part of the world, where the little black "nothing" dress is the accepted style. You're as young as you ever will be—and some black junior dresses are amazingly young—but as a rule you wear a little red dress, a little beige one or a little green one. You're hovering close to the norm, you won't violate good taste, but you will show your own sense of personal style and you'll be an individual. Fashion has its ins and outs, and that's part of the fun of being female. Still, some fashion conduct holds true. It's better, for example, to be underdressed than overdressed. It's better never to be carelessly dressed. These things are always IN, anywhere, anytime:

- put-togetherness: buttons on, hems sewn in place, stocking seams straight—or *no* seams at all
- clothes that fit. *Find* your size: if you are tall, don't squiggle into a short-waisted size; if you are tiny, look for a junior petite size instead of looking lost or misshapen in a regular size. Try every young department in the store until you find clothes that fit properly.
- neatness; pleats pressed, no smudges on your collar, no spots
- the girl look: it makes boys want to take care of you

These are always OUT:

- sloppiness, clothes held together by means of safety pins and cellophane tape—great *only* for travel emergencies
- clothes that bag or are too tight
- anything soiled (hallowed exception: sneakers.)
- the femme-fatale look: it scares boys
- the chorus-girl look: it makes boys nervous

Here are ins and some outs of various situations:

SCHOOL

In Well-cut separates—skirts, sweaters, blouses—and simple dresses; low-heeled and flat shoes; purses big enough to hold what you need, no more;

tailored jewelry and not too much of it; day-keyed make-up; ditto perfume and cologne.

Out Obviously meant-for-dates dresses—satins and velvets and the like—and low-cut blouses; too-short skirts; too-tight sweaters; teeter-totter heels; festoons of pearls; three-foot-high tote bags and the kind made of lucite with flowers imbedded in it; overemphasized make-up and fragrance; jewelry that rattles.

Note: Some schools and college campuses ban Bermuda shorts, blue jeans, long corduroy pants, knee-capper skirts and other departures from the regular skirt norm. If you're going away to school or going to school in a new town, it's wise to find out what's acceptable before stocking up on school clothes.

DATES

Depends what you're doing. The always INS and always OUTS, listed on the preceding page, apply here because presumably you wish to make a good impression on a boy. Other than that, here's what you might wear:

- for little dates—neighborhood movie, snack, just driving around—what you wear to school, with more feminine jewelry, a velvet bow to replace the barrette in your hair. A softer, dressier-than-school dress. A little perfume or more cologne. Shoes—pumps or skimmers—dressier than moccasins. And they're worn with stockings, not socks. Gloves look pretty.
- for bigger dates—dinner out, a movie downtown—things you wouldn't wear to school. Dressy separates; feminine dresses with little waists and pretty necklines; medium- to high-heeled shoes; stockings, of course; gloves; a smallish purse (easier to hold on your lap in a theater or restaurant than a large tote or satchel); a little perfume; jewelry to complement but not overpower your clothes.
- for an informal dance—anything from a skirt and sweater to the little red wool to a string-strapped silk. You know automatically if the dance is described as a sock hop or, verging more closely toward formality, the annual glee club dance. If in doubt, call a few friends who are going too. They'll be flattered you asked them and feel terribly fashion-wise in giving advice.
- for a prom or other formal dance—you wear an evening dress. (Neither the dress nor the dance itself is a "formal." This is a trade word used by people in the fashion business. You wouldn't use it any more than you'd wash out your "hosiery" or buy some new "millinery.") The dress can be long or short, covered up or modestly bared; it should simply be the most smashing dress you can find. (A few very special dances or proms are by tradition long-dress dances—gala parties, charity balls and benefits. This changes as fashion changes, however.)

A few special words

- Never waltz out the door in a brand-new evening dress without giving it a trial run—complete with all the underpinnings and outer trimmings—a few days before the dance.
- Be wary of costume details which might make you nervous. For instance, the tulle stole which came with your new dress. It looks enchanting when you stand all collected and serene in front of your bedroom mirror. But if it's likely to go flying off your shoulder like a distress signal the minute you try a merengue, leave it home. Or practice and practice dancing, stooping, sitting, rising with it, until you master its graceful art.

  Same thing with a hoop. Wear it up and down stairs, in and out of a few doors at home before the Big Night.
- Are your shoes in shape? If they got a bit muddy at the last dance, now's the time to repair the damage with cleaning fluid and maybe a touch-up of dye for fabric shoes—or leather cleaner for kid shoes.
- What will you wear as a wrap? It isn't necessary to borrow Aunt Ethel's mink. Costly furs look silly on a teen-ager. Wear a short jacket—or make a stole of plushy fake fur and line it to match or complement your dress. Or even wear your Sunday-Best coat. If it rains, don't be ashamed to wear a raincoat and galoshes—carrying your dancing shoes in a plastic bag.
- If long white gloves are part of the effect, try to keep them spotless. Take them off if they get soiled; no gloves at all are better than grubby ones. Take them off when you eat, but leave them on for sipping punch.
- Easy on the jewelry. Too much flash and dazzle make you look more like a chandelier than a girl. Also, if you wear a necklace, pin, rings and bracelet with your really fabulous earrings, you lose the impact of the earrings.

DOWNTOWN

When shopping or visiting the art museum for your term paper, wear school clothes or a simple dress or suit. No shorts, sneakers, grubby raincoats or beatnik pants.

ON THE JOB

You dress a little more formally than you would at school because you're in a more adult world. No socks are worn in an office. Certainly no shorts or sneakers. Avoid clanking jewelry, heavy make-up, too much perfume, low-cut or sheer blouses. If you have a date right after business hours, content yourself with a simple dress and a switch of accessories in the ladies' room. If you go all out with frills at nine in the morning, you won't feel too fresh and pretty by five anyway.

TRAVELING

On a plane or a train, wear wrinkle-proof clothes of the downtown or on-the-job variety. Nothing *bouffant,* sheer or fussy—or anything that's likely to get limp when you sit on it for a few hours. Take a purse big enough to hold what you need, roomy enough to accommodate the items you want to freshen and repair make-up.

In a car you wear shorts or slacks (neat ones) unless your destination is a downtown hotel or some other place you would normally wear a skirt. If you plan to visit all those places where Washington slept, wear a skirt or toss one in the back seat so you can put it on over shorts.

SUNDAY BEST

These clothes overlap a little with downtown, on-the-job and little- to medium-date clothes. A suit, a simple but pretty dress, dressy separates. Medium to high heels. For church, a hat, lace mantilla or veil wisp. Not a kerchief. And, of course, don't wear low-cut dresses or sports clothes in church.

WEDDINGS

Morning and afternoon weddings differ only slightly in formality, with the latter being dressier. Wear a suit (not a rough, tweedy one, though), any of your Sunday-Best or medium- to big-date clothes. You'll need a hat or veil, of course. If a hat, make it festive—flowery, maybe. For an evening wedding, you dress more formally, in a big-date dress or something between that and what you might wear to a prom. Use discretion here: you could wear a short evening dress of velvet with shoestring straps but not a long tulle one with acres of skirt. Don't wear fluffy white; you'll compete with the bride. And don't be so dressed up you compete with the bridesmaids either! Here, too, you'll need something on your head. Since most hats look odd with party dresses, wear a veil or headband. And if your dress is rather bare, you'll want a wrap or cover-up to wear for the religious ceremony.

P.S. on weddings. Guests shouldn't wear real flowers. That's the wedding party's privilege.

FUNERALS

Black is the traditional color of mourning in our society, but most teen-agers' black dresses are party dresses. If you haven't a Sunday-Best sort of black dress, wear something conservative in navy, gray, brown or deep green. No gay plaids or prints. If your one and only coat is Kelly green, borrow a darker one from a friend. For a church service you certainly need a hat; you might wear one to a service held in a funeral home, as an added mark of respect.

FASHION AT YOUR FINGER TIPS

This means gloves and bags. When you're in that middle age between childhood and being grown up, both are nuisances that parents urge on you. When you've developed your own special style, you can't live without either.

Gloves add a brisk, smart flourish to whatever you're wearing—a suit, an afternoon or evening dress, riding or (even though on one hand only) golf clothes. They have the same kind of immaculate, staccato chic that white spats give a band of Scottish pipers marching down the street. Gloves are stylish only when they are spanking clean, in perfect repair. Wrist-length gloves, plain or with the simplest stitching, are perfect—and you have a fabulous selection of cottons, nylons, knits, wools and leathers to build your glove wardrobe from. Some ceremonious occasions—a coming-out party, a ball—may demand long gloves; be sure they fit and remember never to jam the hand part of the glove into a lump on your wrist so you can eat supper. (Take them off.)

Handbags become a way of life, as your life gets busier and busier. Choose the right size for each occasion. With all those books, you don't need a very big one for school; a soft pouch or satchel will hold make-up, money, even a small notebook. When you're traveling, shopping, visiting, a reasonable-size tote bag will hold paperback books, small purchases, knitting—even your lunch. On a date take a little clutch bag or one with a chain or handle if you dance a lot—one just big enough to hold make-up, tissues, hanky, mad money. When the pressure's really on—two suitcases, a magazine, a stuffed toy and your little nephew by the hand—remember that an over-the-shoulder bag has an almost tranquilizing effect.

SPORTS CLOTHES

The good sports look is clean, crisp, uncluttered. A bathing suit might be all eyelet trimming, but it could still give the proper effect by dint of its well-cut shape. In choosing sportswear, avoid clothes that won't let you move easily. Leave the jewelry at home. Don't wear beaded sweaters or other evening wear. Look for clothes that will appear almost as fresh after the third set of tennis or the tenth schuss down the mountain as they did when you started out.

- *Tennis* Shorts, shirts with plenty of arm room or no sleeves at all, socks and sneakers should equip you nicely. The sneakers are essential; other shoes ruin a tennis court. Many tennis and country clubs ban all colors but white on their courts, so it's wise to make your sneakers and socks white—and keep them that way—and include at least one pair of white shorts and one white shirt in your wardrobe. Or, if you're a mite hippy, get a tennis dress: this short-skirted white dress with undershorts to match is so flattering even your game will look better!

- *Golf* Shorts and a shirt—in any pretty color—invisible socks (cut not to show above the shoes) and spiked golf shoes are the classic outfit. You vary it according to your needs. Hot weather? Wear a shady hat that won't interfere with your swing but will protect your eyes and let you tuck your hair up inside it. Also—an absorbent towel neatly draped inside the collar of your shirt marks you as A Player. Sharp, cold weather? This is the day for knee socks and wool shorts or a skirt; wear a cardigan sweater and have a lightweight windbreaker handy. A water-repellent cap or hat is canny to have in your golf bag. Not too slim . . . hate shorts? Wear culottes, a knee-capper skirt or a short skirt. Or—prettiest of all on the links—a tennis dress. Some juniors play golf in sneakers and gym socks. Just don't wear the gym socks with golf shoes. You need a pocket to hold tees and a spare golf ball or two; other things—sunglasses, comb, lipstick—can go in your golf bag. A golf glove will keep you from getting blisters.
- *Skiing* In this sport your fashion object is to keep warm as well as winsome. Ski clothes are so downright bewitching you could spend your entire clothes allowance (or Christmas wishes) on them. Try to resist temptation, because the more important part of a skier's accouterments is her equipment: hardy, beautifully fitting boots; light, sturdy poles; good skis with efficient breakaway bindings. And none of the afore-mentioned is exactly given away in ski shops. For clothing you need long underwear or warm, full-length leotards; one or more sweaters and/or wool or cotton shirts, depending on your individual thermostat; one heavy and one thin pair of socks (to be worn *inside* your ski pants); ski pants (the stretch kind are most flattering and come in all price ranges); a parka; skiing gloves or mittens and leather-palmed poplin overmitts; and something to keep your ears warm. This last can be the hood of your parka, a wool headband in a blue that matches your eyes (for three dollars) or a towering fur hat (for forty). If you cannot afford all this, don't fret. There is an inverse snobbism among skiers, and old clothes—even baggy, grade-school ski pants of the Hans Brinker sort—are quite acceptable. Some people ski in jeans. Just wear clothes which are warm, lightweight, easy to move in, and waterproof—unless you plan never to fall down! A word on stretch pants: they should be tight, but not leotard-tight.

- *Sailing* Shorts or duck pants, a bathing suit. Also, those sneaker-type shoes with little slits in the soles: they help grip the deck well. A waterproof jacket to protect you from spray. Nothing fancy or tangly. No big beach hats; they might blow away. Sailing hat, a headband, a scarf.
- *Riding* Whether you wear frontier pants and a plaid shirt or a riding habit—complete with jodhpurs or breeches and jacket, white shirt, stock or tie and velvet hat—omit all jewelry. Exceptions: your watch, your class ring, a gold safety pin in your stock. Woodsy colors look better for jacket and breeches or jodhpurs than pale pastels.
- *Ice Skating* Skating indoors? Leotards, a short skirt and a sweater will be comfortable. Outdoors? The same costume, or a short skating dress, will suit if you're an energetic skater or are practicing your figures. Otherwise, be comfortable in leotards and a street-length skirt or slacks and a heavy sweater or your ski parka. *Must* on the ice: wear brief, colored underpants (red, navy, black, green) *over* leotards or you'll look like an undressed department-store mannequin should you take a spill on the ice. Fancy skaters wear white gloves when they skate; all sensible skaters wear some kind of gloves or mittens to avoid painful ice burns if they should skid across the ice, hands down. A warm cap, wool headband or ear muffs will comfort you outdoors. Girls wear white skates, boys black. Pompons, toe muffs or jingle bells to decorate your skates are considered in poor taste by serious skaters.
- *Bowling* Shorts, slacks, a knee-capper or any easy-moving skirt, because you have to move. Be sure you look well from behind, because that's where you will be seen. Do wear bowling shoes; they have a sliding sole on the right foot and a braking sole on the left and can be rented at alleys.
- *Roller Skating* Wear whatever you'd wear for a little date, provided it's easy to move in. Be sure your underpinnings are above reproach; you might fall head over heels.
- *On the Beach* A bathing suit should show off your figure—but not make a neon display of it. Immodesty is never fashion, and most boys, though they like to whistle at three inches of bikini down the beach, get a bit red about the ears when they have to introduce the bikini-wearers as their dates. Make sure your suit fits, particularly at the crotch and across the bosom when you bend over. Be sure you can run, stretch comfortably, play with a beach ball, as well as sit in it. (You can try this out in pantomime in the dressing room when you buy the suit. Better do it, because bathing suits, like girdles, are nonreturnable.) Beware of the bra that's boned too obviously or has a cup too big for you. Unless it comes with skillful padding, it will only make you look under- rather than well-endowed.

Always OUTS—a final batch:

- evening-dress fabrics—satin, chiffon, organza, peau de soie, tulle—by daylight
- hats after dark—unless they are those little wisps of veil you might wear to an evening wedding or dinner at a dress-up restaurant
- socks with skimmers or medium- or high-heeled shoes
- leotards with high-heeled shoes
- moccasins with Sunday-Best
- sneakers ditto
- watches or rings worn *outside* of gloves (To make a bulky ring fit under a glove, turn it around so the stone is on the palm side of your hand.)
- bras with pointed cups, especially with a sweater
- motorcycle jackets or the kind with "West Side Swells" emblazoned on the back
- drooping slip straps (Secure them to your dress at the shoulder with little clips or sew those ribbon and snap slip-strap holders into your dresses.)
- dresses or blouses so sheer they reveal your underwear (Exception: sheer dresses with attached camisoles or linings. Wear a petticoat rather than a slip with these or you'll have a confusion of necklines.)
- plaids with prints, stripes with prints—unless you're very high-fashion and know just how to handle such effects
- oddly assorted jewelry—chunky silver bracelets with rhinestone-and-pearl drop earrings, for instance
- ditto accessories—a wide saddle-leather belt and a satin clutch bag
- hairdos whose structure shows: a barrette, headband or ribbon looks prettier than a collection of bobby pins
- tight kid gloves, dark silk suits and other obviously city-wear garments in the country
- pin curls, rollers and other beauty aids in public (If you must go out with your hair set, cover your head with a kerchief.)
- shorts, blue jeans, ruffly dirndls and other obviously country-wear garments in the city

Always IN The kind of care that keeps your clothes looking as though you'd just shaken the store's tissue paper out of them. You don't have to work very hard these days to make that really flawless look a part of your fashion personality. Many fabrics and finishes almost take care of themselves; modern washers, dryers and steam irons do what remains to be done with beautiful efficiency.

Clean clothes are as basic a part of your attractiveness as having a smile that dazzles. You never put anything back in your closet that will look less than fresh the next time you want to wear it. Maybe all you need to do is a quick repair job with a good cleaning fluid or spot stick or even a damp cloth. Save the fabric tags that come with new clothes and mark on them the garments they go with. When total immersion is necessary, you'll know whether a garment should be dry-cleaned, washed and dried by machine, washed by hand and machine-dried (as most pleated synthetics should be), washed by machine and drip-dried, or washed by hand and drip-dried. You can't possibly remember a choice of that many details for everything you own!

Mend matters before it's too late. The button should be reinforced before you lose it, the hem should be repaired when only a few stitches are needed—and so should the seam.

Pressing is not much of a business for a girl any more; still, even wrinkle-shedding fabrics do get creases around the middle and around the hem at the back of the skirt if you sit in them long. Touch out the creases with your steam iron *unless* the fabric is soiled (the heat of the iron will help entrench the smudges). Did you know that many wrinkles in modern fabrics will come out quickly if you put the dress, blouse or whatever in your dryer for five or ten minutes and set it on low?

Heaven for leather—special waxes, sprays and creams that mellow the leather and give it a satiny luster when you buff it. Read the labels; you'll find these for shoes, handbags, belts, gloves, jackets. When you're in a hurry, there are many kinds of self-polishing liquids: some reinstate the color, some just shine. Patent leather—plastic or the real thing—needs coddling with a special polish that combats cracking; battered patent gets a new life with self-polishing patent-leather polish. Nappy leathers, such as suède and rough cowhide, thrive on regular brushing, always in the same direction. Shiny spots can be erased by rubbing them gently with an emery board.

Insurance that you'll be nicely turned out from head to foot: a full-length mirror.

When do you wear flowers? There are really only two occasions when good manners say not to—one is when you're a guest at a wedding where flowers should be worn only by members of the wedding; the other is at funerals. But you're free as can be to pin a cornflower on your golf shirt, a carnation on a tweed coat or wear a headband of flowers instead of a hat to a tea. Main thing is to choose a suitable kind of flower for the time and place—you wouldn't wear a formal, jewel-like flower (a camellia, gardenia or orchid, for example) with sports clothes, school clothes or in the morning.

If your beau asks you what kind of flowers you'd like for a dance, you can choose the traditional shoulder corsage—wear it on the right shoulder so it won't get crushed when you dance—or you can ask him to please bring you flowers to pin on your bag, on a ribbon for your neck or your wrist or to clip to your hair. It will be a big help to him and the florist if you tell him the color of your dress—and perhaps the kinds of flowers you like best: miniature carnations or roses, any white flowers, sing-song girl chrysanthemums to clip behind your ears, whatever goes well with you and the dress you plan to wear.

One of the nicest compliments you can pay him is to take good care of the posies so you can wear them again when you go out with him. Tips:

- wear the flowers heads-up, the way they grow; if you wear them upside-down, moisture tends to fall out and the flowers wither
- in cold weather, carry flowers to the party and put them on there
- never, of course, cover flowers with a coat or wrap
- gardenias and violets can be saved for another day if you sprinkle them with water, wrap them loosely in waxed paper or plastic wrap and put them in the refrigerator
- flowers with tube stems—roses, chrysanthemums, carnations and orchids—should have the tape and wire removed. Then trim a quarter-inch off the stem—under water, to keep air from getting in and blocking the tube. After you trim them, dip stems in hot water to make them expand and drink in more water. Then put them in cool water until the flowers perk up and look fresh. Keep them in the refrigerator
- once you've finished wearing the flowers, float them in a low bowl on your dressing table. Nice memories!

If he's a very special fellow, you may want to have a boutonniere to pin on his dinner coat when he calls for you. For a big dance you can get a dark red or white carnation from the florist. On lesser occasions, a bachelor button or pompon from your garden. Buttonholes, as these small lapel flowers used to be called, are a nice way to tell the boy you're fond of him.

21. Presents That Are Perfect

Starting with the tie rack you made for father as a child, you've probably loved the whole idea of presents and the fun of deciding what to give people you love. Not that there aren't some perplexing moments mixed in with the fun: if you're short of money, the right thing may be harder to find. Choosing a present for a boy may be difficult because you want it to be so perfect. The first wedding presents you buy may cause you a worry or two about your own taste in this very formal moment of decision. Or maybe the question is whether you should give a present at all. And then there is the perplexity of the present you're not quite sure you should keep. The time-tested rules about presents are these:

1. You don't give a present that would embarrass the one you're giving it to. Embarrassment can be caused by a present that's obviously too expensive:

- The friend might be distressed that you'd spent far more than you could afford.
- If the occasion were an exchange of Christmas presents, the friend might be unhappy because your present made hers (or his) look insignificant.
- The friend might have a much smaller allowance than you and be hurt to have the difference underlined by your Lady-Bountiful contribution —even if it's skis or a sweater set you know she longs to have. (The best you can do here is to give her yours—you get new skis from your family —or say you know the color of the sweater set is her favorite blue.)

Or embarrassment can be caused by a present that's too personal:

- A boy might think that you were taking the romance too seriously or that he'd given you the idea that he was taking it more seriously than he actually is.
- A boy might not want others—his family, friends—to think you two were close enough to justify a very personal present—such as a sports jacket; a suit; underwear; jewelry; any present with a double meaning; books or records with amorous titles and tasteless contents; anything engraved, printed or embroidered that might give an outsider a poor impression; or any message you write inside a book which might be innocent enough when explained—"Darling, I'll never forget our wonderful night at the Middletown-Hilton! All my love always, Sue" (which merely means the fraternity dance when he finally got around to pinning Sue—but just think what his Aunt Hilda could make out of that inscription without the explanation!)

All this applies, of course, to presents you give anyone—older or younger, male or female. And it applies every bit as much to boys and their presents.

2. You don't accept a present that might cause you embarrassment:
   - Money is the obvious first mention. You do, of course, take it gladly from family, godparents, long-time older family friends who are more or less adopted relatives. You also take gift certificates which let you pick out the present you'd like.
   - Something the giver has no right to give—family jewelry, unless you're engaged; something that belongs to another member of the giver's family, unless you're sure it's free and clear (he shouldn't give you the golf clubs his sister hardly ever uses, as an example, unless you know she approves).
   - Any of the personal presents listed above and clothing, underwear and the like. *Kind solution:* don't cut the boy to the quick if you think he meant well. After all, not many boys are likely to bring on the classic unacceptable mink coat or box of black lingerie. He probably is pretty uncertain in the decision division himself, so consider thanking him and tucking the present away. Somehow, thereafter, show, talk about and make a quiet point of any less personal or less expensive present he might have given—something your brother just bought for his girl or something your sister thinks her beau will give her.

     Thought: Styles change but charm bracelets endure—probably because a charm is a present one can give with confidence and because it will be worn and loved even, alas, when the giver is remembered only hazily. It's pretty hard for a charm to infringe on either one of the time-tested rules about presents.

Here are solutions to some less formidable but equally perplexing problems we've been asked about:

You have a new beau who'll be graduated this month. Do you give him a graduation present?

Yes, if he's invited you to his graduation. If he hasn't, better just send him a card. If you're both being graduated from the same school—and if he's asked you to a party after the ceremony—then you might have a small present ready to give him when he takes you home. Give it to him then if he's given you a graduation present; if he hasn't, neither of you will be embarrassed and you can save the present for another occasion.

One of your friends, a girl, gave you a birthday present. Do you give her one?

It would be nice, but you don't have to. If you're not enthusiastic about exchanging birthday presents, why not take her to lunch or to the movies?

It's his birthday and you haven't known him long. Should you give him a present?

It's really better to wait until he's given you a birthday, Christmas or Valentine's Day present; a card would let him know you remembered. Or give a party for him; that isn't rushing him quite so heavily.

You and your cousin have always exchanged Christmas presents. Now that she's married, do you send something she and her husband can use—or keep on sending a personal present?

Her husband would feel more welcome in the family—and your cousin would appreciate this thought too—if you sent something she would like and he could share. A book, a record, cheese—that sort of thing.

He's in the service and you send him boxes of food during the year. What could you send for Christmas that would be different—and yet something he'd use?

Books, lots of paperback books, a subscription to a magazine or newspaper, a pipe, a lighter, a billfold, a money clip, a small picture of you in a folding leather frame.

Should you give a boy your picture?

Yes, if he's asked for it—or hinted but is too shy to ask outright. You can always desentimentalize it with a light message on a card: "For Jack—Don't want you to forget me! Love, Sue." Good to keep in mind is not *to write some undying message across the corner; you may defeat the purpose of keeping your face before him if the message would cause his family or friends to tease.*

Your father says he doesn't want a present. Do you give him one anyway?

Most fathers say that they don't want presents at Christmas, birthdays, Father's Day—that there's nothing *they need. But who gets the most pleasure opening packages marked "To Dad with love"? Give him a present, whatever he says; just be sure he doesn't pay for it when the bill comes in.*

You have a good friend who is Jewish: may you give her a Christmas present and send her parents, who have been hospitable to you, a Christmas card?

Yes. In the Jewish religion there is a festival of lights, called Hanukkah, that is celebrated around Christmas and is a time of present-giving too. Choose wrapping paper with candles on it—or any pretty, nonreligious design—and just sign your name and "with love." Many cards say "Season's Greetings" so they can be sent to members of other faiths; the design can indicate peace and goodwill rather than specific symbols of the Christian religion.

You get an unexpected Christmas present from someone. Do you rush out and send one that's obviously "in return"?

No, it's best to accept graciously with prompt thanks, and perhaps at New Year's to send a gift of home-made food—a special cake, bread, candy or cookies you've prepared—to the person whose gift you hadn't expected at Christmas. Or flowers are a lovely thought to send an older person. Accompany your present with a cheery note expressing your good wishes to the recipient for the New Year (and keep this separate from your note of thanks for the Christmas gift).

Are spur-of-the-moment presents all right to give?

They're fun to give, especially at Christmas. Make it an outright gesture, with a little note, "I saw this when I was shopping and couldn't resist sending it to you! Merry Christmas and love . . ."

How to stop exchanging birthday and Christmas presents with a friend you seldom see.

Stop sending them, but continue sending friendly cards; she will very likely be glad to end the exchange too. Sometimes, if you do write to each other, it's possible to say, gently, that you think she might like to give up exchanging presents and you would be willing to. That leaves the final decision up to her.

How to stop exchanging Christmas cards.

This one's easy. Don't quaver and rush a card in return to someone you had trimmed off your list.

Should you give an engagement present to a close friend?

It isn't necessary—and, since you'll probably be asked to her wedding and to one or two showers as well, you would be wise to save your money.

Each of your parents says "Oh, please don't give me a present!" when it's Mother's or Father's Day. Should you anyway?

You'll probably feel dreadful if you don't. Perhaps you'll find the ideal answer in the list of presents called MORE YOU THAN MONEY *on page 179.*

Let's name names of presents that are perfect for different celebrations:

FOR A SHOWER Sometimes you're invited to a shower with a theme; the two most popular themes are lingerie and kitchen things. When you're the hostess, it helps everyone if you give guests an idea of the style and colors for any shower with a household theme. Write across the bottom of the invitation, "Mary wants a modern house" or "They've just found an apartment; the bathroom is mostly blue." Here are suggestions of shower gifts, centered around themes you might also use for a shower you give:

kitchen aids under a dollar muffin tins, paperback cookbooks, cheese and vegetable graters, carrot peelers, nutcrackers, can openers, steel or bright plastic measuring spoons and cups, dish towels, egg slicers, funnels, lemon squeezers, spoon holders, knife sharpeners, silver-polishing cloths or paper sheets, sauce stirrers, cooking spoons and strainers, cutting boards

linens general way of describing plastic, straw and other wipe-clean table mats; kitchen and guest towels; paper napkins in dinner, lunch and hors d'oeuvre size; coasters; sets of pillowcases and towels

guest supplies a luggage rack; a fancy hatstand; pretty soap; hangers covered in velvet, quilted chintz or plastic; skirt and blouse hangers; handbag hangers, shoe bags and racks; other closet equipment, including yards of shelf edging

easy housekeeping collection, which might be assembled by a bride's married friends or by friends of her mother's—a sewing kit, kitchen shears, treated dusting and polishing cloths, rubber gloves, special dusters for furniture and the Venetian blinds, the best silver and furniture polish, push-button glass and porcelain cleaner, tarnish-retarding spray for silver, a basket with a handle to carry cleaning supplies around in

one big present contributed to by all friends at the shower—an electric grill; a blanket; a place setting of the bride's silver, glass or china pattern; a supply of towels and washcloths in her favorite olive green or sky blue; an electric furniture buffer or coffee maker

entertainment supplies coasters; ash trays; glasses they won't mind having broken at a party; little dishes for peanuts, olives, cherry tomatoes—perhaps oriental rice bowls or handleless teacups

records It might be nice to ask each guest to indicate the store where the record was bought, in case of duplicates

gourmet foods or special snacks in long-keeping jars or tins; nothing perishable

desk doodads Anything from paperweights to sharp scissors to stickers with the couple's new joint name and address

the start of a garden if they'll have a house—seeds, bulbs, trowels, gloves, a watering can

Showers are best when the presents are imaginative, practical and inexpensive—unless it's a one-big-present party. Hostesses should remember that close friends of the bride or groom—especially members of the wedding—ruefully find that friendship is dear in terms of money. It's easy to see why a bridesmaid—faced with buying a wedding present, her dress plus shoes dyed to match and her share of the joint bridesmaids' present to the bride—shudders when she receives a bid to a shower. A good way to keep shower costs within reason is to give everyone the same low price ceiling when you send the invitations.

As you know, shower presents are opened all at once with all the guests on hand—so it's no secret when the bride-to-be gets a duplicate of your present. If she's struggling to look delighted with six rose-sprigged petticoats, do urge her later to please return the one you gave her. You wanted to give her a nice present, and you did, but no girl can possibly use six rose-sprigged petticoats.

FOR A WEDDING Here again, do urge a friend to return your present if she's received many duplicates. She may have to keep and use three of the vegetable dishes (yours was the fourth) because they came from, respectively, her grandmother, a close business friend of her father's and her sister-in-law. She'll bless you for saying she can return yours.

One way to avoid duplications is to ask the bride if she has registered at any store. Most good stores which sell china, glass and silver have bridal registries—a wonderful means of finding out what the bride wants. She goes to the store, chooses the silver, glass and china patterns she would like to have, and perhaps accessories, such as casseroles, candlesticks, and serving dishes. Then she tells the store's bridal consultant—or whatever title the employee who takes care of the gift registry is given—what she's chosen, and the consultant records the bride's name and address and the date of her wedding on a card and usually adds her future name and address as well. Friends visiting the store talk with the consultant—or look in the register—and discover that Susan has all the china she needs but would love a serving spoon or a few goblets in the such-and-such pattern. As presents are ordered for Susan, the consultant checks them off, preventing duplications and making it possible for future shoppers to know what still is needed. This system makes it very comfortable for you to give Susan just what she wants within the limits of your budget. If yours is to be an inexpensive present, you send her a teaspoon or a butter plate or two. If you're splurging, you send a place setting.

Many friends are reluctant to send a bride part of a set of silver, china or glass; they might want to find a one-of-a-kind present so the bride will remember who gave it to her. What they forget is that a bride does remember with grateful affection those who make it possible for her to set her table with things she loves.

More thought than money ideas for wedding presents:

- a pair of ash trays in the bride's favorite color
- scrapbook for bride and groom to fill with shared memories
- a sturdy scratchproof tray of plastic, metal or wood
- something you've made: an embroidered blanket cover for special guests, store-bought linens which you've initialed in a color that goes with the bride's china
- an unusual old china shaving mug, to be used for cigarettes, flowers or pencils; or an old covered soap dish, to be used for cigarettes
- a ceramic saucepan which goes in the oven or over a flame and holds vegetables for two
- snapshots of the wedding—and the negatives

  (Photos are very welcome wedding presents. If you have a color snapshot of the couple taken before the wedding, you might enlarge and frame it and give it as your present. In most cases it will mean more to them than their posed wedding portrait.)

FOR THE BABY You don't have to send a present when you get a birth announcement any more than you do when a wedding announcement arrives. But if a relative or close friend is the new mother, you may want to. A godmother might give the traditional silver mug or porringer, engraved with the baby's initials and date of birth. (Don't be crushed to find your godchild being fed from plastic. The mother will keep your present proudly polished and on view, and when the child grows up the mug will hold pencils or cigarettes and the porringer will be filled with candies or nuts.)

Good baby and baby-shower presents are clothes, especially the easy-care kind—no-iron or knitted wrappers, dresses, little suits, sweaters, sun suits. Size markings on infants' clothing don't jibe with the child's age, so ask for a dress or whatever to fit a child "up to three months" or "six months." Terry bibs, plastic bib aprons, crib and bath toys are easy to choose. Slightly older choices—such as rag books, blocks and pull toys—are distinctive and will be used before anyone can believe the baby is nearly a year old!

Second, third and fourth babies rarely receive the presents showered on a first child, so it's nice to remember them too—or to give the mother a present instead. A read-it-in-snatches book (a collection of light verse or short stories, perhaps) or a bottle of really heady cologne is a great morale-raiser for a girl with a houseful of preschoolers.

Let's name names of presents that are perfect at Christmas and birthdays for different people on your list:

FOR OLDER PEOPLE, teachers, bosses, friends who are not members of your family:

- something you make; see page 178
- something special you know they like—a little package of very good tea; cheese (a round of Brie, Camembert or Muenster, perhaps); some marvelous fruit, especially in winter
- flowers, best of all in an arrangement you've fixed yourself
- a book of special interest

FOR A GIRL the best choice is often anything you'd love to have yourself—unless she has a special hobby or collection or has talked about wanting a special perfume or a yellow shirt or whatever. Things we know you like:

- stuffed animals, large or small—fey, fake or almost real
- records
- sweaters, blouses, scarves and belts
- gloves, bags, stockings
- lovely accessories, such as bracelets, beads, earrings, odd slippers, perfume or cologne
- writing paper, a pen, an address book
- games
- a piece of silver, china or glass or linens for a treasure chest
- things for the bag—a billfold, compact, comb-and-brush set, pocket perfume

FOR THE FAMILY the best choice is often something you make or something special you do; see more of this on pages 178 and 179. As often as not, members of a family *say* what they want, and there you are. Any of the presents you'd give a girl would be the kind of thing for your mother, an aunt or grandmother (except for the stuffed animals!). Most of the presents you'd give a boy (this follows) would be fine for your father or your uncle; the style might vary, of course. And you might spend a little more on your family, especially if you and a sister or brother pooled your money for something you knew was very much wanted.

FOR A BOY a little alert detective work makes your choice easier. *Listen* to what his interests are; *notice* things that attract him when you look at a magazine or television or a shopwindow together; *remember* he's not wearing his watch because the strap broke; *make a mental note* when the cover of his tennis-racket case splits; *don't* give him the "Romeo and Juliet Overture" when he's crazy about show music. And if you're still blank for inspiration, try one of these:

- something for his car—flashlight, map case, special cleaning cloth or sponge, rubber floor mats
- something for his dog—collar, blanket, coat, new bed cushion, toy
- something for his bike—tool kit, wire basket to hold schoolbooks, new bell or tire
- sports equipment—bowling shoes or bag; tennis balls and new racket case; golf balls, golf glove, a marker to chalk the spot where his ball lands on the green; a nylon line for his boat; fishing lures or flies
- a book—new or the definitive one—about any sport that's caught his fancy; buy this weeks ahead, because sometimes books on special sports are not kept in stock and have to be ordered
- a pewter tankard, a pocket-size chess set, a good slide rule, a pocket postal scale, a new crossword book and a tumbler filled with #2 pencils
- a lighter, a pipe, a tobacco pouch, a huge ash tray, a good-looking glass jar filled with match books
- an initialed belt, a pigskin or saddle-leather billfold, a tie case
- cuff links, a fountain pen, after-shave lotion
- linen handkerchiefs with his monogram, a monogrammed key chain, a Shetland pullover
- film for his camera, an album for snapshots, plus your offer to help him fill it

PRESENTS YOU MAKE, some in minutes, some in months. Ideas for everyone on your list:

- socks in his favorite color or Argyles; a helmet to wear skating, skiing or merely walking to school; numbered mitts for his golf clubs
- a sports tray: fasten ticket stubs, the cover of the program for the big game, photographs from inside the program or a magazine, school stickers to a metal tray, using rubber cement; when dry, spray with a clear plastic spray from a paint or art-supply store
- a menu memo: fasten a pad of paper to a small cutting board with plastic tape (back part of the strip with paper so the pad slides in and out without sticking); make a similar paper-backed loop at the top for the pencil; trim with wide dark-green and narrow red strips of tape
- giant blocks, for toys or paperweights: have a lumberyard slice a piece of "four-by-four" into cubes; sand, smooth raw edges and snub corners with medium-grade sandpaper; paint, decorate with tape—alphabet letters on two sides, cutouts (apples or cats) on other sides
- blushing-beauty box: paint biscuit tin; fasten rows of rickrack "curls" with fabric glue; snip mouth and lashes from colored plastic tape; add a bright bow or two

- something to nibble: oatmeal lace cookies, brownies, fancy meringues squeezed through a pastry tube, miniature fruitcakes, tiny frosted cupcakes from a mix

MORE YOU THAN MONEY presents—the best of all. After you make your list of things for family and friends, make a second list of ways you can give of your time and your talents.

- Surprise your mother or sister by offering to fix the refreshments for her next party. Tape your offer to a small toy rolling pin and hang it on the Christmas tree.
- If you have your driver's license, tag a tiny red toy car with your pledge to serve as the family chauffeur half a dozen Saturday mornings. (This handsome idea will get the backlog of errands done.)
- Can you type? Give your father three Saturday mornings' worth of typing service—to be claimed whenever he needs them. Or give your beau or brother a certificate on which you promise to type his term paper.
- Offer to get Sunday-night supper every other Sunday for two months.
- Or do the dinner dishes for your mother during January.
- Tie "walking papers" to a dog biscuit with a silly green bow, offering to walk the dog at night for a month.
- Give your young sister her first home permanent.
- Teach your brother the two-step (patiently, even if you think he'll never learn).
- Baby-sit with younger members of the family four weekend nights for your parents.

All year long keep tabs on the people closest to you. Put index cards, with each dear one's name written at the top of a card, in your desk. When your uncle says he's always wanted to try painting, write that on his card; maybe at Christmas you and your brother could give him a modest outfit of paints, brushes and canvas. Notes on other cards may not mean much, taken one by one, but the sum of tabs on the card for your beau may add up to . . . likes jazz . . . got new record player for birthday . . . prefers piano to other instruments; always wanted to play . . . great for George Shearing . . . his family has just inherited piano . . . they have had piano tuned. Your present: some Shearing records and a good instruction book showing simplified chord method of learning to play the piano. Your father may have hankered for a jeweler's loupe (not too far out; natural stones and some rocks and pebbles are beautiful magnified) and talked about it in July; you look at the card in November and then find one at an auction or secondhand shop—or through your jeweler. Put your heart and mind—*as well as your money*—to choosing a present and it's fairly sure to be perfect.

22. The ABC's Of Letters

Mail call—at home, at school, in the Army—is a highlight of the day. Letters bring news, give you a chance to visit with a friend. They bring pleasure . . . in a birthday card, a clipping that makes you laugh, an invitation. Letters carry messages, send reminders, give thanks, do errands and even patch up quarrels. Many of them are treasured over the years, to be read and reread, as they keep the memories of happy times alive.

Each letter is a bit of your own personality put on paper: you want it to picture what you are really like as it accomplishes its purpose. In the pages that follow, you'll find ways to write letters, what to put in them and what to put the message on—plus the basic rules of letter-writing. Equally important (and more fun), you'll find ways to make your letters as individual as you are.

WHAT WILL YOU SAY?

Most people love to write newsy, everyday letters; others, although they can spend hours on the telephone talking with a friend, go blank when they must *write.*

You may wail, "I have nothing to write!" But a friend who recently moved away or is out of town for the summer is as interested that you have gained five pounds or have a new beau as if she were still around the corner. Write about what happened yesterday, books you've read, movies you've seen, ideas you've had. Add clippings of interest to you both, such as the announcement of a friend's wedding snipped from the local paper. Or join with the crowd in writing a "round robin" letter to which everyone contributes a paragraph.

Be spontaneous about letters. If the reason you're writing Susie is to tell her "I've been accepted at college!" don't ruin the effect by starting the letter with a trite "The weather is lovely here today." Feel free to use contractions, such as "I'm" and "you're" . . . but never use faulty grammar. Happily, most of you can write lively letters.

If you must write bad news, do it with tact and good sense. Prevent worry by telling no more than you must, and no less. If you write, "Hugh was in a terrible automobile accident" without adding that he escaped with minor cuts, you could make your reader frantic. Want to pour your sorrows into the ear of a trusted friend? It's usually wiser not to, but if you must get your feelings down on paper, do so—then tear up the paper or wait a day or two and read it again before mailing it. If you send it, your problems may vanish—to remain only in the worried mind of your friend. Keep *all* touchy letters overnight before mailing them, to judge, later, whether you really meant every word you wrote.

It's a thoughtful habit to write not only when you have news to relay or a letter to answer but also when good or bad things happen to family or friends. Write cheery notes to people who are sick (to a child, homebound with chicken pox, you could send a riddle one day, its answer the next, provided that you remember to mail *both* letters!). Write on happy occasions, too. A letter is a wonderfully personal expression of birthday congratulations or of good wishes for a just-engaged friend.

Letters to boys You don't need to send a literary masterpiece; if he likes you in person, he will like you on paper!

"Dear Tom" and "Love" are acceptable and ordinary ways to begin and end a letter to a boy. "Darling" and "All my love" should be used only when you mean them. If you feel shy about saying "Dear" and "Love," start with "Hi!" and end with "Best." But don't omit the salutation or the conclusion from a letter or the boy you write to will be searching furiously for pages that never existed. What to write? Just what you would say if you were talking . . . little news and big news; questions about his interests, hobbies, job, school; comments on anything from a football game to a U.N. decision; a few nice words about *him* (but not a deluge of obvious flattery). Tell him you love him if you really do and if you know he wants to hear it, but don't swear undying devotion if what you are really offering (or what he is really accepting) is only a little more than friendship.

Since boys are people, after all, they appreciate swift acceptances and regrets to invitations, an enthusiastic thank-you note after a college weekend, and, sometimes, thank-you's for flowers, presents and dances.

What about the "Dear John" letter ending your special relationship with a boy? Young men we've polled on this point say frankly that they would rather be dropped in person than in the cowardly and somehow less considerate way—by letter. But if you must write the "Dear John" letter—he's away at school or lives in another town, as he might if he were a summer romance—do it as considerately as possible. Just say that it's really hard for you to keep up a long-distance romance. Sometimes a spasmodic correspondence can be left to die by itself; but if it's been heavy, you have to end it definitely but nicely. Even if, with cause, you're enraged at him, make the letter one you won't be ashamed you sent, once the rage dies down.

Liven up your letters with snapshots, clippings and cartoons. Some of the most delightful letters saved from the past are those of people who drew, as well as wrote, their news—so if you can draw, why not illustrate your letters?

Who writes first? If the boy has asked you to write, go ahead and do it. Make it a brief, nonemotional note—and if he doesn't answer, forget him. Send him a Christmas card if you like—but not just to nudge him with a "Did you get my letter?" or "Don't you remember me, Tom?"

How often? As often as he does, is the answer—except that you know he's a bad correspondent, and so you write a little more.

Letters which must be written: bread-and-butters and other thank-you's; letters of sympathy; answers to formal invitations; other invitations and answers to them. Don't use printed cards for these. If you start off a thank-you letter with "Thank you for the lovely . . ." you have dealt your best hand first and may have nothing to say later.

"Bread-and-Butter" letters It is easy enough to write thanking Susie for the weekend at the beach, but it is a bit harder to write her mother. A simple rule to follow in bread-and-butter letters is this: start with enthusiastic, appreciative words about the visit; follow with some detail of your trip home or news of friends and family which would be of interest to Susie's mother; and close with renewed thanks. Abandon this formula if a lively note, prompted by sheer delight in your visit, flows spontaneously from your pen. "Thank you for the lovely weekend," by itself, will have the sparkle of a burst balloon. Instead, say something like "You and Mr. Anderson did so much to make the weekend absolutely heavenly. . . . The cookout Saturday night was fun. . . ." If you are desperate, phrase your letter as though you were writing Susie instead of her mother. (You can always think of more to say in your thank-you to Susie herself!)

"Bread-and-butters" need not be long, but they must be written whenever your visit is overnight or longer and they must be prompt—within a day after you get home, when you will still be full of the fun of the visit and can write an enthusiastic letter easily. If they are put off, they grow harder to write, especially since they must be written with apologies for their lateness.

"Thank-you's" A present also deserves a quick thank-you, unless you have personally thanked the giver. (An older person likes to be thanked on paper as well as in person.) This letter, too, may be brief—but prompt. Again, don't start "Thank you for the lovely . . ." but say enough to make the giver know you are delighted with it. Occasionally you may receive a present whose purpose is obscure or dubious: a book on beekeeping or one of those blobs of china people love to give as wedding presents. Use all your imagination in thanking tactfully for these. Incidentally, boys—even the ones who dislike sentiment—appreciate light, bright thank-you's for special presents, weekend visits to their colleges.

After a party, any hostess appreciates a quick line of thanks. So does a person who interviews you for a job. Thanking an interviewer not only expresses your appreciation of the chance to talk with him but also leaves him with a favorable impression of you as a nice person to have around.

Always write a thank-you on writing paper—never by way of a printed card. Factory-made thanks don't seem very grateful.

Samples:

Dear Aunt Lucy,

The red poplin mitts are perfect! My old ones were completely worn out, so your present is welcome indeed. They're warm and snug and their color will help the ski patrol find me when I'm lost in a snowbank. So many thanks.

We all wish you could have been here for Christmas. Jack brought a Chinese friend home from college and it was great fun for the rest of us to see how our holiday customs look through foreign eyes.

Come see us soon.

Again, all my thanks for your thought-ful present.

Love,

Enid

In case the present is a horror:

Dear Mrs. Updegraff,

How sweet of you to think of me at my graduation! The crocheted bureau scarf is so beautifully made, etc.

Greeting cards are for fun; they don't do for sympathy. The friend who has just lost someone will be far more consoled by a warm, personal expression of your love and sorrow than by a printed card, no matter how beautiful.

Letters of sympathy are the hardest of all to write and perhaps the most needed. Death is a blow to people, and the more expressions of love and sympathy they receive, the less bereft they feel. When you hear of a death in the family of a relative or friend, try to make your letter as comforting as an arm around the shoulder. A letter of sympathy—and the answer to it—can be very short:

Dear Amy,

I am so sad-- we all are-- about your Uncle Ned. I've adored him as long as I can remember so I think I understand how awfully hard this is for you. Can I do anything? Mother and Daddy suggested that you might like to come and stay with us next week. I'll call you about it Thursday. Meantime we send you all our love--

Devotedly,

Enid

Answers to letters of sympathy are not necessarily prompt, not only because the family is involved with so many sad details, but also because the sense of loss may make answering too hurtful for a time. But a written answer, however delayed, should be sent, rather than one of those form acknowledgments. (An exception would be the case of some prominent figure whose family received hundreds of letters. Even in this case, though, close friends should receive written answers.)

Dear Enid,

Your letter about Uncle Ned was the greatest comfort and I am so grateful to you for writing. You are dear to want me to come next week and I am looking forward to the visit more than I can tell you.

With best love to you, your mother and father,

Amy

Either Enid or Amy might have added, if she wanted to, a sentence or two about some gay thing they and Uncle Ned had done together ("He was so patient about teaching us to play golf" or "Remember that wonderful Labor Day picnic?"). Happy memories help ease the pain of death.

However, as is more often the case, you may have known the person who died only slightly and have little to say; if so, simply tell your friend that you know her uncle's death is a great loss to her and that you hope your love and prayers and those of all her friends will comfort her. Write as you would talk—without empty sentiments like "my heart goes out to you at this time of loss," which you would never *say*. If your letter sounds stiff and inadequate, no matter; it will be read quickly—and the important thing is that it is there to be read.

The written answer to a formal invitation This one is so bound by the rules of etiquette that it may seem hopelessly old-fashioned. But it isn't. The anonymous formality of a boy's dinner jacket is quite proper for a gala dance and doesn't seem old-fashioned at all. And it's the same with formal acknowledgments and regrets.

Your answer to a wedding invitation, which is the sort of formal invitation you are most apt to receive, should be centered on plain white folded-at-the-side paper or your best *conservative* note paper and should follow the invitation itself, even to writing out the date the same way. An invitation to just the church ceremony does not require an answer, but one to the ceremony and/or to the reception (some ceremonies are small, with large receptions following) must be answered in this fashion:

You accept:

Miss Eleanor Brightwaters Tide
accepts with pleasure
Mr. and Mrs. Smith's
kind invitation for
Saturday, the fourth of November

You regret:

Miss Eleanor Brightwaters Tide
regrets
she cannot accept
Mr. and Mrs. Smith's
kind invitation for
Saturday, the fourth of November

Informal invitations are answered informally: "I'd love to come to dinner at six-thirty on the eighth. How nice of you to ask me!" And *promptly*. Is that word beginning to sound repetitious? If so, it is only to make the point that in all letters required by courtesy, promptness is what counts, almost more than what you say and how you say it.

How to write an invitation: see the party section beginning on page 74.

If you receive a formal invitation to a formal dance or tea, you answer it as you would a wedding invitation. The likelihood of getting one of these is rare, but a sorority might send out tea invitations that way.

A final word on all special-occasion letters: they are surrounded by rules of etiquette for the plain reason that all etiquette is simply thoughtfulness formalized by years of custom. Think that through and you will find it less painful to abide by the rules.

Letters to strangers As a soon-to-be-adult, you'll write letters to people outside the circle of friends and family . . . to prospective employers, companies, celebrities.

If you want to write to the President, a TV star, an author, your congressman, feel free to do so! Public persons always appreciate sincere praise, and most are not offended by carefully considered criticism. Depending on the personality of the celebrity and the efficiency of his secretarial staff, you may or may not receive an answer to your letter. If you do get one that seems rather vague, don't be too disappointed. There may be many reasons why the reply can be only in general terms.

If you want to order something by mail—a dress, a college catalogue, an unusual present—be clear about it! If you wish to order a dress, for instance, specify size and color and include a second color choice. Write the address to which it is to be delivered very clearly. Enclose a check or money order unless the dress is to be sent C.O.D. or charged (in which case, give the full name and address as they appear on the charge account). It simply isn't wise to send money through the mails. (A dollar bill might be folded in a letter, or a few coins taped on, but larger amounts should be sent by check or money order.) When typing any business letter, be sure to make a carbon copy for future reference.

If you want to write a letter about a job, it should be written with great care, because it is often a potential employer's only picture of you. Type it if you can, and use your best plain white single sheets of writing paper.

If you are replying to an advertisement, answer the questions it asks truthfully and as thoroughly as possible. In a short paragraph, sum up any pertinent information about your extracurricular activities or about part-time jobs you have held. A prospective employer is interested in the fact that you serve as class secretary: that indicates a certain amount of leadership and responsibility on your part. The manager of a bookshop advertising for a salesclerk wants to know that you belong to your school's literary club: this shows you might sell his books enthusiastically.

Summer and part-time jobs prove you have the initiative to go out and do something constructive. Volunteer work, such as entertaining hospital patients, counts, too, but should be put down as volunteer, not paid, work.

In listing your experience and qualifications, don't be afraid to say that a previous employer complimented you on your skill or loyalty.

If the advertisement asks for references, give them, with addresses. These are not always followed up, but it is better to have the details accurate, just in case. It's courteous to ask the permission, beforehand, of persons whom you wish to list as references.

If you are not answering an advertisement, but writing "blind" to a company which might have an opening for you, find out a few things before you roll a sheet of paper in your typewriter. First of all, find out to whom you should write—the personnel director, a department manager, or whomever. Because people like to be called by name, this is infinitely more productive than writing, "Jones Shoe Company . . . Dear Sirs:" The company telephone operator or some present or past employee can give you this information. Find out what the company does and what opportunities it offers for a person of your age and experience. See if there are possible openings for file clerks, salesgirls. Then write, stating your qualifications and giving some idea of the job they might suit. Let a company know what you could do for it rather than what it might do for you.

It's a good idea to say, "I will call you on Monday to see if I may make an appointment with you." This will leave no doubt in either your mind or that of your prospective employer as to what the next move should be. After an interview, write to the person with whom you talked: thank him briefly for taking time to discuss the opening, or lack of it, with you. This is a gesture which few people observe but which is much appreciated and will serve as a favorable reminder of you.

Added thoughts: If you write to a celebrity or other personality unknown to you and expect an answer, be sure you put your own address on the letter as well as on the envelope. If you want a pen pal, find one through a church group, a school foreign-student program or a club; you could pick up some dubious acquaintances by answering "lonely hearts" in personal columns.

If you receive mail of a questionable nature through an answer to an ad or after clipping a coupon, turn it over, complete with the envelope it came in, to the post office; there's a strong campaign against this sort of thing, and the postal authorities need your help.

LETTER-PERFECT FORM

What goes where on a letter; how do you begin and end? There are easy rules to follow.

The date In the lower left-hand corner of the last page, a little below the signature. Business letters, written on the firm's letterhead, sometimes have the date at the top on the right-hand side of the first page; you can date social letters that way too, if you like. Except for business letters, which require the whole date—September 15, 1962—you usually put Saturday or September 15th.

Your address At the end of the letter, below the date.

Exceptions: If you have writing paper with your address or if the letter is to a friend. Your address also goes on the back flap of the envelope or, to please the post office, in the upper left-hand corner of the front of the envelope

The envelope address Indent it nor not, as you please. In business letters the left margin is usually kept straight because it's easier to type that way. It's better not to use abbreviations—not just because they look hasty but to make the address as clear and quick to read as possible. A correct address includes the name, building number and street (or R.F.D. or postbox number), town and postal-zone number, state, and apartment or floor number if necessary. If the letter is to be sent abroad, add the country.

A nonbusiness letter is addressed like this, without commas:

Miss Barbara Scriven
105 East Elm Road
Terre Haute 3
Indiana

or

Miss Barbara Scriven
  105 East Elm Road
    Terre Haute 3
      Indiana

As you can see, the indented style at the right requires a little planning ahead if the last line is to fit on the envelope . . . even more so if it were going to Massachusetts. A business letter is addressed like this, with commas:

Mr. John J. Anderson, President
The Anderson Company
1200 Lake Shore Drive
Chicago 17, Illinois

Exceptions: A one-word title, such as President, is easy; a longer one can go on a separate line. If the company abbreviates words like *and, company, incorporated* in its name, so can you. If the building name serves as the address, you don't need to add the street number and name. *Addition:* A suite or apartment number goes in the left-hand corner for quicker handling.

Mr. Joseph Stevens
Co-ordinator of Co-operating Commissions
Callaway & Sons, Inc.
Merchandise Mart
Chicago 54, Illinois

Suite 2800

Miss Joan Scriven
  Elmwood Terrace
    Terre Haute 3
      Indiana

Apartment 4F

If you're sending a letter abroad, write the address exactly as the person to whom you write gave it, even if it looks odd to you: Via Appia 18 and *not* 18 Appian Way; a German girl is Fräulein, not Miss. Don't turn town names into English either. A letter addressed to Rome will get to Roma, but one sent to St. Catherine may never find its way to an Italian hamlet called Sta. Caterina. But always write a country's name in English. Don't abbreviate town names. "N.H." may mean New Haven to you, but to the post office it's New Hampshire. And "City" is confusing unless it's part of the town's name.

BEGINNINGS AND ENDINGS

You are always safe if you start a *social* letter with "Dear Lucy," or "Dear Jim," or "Dear Mrs. Brown," and end it "Sincerely." For others, see further. Most people are Miss, Mr., Mrs. on envelopes, but a boy is Master John Smith until his thirteenth birthday. A woman is always addressed by her husband's name: Mrs. John L. Goodrich. It's *never* Mrs. Mary Goodrich unless that is her business name and you are writing her on business at her business address. A widow retains her husband's name: she is Mrs. John L. Goodrich until she dies, unless she remarries. A divorced woman uses a combination of maiden and married names; if her maiden name was Mary Lougee and she married John Goodrich, she is known as Mrs. Lougee Goodrich.

Special people have special titles. Here's a chart to help you use the correct forms of addressing, beginning and closing letters to them—and, for good measure, what to call them when you're speaking to them or referring to them.

The President	Address:	The President The White House Washington, D.C.
	Letter opening:	Dear Mr. President: *or* Mr. President:
	Closing:	Respectfully
	Speak of him as:	The President
	Call him:	Mr. President or Sir
The President's Wife	Address:	Mrs. Kennedy The White House Washington, D.C.
	Letter opening:	Dear Mrs. Kennedy:
	Closing:	Sincerely
	Speak of her as:	Mrs. Kennedy
	Call her:	Mrs. Kennedy
To address them both:		The President and Mrs. Kennedy
United States and *State Senators*	Address:	The Honorable James A. Lee United States Senate Washington, D.C. *or*

		The Honorable James A. Lee State Capitol Albany, New York
	Letter opening:	Dear Senator Lee:
	Closing:	Respectfully
	Speak of him as:	The Senator or Senator Lee
	Call him:	Senator Lee
To address Senator Lee and his wife:		The Honorable James A. Lee and Mrs. Lee
Members of Congress or *State Legislature*	Address:	The Honorable John A. Dix United States House of Representatives Washington, D.C. *or* The Honorable John A. Dix State Capitol Albany, New York
	Letter opening:	Mr. Dix
	Closing:	Respectfully
	Speak of him as:	Mr. Dix
	Call him:	Mr. Dix
To address Mr. Dix and his wife:		The Honorable John A. Dix and Mrs. Dix
Governors:	Address:	The Honorable Albert Kyte Governor of Connecticut The Governor's Mansion Hartford, Connecticut
	Letter opening:	Dear Governor Kyte:
	Closing:	Respectfully
	Speak of him as:	The Governor
	Call him:	Governor Kyte or Sir
To address the Governor and his wife:		The Honorable Albert Kyte and Mrs. Kyte

The Mayor:	Address:	The Honorable Terence Ames Mayor of Terre Haute City Hall Terre Haute 1, Indiana
	Letter opening:	Dear Mayor Ames:
	Closing:	Respectfully
	Speak of him as:	The Mayor or Mayor Ames
	Call him:	Mayor Ames or Sir
To address the Mayor and his wife:		The Honorable Terence Ames and Mrs. Ames
Head of a Government Agency	Address:	Mr. Edward L. Doe, Director The Peace Corps Washington, D.C.
	Letter opening:	Dear Mr. Doe:
	Closing:	Sincerely
	Speak of him as:	Mr. Doe
	Call him:	Mr. Doe
To address Mr. Doe and his wife:		Mr. and Mrs. Edward L. Doe
Doctors of *medicine*—M.D. *dentistry*—D.D.S. *philosophy*—Ph.D.	Address:	Dr. Joseph Glow
	Letter opening:	Dear Dr. Glow:
	Closing:	Sincerely
	Speak of him as:	Dr. Glow
	Call him:	Dr. Glow
To address Dr. Glow and his wife:		Dr. and Mrs. Joseph Glow

Members of the Protestant clergy:

Bishop	Address:	The Right Reverend William B. Adams Bishop of Connecticut
	Letter opening:	Dear Bishop Adams:
	Closing:	Respectfully
	Speak of him as:	Bishop Adams
	Call him:	Bishop Adams

Dean	Address:	The Very Reverend William B. Adams Dean of the Cathedral
	Letter opening:	Dear Dean Adams:
	Closing:	Respectfully
	Speak of him as:	Dean Adams
	Call him:	Dean Adams
Canon	Address:	The Reverend Canon William B. Adams (plus any special title)
	Letter opening:	Dear Canon Adams:
	Closing:	Sincerely
	Speak of him as:	Canon Adams
	Call him:	Canon Adams
Archdeacon	Address:	The Venerable William B. Adams (plus any special title)
	Letter opening:	Dear Archdeacon Adams:
	Closing:	Sincerely
	Speak of him as:	Archdeacon Adams
	Call him:	Archdeacon Adams
Priest	Address:	The Reverend William B. Adams
	Letter opening:	Dear Mr. Adams: (If the priest holds a doctor's degree, write "Dear Dr. Adams:" If he is known as "Father Adams," write "Dear Father Adams:")
	Closing:	Sincerely
	Speak of him as:	Mr. (or Dr. or Father) Adams
	Call him:	Mr. (or Dr. or Father) Adams
Minister	Address:	The Reverend John L. Robinson (plus any title) *or* The Reverend Dr. John L. Robinson
	Letter opening:	Dear Mr. Robinson: *or* Dear Dr. Robinson:
	Closing:	Sincerely
	Speak of him as:	Mr. (or Dr.) Robinson
	Call him:	Mr. (or Dr.) Robinson

To address a clergyman and his wife:	The Reverend John L. Robinson and Mrs. Robinson The Right Reverend William B. Adams and Mrs. Adams

Never speak or refer to a clergyman, Protestant or Roman Catholic, as "Reverend" or "the Reverend." Examples: "Reverend Jones, what time are services Sunday?" or "The Reverend told me the other day . . ." (Think of the word "Reverend" as an adjective, such as "wise." As you wouldn't call a priest or minister "Wise Jones," you shouldn't call him "Reverend Jones.")

Members of the Roman Catholic clergy:

Cardinal	Address:	His Eminence Joseph Cardinal Peters (no commas) Archbishop of New York
	Letter opening:	Your Eminence:
	Closing:	Respectfully
	Speak of him as:	His Eminence or Cardinal Peters
	Call him:	Your Eminence
Archbishop	Address:	The Most Reverend Joseph L. Peters, D.D. Archbishop of New York
	Letter opening:	Your Excellency *:
	Closing:	Respectfully
	Speak of him as:	His Excellency * or Archbishop Peters
	Call him:	Your Excellency *
Bishop	Address:	The Most Reverend Joseph L. Peters, D.D. Bishop of New York
	Letter opening:	Your Excellency:
	Closing:	Respectfully
	Speak of him as:	His Excellency or Bishop Peters
	Call him:	Your Excellency

* The forms "Your Grace" and "His Grace" are still *sometimes* used for Archbishops.

Monsignor	Address:	Right Reverend (or Very Reverend, depending on which is his official title) Monsignor Joseph L. Peters Pastor, St. Barbara's Church
	Letter opening:	Dear Monsignor Peters:
	Closing:	Respectfully
	Speak of him as:	Monsignor Peters
	Call him:	Monsignor Peters
Priest	Address:	The Reverend Joseph L. Peters, S.J. (or other initials indicating his order, if he belongs to one) Pastor, St. Barbara's Church
	Letter opening:	Dear Father Peters:
	Closing:	Sincerely
	Speak of him as:	Father Peters
	Call him:	Father Peters

Members of the Jewish clergy:

Rabbi	Address:	Rabbi David Leiter*
	Letter opening:	Dear Rabbi Leiter *:
	Closing:	Sincerely
	Speak of him as:	Rabbi Leiter *
	Call him:	Rabbi Leiter *
To address Rabbi Leiter and his wife:		Rabbi and Mrs. David Leiter
Cantor	Address:	Cantor Michael Kaufman or The Reverend Michael Kaufman
	Letter opening:	Dear Cantor Kaufman:
	Closing:	Sincerely
	Speak of him as:	Cantor Kaufman
	Call him:	Cantor Kaufman

* If the Rabbi has a doctor's degree (D.D., for example) you may add the letters after his name (Rabbi David Leiter, D.D.) or address him as Dr. David Leiter. In the salutation, as in speaking, you may address him either as Rabbi Leiter or Dr. David Leiter (use the latter if he is customarily known that way; otherwise Rabbi is quite correct even if he has the degree).

Business forms:

Companies	Address:	Lord & Taylor
	Letter opening:	Dear Sirs:
	Closing:	Yours very truly or Sincerely yours
Businesses	Address:	American Automobile Association
	Letter opening:	Dear Sirs:
	Closing:	Sincerely yours
To a specific person in a company	Address:	Mr. Edmond L. Jones Personnel Manager Lord & Taylor
	Letter opening:	Dear Mr. Jones
	Closing:	Yours very truly

If you have only the last name of the business person you're writing to, address the envelope to Lord & Taylor and put *Attention Miss Snodgrass* in the lower left-hand corner of the envelope. Your letter should still open to *Dear Sirs:*—since you are routing the letter to them by way of Miss Snodgrass.

Your signature To friends and relatives, you are "Betty" or "Your loving granddaughter, Betty." To others, "Betty" or "Elizabeth" or "Elizabeth Bassett." Do not add "Miss," even in parentheses, unless you are writing a business letter and you have a name such as Marion or Leslie, which might be mistaken for a boy's. When you marry, you will sign your name "Elizabeth Bassett Smith" or "Betty Smith." If necessary for identification, you will add "(Mrs. John Smith)" just underneath. This is always added on business letters of married women. Never sign a letter merely "Mrs. John Smith."

Nice ways to begin and end a letter "Dear Mrs. Smith," "Dear Sarah," "Dear Sally," "Sally dear," "Dearest Sally," depending on how well you know her. The happy medium between "Sincerely" and "Love" (although the latter is used often for letters to friends) might be "Affectionately," "Devotedly," "Fondly," "With love," "As ever." "As ever" is a good closing for a letter to a contemporary—especially a boy—as it avoids commitment. Closings of the "See you later, alligator" variety are dated the minute you write them.

Sequence of pages There's no special rule; just keep your letter legible and logical.

Folding a letter When a letter is folded, the first page is on the inside, the last page on the outside. Fold the paper to fit the envelop; if it must be folded in thirds, fold the bottom third up first, then fold the top third down over it. Make each fold the same size.

PEN, INK AND PAPERS

The kind you choose—and you can have a variety—should suit both your personality and the purpose of the letter. There are long single sheets for a chatty letter . . . half-size paper or correspondence cards for short notes . . . post cards for brief messages . . . single sheets for business letters . . . double sheets for formal letters. You may want to have colored borders or colored paper, an engraved monogram, or paper printed with your name and address. Colored inks or colored typewriter ribbons, patterned envelope linings—you see them gaily flowered, in stripes and prints—give extra charm to your letters. You can have as much fun choosing your writing paper as you do selecting your clothes. You can haunt the junk stores for old post cards that say "Bessie at the Thousand Islands" or "Louisiana Purchase Exposition of 1903" —fun for quick notes to close friends, some invitations. There are cards and notes printed with butterflies, flowers or birds—some with oriental line drawings—that suit a brief letter, an informal invitation or its acceptance, a thank-you to a close friend.

Business letters are staid—plain white, gray or blue paper. Formal invitations and acceptances, letters of thanks for wedding presents, and letters of sympathy require your best, most conservative paper—usually white, ivory or gray double sheets that fold in half and, almost certainly, black ink in your pen. This stationery is doubly handsome if it's engraved with your monogram or a single-line house address. Some families bent on genealogy have a die cut from the family coat of arms, and this looks particularly handsome if it's blind-stamped without colored ink.

To avoid (not always easy because these are *always* in stock): gold and silver—anywhere (on borders, brightening up the flower design, in the envelope linings); bizarre colors, such as fuchsia, and deckle edges, except in very expensive paper; kittens, sequins, witty sayings.

School, sorority or club paper is in good taste for all except formal letters.

Don't forget: portable packages of writing paper and envelopes (desk and paper all in one, and you can take it with you—on the bus, to the dentist's waiting room); those sheets of paper that fold up into an envelope; self-seal envelopes when you're sending a large batch of mail.

ENGRAVED AND PRINTED PAPER

Stationers have all sorts, including some horrors from the best houses. If you go all out for a three-initial engraved monogram die, pick a classic design you won't tire of; you'll use it till you marry. With a monogram die you have to buy good paper (usually pure rag), and there's a stamping charge besides. Nice monograms are these:

Writing paper should be engraved, but thermography (a process which closely simulates engraving) is acceptable on wedding invitations. (The cost of engraving these can be astronomical.)

Paper printed with your name and address, usually across the top of a sheet, is much less expensive than engraved paper and very good-looking; search for simple block lettering, plain vellum or kid paper or the kind with a horizontal hairline stripe.

Colors for monogramming or printing: The neutrals—white (pretty for the young) or gray, a color to contrast with the paper or match the border, or the same color as the paper, but either a shade lighter or a shade darker.

Visiting cards Once these were left when you paid a call, according to a set of rigid rules. Now their main use is as enclosures with presents—hardly a must, however, unless most of your friends use them. Visiting cards are always engraved, either in script or a plain Roman-style lettering, on a stiff white kid-finish card or a thinner parchment card. You may have envelopes to match, without any engraving, of course. Cards for a girl over fourteen read "Miss Anne Louise Brainard" and are slightly smaller than women's cards, not so small as men's cards. When you enclose one, you draw a pen line through the "Miss" except for a wedding present; you may add a written message if you like. The little envelope (your own, the store's or the florist's) is briefly addressed to "Mrs. Hall," "Miss Wilmerding," "Master Alan Brown" or "For Susan" (to a little girl).

Informals are small top-fold note paper or cards that are used for short notes, invitations and acceptances. The name is engraved on the front, as on a visiting card, but an informal is not a substitute for a visiting card. (A blank card can substitute as an enclosure with a present.)

THE LOOKS OF A LETTER

Plan to leave fairly wide margins at the top, bottom and sides of your pages; they look neater than narrow, cramped ones. If you invariably forget and write to the edge of the paper, possibly on a downhill or uphill slant, take a piece of sturdy white paper and cut it to the same size as your writing paper. With ink, draw heavy margin and line rules on it for a guide. When the ink is dry, slip the guide under your writing paper. Make a similar guide for envelopes. After using them for a while, you can probably discard the guides. Sometimes the reason handwriting is illegible is haste—forgetting to dot the i's and cross the t's and scribbling the e's, i's, m's, n's, u's, v's, w's, a's and o's so they can't be told apart. Then again, you may be using the wrong pen point: if your writing is tiny, a fine point will show it off to advantage and a ball point can serve you well; if you have a positive, bold script, the character of your writing will show best with a broad-point ink pen. In most cases, an ink pen is better suited to formal and business letters—and those with cartridges eliminate the mess associated with fountain pens.

To type or not to type Typing saves time; for informal and business letters, it's considerate and convenient. Even when they are done quickly, typewritten letters usually look neat and legible. You don't type invitations, acceptances, regrets, letters of thanks and sympathy.

Be sure to sign a typewritten letter in your handwriting. (In business letters, you type your name just below your signature.) It's perfectly proper to type the salutation and complimentary close, even when it's "love." Use paper designed for typewritten correspondence: there's a wide choice of pretty and easy-to-erase paper made specially for this. Any thinnish, good-quality paper which will roll into a typewriter is fine for typewritten letters. Don't get folded-at-the-side paper or heavy envelopes if you plan to type; it won't roll.

Nice ideas to make letter-writing fun: notary and legal seals to use on the backs of envelopes; sealing wax, in which you can press your class ring; seals of flowers or butterflies. (All these are for social correspondence only.)

GREETING CARDS

These may be sent instead of a note where the light touch is required. But don't send sympathy cards (write a note instead) . . . or printed thank-you cards (again, a note is in order) . . . and don't send the kind of humorous cards that carry a bitter sting to anyone who might take offense and mistake what you think is wit for an insult.

At Christmas, it's perfectly correct to have your name printed or engraved on your cards if you have a large quantity to send. (Your name should be printed in full—first and last, without a "Miss" preceding it; you can use a middle name or initial, but unless people ordinarily use this form in addressing you—such as Betty Lou, Mary S.—it sounds rather stiff . . . and, please, no printed nicknames.) It's a more caring touch, however, to sign your cards yourself and scribble a brief message on those going to faraway friends and relatives who'd appreciate a bit of news about you, or a special, affectionate greeting. Let your cards express your best taste . . . choose art that is well-done, whether it is humorous or dignified . . . greetings that are nicely printed and sincerely and simply expressed (such as the cards distributed by UNICEF, which are always outstanding in appearance and carry the message for peace in many languages).

23. Getting Along Successfully In A Job

Your family has just given their consent for you to look for a job—the most exciting news you've had in a long time. The word gets around, and your friends' question-for-the-day is "Are you really going to work?" Are you? Will you be one of those young people whose interest in a job is equally divided between the money and the fringe benefits—the kind one employment director describes as "just a body at a desk"? Or are you going to work? Are you eager to do a good job and to learn to do a bigger one? Will you be businesslike about business?

If the answers to the last three questions above are "yes," you're the kind of employee that companies want. They can't promote machines—only people. While you may not be planning on a lifetime business career, the years you do work can be very rewarding. You'll be proud of the progress you make, the interests and skills you develop; perhaps one day you'll be proud that your business ability has helped pay the way for your husband to finish law school.

Finding a job It helps if you have learned your lessons in school before you apply. You need to *know* arithmetic, grammar, spelling, punctuation. It helps a great deal if you have learned to type (a minimum of 30 words a minute is required for a beginner's job) and maybe to use a simple computing machine. If your high school doesn't include these last two courses in the curriculum, you might make one or both a summer project or, if your schoolwork permits, go to a business school after classes. Have your Social Security card and résumé ready to take with you on your job hunt. Never made a résumé? Most firms ask to see this brief typewritten history of your life when you apply for a job; sometimes a firm keeps the résumé, so it's a good idea to have several carbon copies. These are the facts you put in:

- your name, address and telephone number
- the date and place of your birth
- your Social Security number
- your typing speed
- the names and addresses of the schools you've gone to
- any course, academic or commercial, which might have some tie-in with the job you're applying for
- extracurricular activities, if they are pertinent: school paper, yes; sophomore hazing committee, no; captain of the tennis team, yes
- previous jobs—summer, part-time, even baby-sitting, if you've gone to one family for a year or more. Give the names, addresses and telephone num-

bers of employers; the names of your immediate superiors in business firms, and the lengths of time you were employed.

- personal references—not relatives, but a clergyman, teachers, friends of your family (particularly business friends of your father's), or employees of the company where you're asking for a job. (Ask their permission first.)

Start with a survey of jobs you might be able to get. A small notebook is a businesslike way to keep the information you gather. Put your name, address and phone number on the first page. Fill the book with the information you glean from teachers, neighbors, friends, relatives: jot down the kinds of jobs your friends have, the names of companies that might employ you, the kinds of work your teachers think you are particularly suited for, perhaps some leads to jobs that are open right now. Go to the public library and see if you can dig out the names of advertising agencies, retail stores and industrial concerns from the various business directories. Other sources might be the local office of your state's employment service and the placement services sponsored by Y's, advertising and publicity clubs, and trade associations. In every case, *try to get the name of someone in the company to see*—an executive or the head of personnel.

The classified section of a newspaper may give you your best leads. Follow the exact procedures specified in the ads, whether they tell you to phone, write or come in person Wednesday morning only. (If you can't take direction, you'll be a difficult employee to work with.)

Employment agencies might be useful to you too; read the kinds of jobs listed in the agency ads that often appear in the classified section. Employment-agency fees are regulated by state law and differ from state to state; usually they're about a week's salary for jobs that pay less than $60 a week. You pay the fee *only* when and if you take a job to which the agency gave you a lead.

How should you look when you apply for a job? We asked two personnel experts about this—at one of the world's largest department stores and at a multimillion-dollar organization that hires both office and field workers. Their advice is to look well pressed, not heavily made-up, to have clean fingernails—and never to run over after classes in just what you wore all day at school. At least include pumps and hose in your ensemble and make sure your hair is neat. You manage to put on pumps and stockings for a date, so you can do it for an interview, the department-store expert pointed out. She said applicants *had* arrived in shorts with their hair in curlers. From this you see that you'll stand out in a crowd of job seekers if you wear a suit or a dress with sleeves and a conservative neckline—*pressed*—pumps with medium heels—*shined*—and straight-seamed or seamless stockings. More about the right clothes for business on page 162.

How do you get an interview? If you're applying to a small or medium-size firm, call for an appointment. If you're answering an ad, do what it says. If someone you know arranges an interview for you, be sure you get the address and the time accurately.

Allow extra time to get to your interview. It's inevitable that, when you have to get somewhere on time, the elevator is stuck or the traffic jams up—and you arrive too late to get the job or too frantic after the scrambling to sound as if you could handle it.

Go alone when you apply for a job rather than with a gaggle of friends. Or even with one friend. Reason: you're apt to giggle nervously or let one bold soul act as your spokesman. The interviewer can't immediately sort out one good from one bad in the group and is apt to dismiss you all with a "Sorry, no openings." It's as unwise to job-hunt with a group of other girls as it is to huddle with other girls at a dance: no one will try to break into the group to find *you.* (Of course you're a bit scared to go alone. Like your first dive off the high board, you might as well get it over with.)

When you arrive you'll probably have to explain yourself to a receptionist. Wait in front of her desk until she looks up from whatever work she's doing and say, "Good morning; I'm Susan Hamilton and I have an appointment with Mr. Evans at ten." She'll ask you to wait and probably phone Mr. Evans's office to say that there's a Miss Hamilton to see him. You then sit down, read a magazine or review your résumé and your ideas about the kind of work you'd like and the money you expect to get. If, after fifteen minutes, you are still waiting, you might remind the receptionist politely that you're there. You ask, "Do you think Mr. Evans will be busy much longer?" She may give you some disconcerting answer like "Oh—I forgot all about you!" and you will be glad you spoke up because Mr. Evans may have been wondering where *you* are.

Either a secretary will come out and guide you to Mr. Evans's office or you'll be told, "You can go on in now. It's the second door on the left." Walk in, closing the door after you. Mr. Evans may get up and offer you a chair; then again he may just keep on signing letters and leave you standing. Don't sit down until he asks you to, though.

An application blank may be handed to you sometime during the interview. You'll seem much more efficient if you have your own pen; otherwise you may have to borrow a pencil and the result will be a smudgy application. Look at each question carefully before filling it in; your application will look much neater if you haven't hastily put your telephone number in the space for city and postal-zone number and drawn all those arrows over the top of the page. Complete all the answers and sign the form if it says to. If there's a question you can't answer ("What foreign languages do you speak?"), write "none" or draw a line through the space given for answering—just to show you've focused on the question. The interviewer or prospective employer can tell a great deal about you by the way you fill out this business form; you don't want his first opinion to be *careless, doesn't pay attention to directions.*

Taking some tests may be part of the interview. Don't balk at them or hedge timidly with a "Well, what *kind* of tests?" Even if you feel those trembling hands couldn't type ten words a minute, sound competent with a "Yes, of course" when you're asked. Interviewers allow for nervousness and lack of experience. You may also be given some psychological tests with questions that sound pretty silly to you. Answer them as sensibly and accurately as you can; don't spend so long over one stickler of a question that you have to rush through the rest, since these tests are often timed. Above all, don't let your funny bone interfere with the answers you write down.

Be extra polite In case of doubt, err on the side of overpoliteness. The interviewer will be impressed. Say "Good morning" and "Thank you, Mr. Evans." It's a very nice touch to remember the interviewer's name.

If you are asked to smoke during the interview, resist the offer. It looks too casual and, besides, you might be nervous and shake ashes all over.

Know when to ask questions It's not your place to start the interview, so let him take the lead. You don't want to be a mouse; nor do you want to be aggressive about selling yourself. Most business people like to find out about you in their own way, so respond to the leads given you by the interviewer. Speak clearly; don't interrupt. If he throws some puzzler of a question at you, answer it if you can—or say, "I'd have to think that over before answering it, Mr. Evans." Interviewers ask odd questions for many reasons—to test your poise, to see whether you think about questions or just babble an answer, and sometimes just to liven up a dull morning. If you suspect a question was asked in fun, add a half-smile to your have-to-think-that-over answer. The personnel man, if in a pixy mood, will appreciate your having a sense of humor; if the question was really a serious one, the half-smile will commit you only to looking pleasant.

Sample puzzler questions:

> Do you prefer things to people, Miss Hamilton?
> Do you think you would like working for several people at the same time?
> Would you rather work for a man or a woman?
> What do you really hope to make of your life?
> Have you ever tried modeling?
> A girl like you ought to get married and have a home and children. Don't you agree?

When it's your turn to ask questions, the first ones you ask should center around the kind of work you'd be doing, what job you might be able to progress to from it, the kind of training you'd need for advancement—books you might read or special courses. Questions about salary, working hours, vacations, health and insurance benefits are in order, but the order they come in is *last*. A prospective employer is much more concerned with what you will give the company than what you hope to get. (Shining example of the wrong way to start an interview: the engineering-school graduate, aged 23, who asked briskly, "Sir, my first question is, What plan does your company provide for retirement at age 65?")

If you're offered the job, you don't have to make the decision then and there. Just say, "Thank you very much. I'd like to think about it overnight. Is it agreeable to you if I let you know tomorrow?"

Whether or not you take the job, or whether you're offered one, you thank the interviewer and write him a thank-you note. This is particularly important if you have been referred by another employee or a friend. As an example: a long-time saleswoman in a department store calls the personnel department and says she has a niece who is looking for a job. The personnel interviewer makes an all-out effort to find the niece a job because she values the saleswoman. A pleasant interview follows, but there is no job at the time. When the thank-you letter arrives, the interviewer thinks to herself, "What a nice letter. There wasn't a job when I talked to this girl, but the dress buyer just told me she has two openings in her office. I'll look up the girl's application form and see if we can't hire her."

On the job Just as you allowed extra time to get to your interview, allow it for getting to work on time—every day. In addition to the peace of mind this gives you, it's the kind of thing employers notice. Bosses and supervisors often come in early to get important work done before the day's phone calls, meetings and appointments begin. Any small extra job you do—getting coffee, looking up an address, typing a memo—will be noticed by your employer—and so will you. ("Nice girl, that Miss Hamilton." "Have to get this memo to J.B. before nine; that Hamilton girl is always in early." "Miss Hamilton does a lot of extra work for me; she certainly deserves a raise." "Yes, J.B., you couldn't find a nicer, more dependable assistant secretary than Miss Hamilton. In this office at 8:45 every day of the week." *Congratulations, Miss Hamilton.*) One reason our Miss Hamilton made herself noticed by her boss is that most teen-age employees have a poor record when it comes to being absent and late. Absenteeism is one of the chief reasons for firing teens. (If you're ill, call up; don't just not show.) Another reason is being woolly-headed about the time spent on coffee breaks and lunch hours; the teen tendency is to shop, talk, wander and drift back, saying, "How did it get to be so *late*?" Trying to leave early is also frowned on. A business firm in the Midwest, plagued by its employees' lighthearted attitude toward getting the work out, put this memorandum on the bulletin board:

> MEMO TO ALL EMPLOYEES:
>
> At present we have a heavy demand of orders from our customers and we are several weeks behind in meeting these orders. In between arriving late, taking time for the morning coffee break, the lunch break, frequent trips to the water cooler, the afternoon coffee break and leaving early, the management would like to suggest that our loyal employees concentrate greater effort on that period of the day which will henceforth be referred to as the work break.

Maintain good personal relationships with your supervisor and with other employees; failing to do this is another major reason for firings. Begin your day with brief, smiling good-mornings—to everyone, including the newspaperman and the elevator man. Follow the office code of ethics: you don't gossip or talk behind anyone's back. You don't discuss salaries with other employees. You don't shift the blame for a mistake to someone else. You try to keep discussions of your background and social life on the average of the group you're with. (So your mother *is* going to be next president of the Junior League; you can say she does a lot of volunteer work in the hospital or something else accurate but not too informative. Or if she works a long, hard day in a gift shop and the other mothers don't have to work, talk about her interest in Early American glass.) You don't go over someone's head, bypassing your immediate supervisor with a complaint or a criticism to a senior executive. You are loyal to your company: disloyalty includes criticizing the company, revealing its plans or private information to outsiders, stirring up discontent among other employees, and failing to do a conscientious job during the work period.

Doctor, lawyer, merchant and every other employer we've talked to listed the following complaints in describing the employee nobody wants:

- can't get a telephone message straight or forgets to deliver it
- gets and makes too many personal calls
- doesn't check work; never reads a letter over before bringing it in
- cocky attitude; short with strangers
- takes no interest in the appearance of the office; has to be constantly reminded to straighten mine up after a meeting
- leaves a litter of lipstick-smeared coffee containers, crumbled bits of doughnuts, unemptied ash trays on her own desk
- has plenty of time to conduct an office romance with one of the trainees, no time to get my charts out for the afternoon or have materials I may need at her finger tips
- invariably manages to interrupt when I'm talking to one of my partners; question is usually one she could have answered herself
- feels if I have a two-hour business lunch, she can stay out that long too
- starts getting ready to leave fifteen minutes before the gong
- on the other hand, has never been known to stay a few minutes *after* the gong to finish up a job she's doing
- and acts as though I'd shot her mother if I ask her to stay a few minutes to get out an unexpected but important letter
- expects me to make it up by driving her home—asks, as a matter of fact
- seems to think the company owes her a job

Diagnosis: Unproductive member of corporate body
Condition: Hopeless
Recommendation: Immediate severance

Baby-sitting, your first job perhaps, is one of the most important ones you'll ever have. When a mother hires you to take care of her children, she wants you to do a double job—to keep them safe and to keep them happy. To meet a trust like this, you need to be very businesslike—not just about your responsibility to the mother and children but also about the mother's responsibility to you. This is the way we see it:

IT'S UP TO YOU

- to arrive on time; if it's a first visit, to come early so you can make friends with the children before the parents leave
- to arrive in good health: don't report with a cold—it's not good for the children's health.
- to do your best to produce another responsible sitter if you have to break the date.
- to make a check list of things you'll need to know: the children's bedtime, where night clothes and diapers are kept, the time for feedings or meals you'll give the children, how to work any appliances you'll use, any rituals leading up to bedtime.
- to stay until they get back
- not to invite your friends over, unless you have specific permission for a specific *girl* to come
- to stay awake
- to check on the children from time to time once they're asleep
- to keep the outside doors locked
- to make any necessary phone calls brief
- not to complain about the children (when Mamma's away, the mice *will* play), but to report any mischief that might have some aftereffect or for

IT'S UP TO THE MOTHER

- to stay long enough to give you your instructions instead of flying out with a " 'By, darlings!" as you walk in the door
- to cancel the job if she has a sick child: you should not be expected to tackle this kind of problem
- to let you know when she has to cancel the job—as soon as possible, so you can make other plans
- to show you how to work the range and the television set
- to tell you whether to put dishes you use in the dishwasher or to do them by hand
- to tell you what you may not use —the phonograph, for example
- to tell you which child has homework to do, which ones may watch television and for how long, the address and phone number where you can reach them, the doctor's name and number, the approximate time they expect to be home
- to call you if they decide to stay out an hour longer than planned
- to pay you an agreed-upon sum per hour
- to pay you a slight extra fee for feeding, bathing and dressing the children, if that's the custom in your community
- to pay you extra if she asks you to wash the family dishes or do any other household chore

IT'S UP TO YOU	IT'S UP TO THE MOTHER
which you might otherwise be accountable.	
❦ to report any damage you're responsible for and offer to have the item repaired or replaced	
❦ to call your family if, for some unexpected reason, the parents can't take you home	❦ to take you home when your assignment is late in the evening
❦ to thank the parents for asking you to sit for them and for taking you home	❦ to thank you for coming

A good job well done is the ideal for any kind of employment—baby-sitting, part-time, full-time. Not every job turns out happily, no matter how well you try to do it. The employer may not be doing his part to make it a good job. Perhaps the kind of work truly doesn't interest you or you feel there's no opportunity to learn or to advance. *Before* you decide to leave, talk to your boss about what your future in the firm might be and what you could do both on the job and in your free time to make you eligible for different work or a better job. *If* you decide to leave, be a good enough businesswoman to have another job lined up before you give notice. When you accept another job, arrange to give at least a week's notice so your spot can be filled. The day you leave, say good-by pleasantly to those you've worked with, knowing you've been businesslike about resigning and about your own business career.

24. The Formalities Of Life

Some of the events and milestones of living are marked by ceremonies that are stately, dignified and carefully planned. They are often very beautiful to see and hear, and they are *always* packed with protocol. This briefing will help you know what takes place and what will be expected of you.

BANQUETS

You just might find yourself attending a large public dinner or banquet. Your usual good restaurant manners will stand you in good stead here. A few added tips:

- There will be no one to seat you, so just walk to the table assigned to you. Sit down, introduce yourself, and chat pleasantly with your tablemates. If no table is assigned, join a congenial-looking group already seated, asking first, "May I sit here?" Ask "Is this seat taken?" before you claim it. (Whenever you *are* assigned a table, stay at it. Switching from an assigned table confuses the banquet committee.)
- Service at banquets is often hurried so that there will be time for speeches or a stage presentation. Co-operate by refraining from asking the waiter for special services. If a fruit cocktail is placed before you and you don't happen to like fruit cocktail, leave it on your plate. The waiter will remove it when he brings the next course. However, if your religion says it's a fish day and only meat is served, you may ask the waiter for a substitute. Hotels and restaurants catering banquets are prepared for this and always have fish or eggs ready.
- The "distinguished guests" at the speakers' table or on the dais (raised platform at one end of the room) are sometimes seated after everyone else. When this is the case, one often rises and remains standing until these guests have been seated. However, this may not be expected at the banquet you attend, so watch other tables for your cue. If a clergyman is at the speakers' table, he may be called on to say grace before dinner. Stand (if others are doing so) and bow your head.
- If the toastmaster has a list of names of "distinguished guests and committee chairmen who did so much to make this dinner a success" and requests that you "please hold your applause until I have finished reading," please do so.
- Silence, please, during the speeches or entertainment—except, of course, for laughter where it is indicated.
- And please hear the speeches out. If you must leave before the program is over, do it between speeches or acts, while the group is still applauding.

- If you see a card on your table reading "gratuities have been arranged by the committee" or "by your host" or if the banquet is held in a school hall, museum or club, you don't leave a tip.

TEAS

Perhaps a faculty or a church tea or one given in the grand old manner by a friend of your mother's.

- Leave your coat and gloves wherever the hostess indicates. You may carry your purse with you, but it's best to have your hands free to juggle cups, saucers and little cakes.
- Unless there are tables to sit at (and this is rare), you stand to drink your tea and eat whatever little delicacies are provided. You approach the tea table and ask whoever is pouring, whether you know her or not, for tea "with lemon, please" or "with a little sugar and milk" or however you like it. (Often coffee or hot chocolate is served as well.) Since being asked to pour at a tea in a private home is an honor, you may assume that the pourer is a close friend of the hostess or of her daughter. If she is a good friend of yours, also, stop and chat a minute but not so long that you keep her from pouring for other guests. And never hover over the table too long, nibbling every goody in sight.
- When you have finished your tea, leave cup, saucer and napkin on a sideboard or side table. It's nicer not to leave it on the tea table, since that has been carefully set with the best clean china and one used teacup can spoil the effect.
- Of course, greet your hostess on entering, thank her on leaving, and be sure to chat with any guest of honor. If you are at a loss as to what to say to your hostess, you can tell her how pretty the house looks or how good the cakes were. Hostesses always love praise.

RECEPTION LINES

You find these at many school and church parties, business dinners, convention banquets, large dances, coming-out parties and wedding receptions.

- Give your name to the first person in line—Anne Evans. An older married woman might identify herself as Mrs. Cox.
- Then you say some pleasantry—"Good evening" . . . "What a wonderful idea this party is" . . . "The flowers are lovely"—to this first person, who will hand you on to the next in line, saying, "Mrs. Jones, this is Miss Evans (or Anne Evans)."

- You go on down the line, shaking hands and saying little pleasant nothings. Never talk at length, as you will hold up the others waiting in line.
- If the first person in line looks like a butler, he is probably a professional announcer and will incline his head in a practiced way to get your name. Just give him your name—no hand, no "good evening."

COMING-OUT PARTIES

The young lady of Victorian and Edwardian days was kept under wraps—in the schoolroom, away at school or being "finished" abroad—until her family brought her out to meet their friends and, more important, their friends' eligible sons. Intention: matrimony. If the eligible daughter failed to receive an offer during her first season, all concerned were a little uneasy about her future life, since marriage was the chief vocation for a girl. Unless she married, she faced the bleakness of being a maiden aunt/built-in baby sitter (if she had any family) or a governess (if she had to provide for her own support).

Today, girls look forward to college or specialized training and a job, as well as marriage, so coming-out parties—having lost their original earnest purpose—are among life's gayer ceremonies.

The parties take many forms. Parents or grandparents may give a dance to present a daughter to their friends; several sets of parents may give a dance together to present their daughters; or a dozen or more girls may make their debuts at a large dance under the sponsorship of a charity. Traditionally, debuts were an evening dance, a tea dance or a tea. Now, in many communities, one group ball is held, perhaps at a club or hotel, and a series of small parties is given by the parents of the debutantes—crowding the calendar with buffet lunches followed by dancing and going on into a round of tea dances, dinner dances and supper dances. The season and the climate offer many chances for variations of the traditional party too: tents may be set up for outdoor dancing in good weather. A family who spends summers out of town sometimes gives an outdoor party for country friends and another party in town during the Thanksgiving or Christmas holidays.

Each debutante usually asks three or more boys to be her escorts, thus providing a stag line. Each escort sends flowers to the girl who asked him. The father of the girl being presented also sends her flowers, and these are the ones she wears, so her escorts often send baskets of flowers, which are banked near the receiving line.

At a private party, the parents and their daughter—perhaps the grandparents too—form the receiving line and greet guests as they arrive. At a group debut, the girls being presented form the receiving line along with members of the board of the sponsoring charity and/or the girls' parents.

The escort's duties at the party are to dance frequently with the girl who brought him and to dance with the girl being presented; with her mother, grandmothers and sisters; with his date's mother, grandmothers and sisters; and with all the debs of the season. Many of these duty dances can be accomplished while those in the receiving line are still greeting guests. After all the guests have been received, the party girl dances her first dance alone on the floor with her father. In many group debuts this becomes a very pretty production as the girls form a line on the dance floor, curtsy to the guests and then dance with their fathers.

At an evening dance, debutantes have no choice of colors to wear—it's *white* only—but gloves and hemlines may be long or short, depending on the fashion of the year and the custom of the community. At daytime dances or teas, a girl may choose any light color that appeals to her; the one rule is no extremely sophisticated styles or colors. White tie and tails are usually worn by men at evening debuts, but this may vary in your part of the world.

WEDDINGS

First of all, how to answer the invitation: you answer it just as you do any formal invitation, in the manner shown on page 185. If the invitation comes in the form of a note sent by the bride's mother you answer this way:

Dear Mrs. Cox,
How nice of you to ask me to Anne's wedding! Of course I will be delighted to come on the twenty-fourth, and stay for the reception.
Love,
Enid

or if you cannot accept

Dear Mrs. Cox,

You were so thoughtful to ask me to Anne's wedding.. I hate to have to miss it.

The whole family is going to my Grandmother's for Thanksgiving and mother says I simply can't be excused.

I know it will be a beautiful wedding, and Anne the prettiest bride ever.

Much love to you all. I'll be thinking of you on the twenty-fourth.

Enid

If you receive a formal invitation to the church ceremony only, with no mention made of a reception, you needn't answer at all. You must answer an invitation to the reception only, to the ceremony and reception, and to a small home or rectory wedding, simply to let the bride's family know—well beforehand!—how many people are coming.

What to wear: read all about this beginning on page 163.

At the church wedding

- Arrive at least fifteen minutes ahead of the hour called for the wedding. The wedding must start on time, especially in busy city churches, where several weddings may be held in one morning or afternoon, and the wedding cannot start until guests and families are seated.

- Chat with friends, if you like, outside the church. Don't create a hubbub of conversation in the vestibule.
- Wait at the inner door of the church for an usher to seat you. He will walk up, offer his arm and escort you to a seat. Most likely he will ask, if he doesn't know, whether you are a friend of the bride or of the groom. (Traditionally, the bride's friends sit on the left side, as you face the altar or pulpit, and the groom's on the right.) If he forgets, just tell him, "I'm a friend of Sally's" or "of Bob's."
- Technically, you needn't give up an aisle seat at a wedding for a late-comer, but it's a nice thing to do if the late-comer is an older person.
- You may nod to friends or talk very quietly to those in your pew, but don't carry on loud conversations. You're in church, after all!
- After guests have been seated and relatives of the bride and groom ushered to the front pews, the wedding march is begun. Late-comers are no longer seated; they should remain in the vestibule until the wedding procession has marched all the way down the aisle, then silently find themselves seats in the very back of the church.
- When you hear the wedding march, stand and face the aisle to watch the procession.
- During the ceremony, follow the lead of other guests if you are in a church whose service is unfamiliar to you. You need not kneel, cross yourself or sing hymns if these are not your own customs. Just stand when the others do, and sit when they do, respecting the customs of the church you are in.
- After the ceremony, the wedding party leaves; then ushers return to escort relatives from the front pews. When all relatives have left, the front pews take the lead toward the exit and each row follows. If the aisles are ribboned, you'll get the cue as the ribbon holding your pew is turned back.

THE WEDDING PARTY

This is the usual order of the processional and recessional in Protestant, Catholic and Jewish weddings. They may vary, depending on the church, the number of people in the bridal party and any number of other factors, but in general they take this form:

Processional (the walk down the aisle)

- Ushers, paired according to height, with the shortest first.
- Bridesmaids, paired according to height, with the shortest first.
- The maid or matron of honor. If there are both, the one who will serve as the bride's actual witness will probably walk last.
- The flower girl or ring bearer, if any.

- The bride and her father, or whoever else is "giving her away." The groom and best man wait for the wedding party at the foot of the aisle.

Recessional (the walk up the aisle, after the wedding)

- The bride and groom.
- The flower girl and ring bearer, unless they have been wisely seated in a family pew before the ceremony itself.
- The bride's ranking attendant (her witness—maid or matron of honor) and the best man.
- Bridesmaids and ushers: they may walk as couples, or singly, or may be paired as they were in the processional.

THE EPISCOPAL WEDDING

In the Episcopal Church, weddings take place in the morning or afternoon or, occasionally, at candlelight services in the evening. If both bride and groom are members of the Episcopal Church and the wedding is held in the morning, it is often followed with the celebration of the Holy Communion or "Nuptial Eucharist." After the wedding procession, a betrothal ceremony takes place at the chancel steps. At this time the bride is given by her father to the priest; he, in turn, bestows her on the groom, and the father retires to his pew.

Then the couple, accompanied by the best man and maid or matron of honor, goes to the altar rail to be married. Vows are exchanged and the ring or rings blessed, and a blessing is given by the priest.

Guests stand throughout the betrothal and marriage ceremonies, kneel during the Communion service, if it follows (and if it is a part of their own religious practice to kneel; otherwise they may remain seated). If you are in doubt as to when to stand or kneel, watch other guests.

The words of the marriage and Communion services and the special Collect, Epistle and Gospel used for the Nuptial Eucharist can be found in The Book of Common Prayer. (In most churches there are a few copies in each pew.)

THE ROMAN CATHOLIC WEDDING

When one Roman Catholic marries another, they are ordinarily married in the morning, with a Nuptial Mass immediately following the ceremony itself. The wedding party walks down the aisle, as in other church ceremonies, but the bride's father does not vocally "give her away" as he does in Protestant weddings. He escorts her to the foot of the aisle, where the groom and best man are waiting. Then the groom takes the bride's arm and her father joins her mother in the front left-hand pew.

Bride and groom, best man and maid or matron of honor go through the altar rail into the sanctuary for the wedding, accompanied by the remainder of the wedding party, if there is space enough. The priest gives a very brief talk on the importance and duties of marriage; vows are exchanged and the wedding ring or rings blessed. Mass follows. Twice, toward its end, it is interrupted as the priest turns to confer special blessings on the newly married couple. The first of these is principally for the bride, the second for both bride and groom. The priest may read a Papal Blessing after Mass.

At some weddings, after Mass, the bride will turn and walk alone to an altar at the left of the main altar to offer her bouquet to the Madonna. She prays a minute there, then returns to her husband for the recessional.

At a Nuptial Mass you may find, in your pew, leaflets containing the words of both the marriage ceremony and the Mass in English. Reading will help you follow, if you are unfamiliar with the service. If the leaflets are imprinted with the names of the bride and groom, they are meant for guests to keep as remembrances of the wedding. In a marriage between Catholic and non-Catholic there is no Nuptial Mass and the wedding ceremony itself usually takes place outside the altar rail.

A QUAKER MARRIAGE

From its beginning, the Society of Friends has stressed the conviction that marriage is an individual commitment to be made in the presence of God and of witnessing friends, with no need of official pronouncements to complete it. But before this public commitment is made on the day of the wedding, the proposed marriage has already received the approval of the Meeting. This approval is given after careful investigation through an appointed committee, thus exhausting all human means to insure the marriage's success.

The wedding itself is a meeting for worship, held after the manner of Friends, within which a marriage takes place. The bridal couple enters the meeting and customarily sits on one of the facing benches. In giving themselves to each other, they eliminate the need for the bride to be given by her father. Likewise, no third person officiates. No bridal party is necessary, although this is commonplace today.

In an atmosphere of quiet and reverence, following a period of worship, the couple rises. Taking each other by the hand, they make their promises in clear, audible tones—first the groom and then the bride. "In the presence of God and these our friends, I take thee . . . to be my wife (husband), promising with Divine assistance to be unto thee a loving and faithful husband (wife) as long as we both shall live." The exchange of rings at this point is customary today, although this is not necessary to Friends' procedure. The couple may salute each other with a kiss. Thus they enter into a binding relationship before God and in the presence of their friends.

When they are seated again, the marriage certificate is brought for the newly married to sign, the bride using her new name. The certificate is read to the meeting by a designated person. This is done with dignity and care in order to contribute to the atmosphere of worship. The meeting then gathers into silence for perhaps half an hour, during which those assembled share in the ceremony through prayer, meditation, and spoken messages.

The person chosen to close the meeting may, if desired, first make an opportunity for the bridal party to withdraw. After the close, those who have been present are asked to sign the certificate as witnesses of the marriage. This certificate becomes a cherished possession in the new home; a copy of it is made for the records of the Monthly Meeting, under the care of which the marriage has taken place. Many of these certificates, handed down for 300 years, have proved to be valuable historical records. Usually a reception for the couple is held either at the Meeting House or at the bride's home.

Because Quakers so revere the sacrament of marriage, they believe that God alone can bless such a union and give significance to such a mystery. The personal promises before God made by bride and groom, together with the certificate signed by them and those present as witnesses, leave the contracting parties little doubt that they have been very thoroughly married when they leave the Meeting House.

THE JEWISH WEDDING

In the Jewish religion there are three groups: the oldest and most traditional is the Orthodox; next is the Conservative; third is the Reform. Wedding ceremonies differ with each group (and even within the group, depending upon the family), but there are basic similarities.

In any of the three groups, weddings usually take place any time from noon on, except for Fridays after sundown and Saturdays before sundown, and major holidays, or periods of national mourning. The wedding may be in a synagogue or temple or in a hotel or private club or home. In some communities there is now a movement away from hotel and club weddings.

Two betrothal benedictions begin the Orthodox and Conservative wedding ceremony. They are followed by the ring ceremony and the reading of the marriage contract, which is in Hebrew and in English translation. After this, the seven marriage benedictions are read or chanted by the cantor and the choir, who may also sing special songs.

At an Orthodox or Conservative ceremony held in a synagogue, the bride stands at the groom's right before the Ark of the Covenant (the equivalent of an altar or communion table). The bride may have a maid or matron of honor and bridesmaids. The parents of both bride and groom often take part in the processional and recessional. At an Orthodox or Conservative wedding—whether or not held in a synagogue—the bride and groom are married beneath a canopy supported by standards. The rabbi, the maid of honor and the best man usually stand with them. In the Reform service, a canopy is not required, although the rabbi may prefer one. The four parents stand with their children. The rabbi faces the bride and groom and, beside or in front of him, there is a small table that holds a cup of wine; there is also a glass wrapped in a napkin. A Reform service sometimes eliminates the glass.

The service is in Hebrew with English interpolations in modern Orthodox and Conservative weddings; a Reform wedding is conducted in English, with only a few of the blessings in Hebrew.

The rabbi blesses the wine and passes the glass to the groom, who takes a sip and gives it to the bride. The ring ceremony follows, and the groom places the ring on the bride's right index finger (she may wear it on the left hand after the ceremony). In the Reform ceremony, the groom places the ring on the bride's left ring finger.

The rabbi then makes a short address to the couple on the sanctity of matrimony.

The wine is again given to the bride and groom, and in the Orthodox and Conservative services the groom crushes a glass under his foot. This custom is sometimes followed at Reform services. The wedding reception follows, and a special nuptial grace is offered after the collation served at Orthodox and Conservative weddings.

Men must wear their own hats or the traditional skullcaps at Orthodox and Conservative services; synagogues have skullcaps for those without hats.

A hotel or club wedding

The ceremony is the same, complete with canopy, if needed. The hotel or club wedding puts ceremony and reception under one roof, which is its advantage. (Recently built Orthodox and Conservative synagogues generally also have facilities for wedding dinners after the ceremony—all under one roof.)

At a home or rectory wedding

Some home or garden weddings are as formal as those in church; in others, processional and recessional, if they occur at all, are somewhat shortened, due to lack of space. No matter how small the wedding, you will probably be ushered or shown to a seat or told where to stand. If the couple does not leave the room after the ceremony but turns around to receive the good wishes of their friends and family, you give them yours, after their relatives have spoken.

In a judge's office

No processional, no recessional; otherwise as above.

At a wedding reception

- The family of the bride is under no obligation to make arrangements for your transportation from church to the place where the reception is to be held. Sometimes they will do so, out of the kindness of their hearts, but it is better for you to take the initiative and find your own ride.
- Allow a little time for the receiving line to form and the posed pictures to be taken. Leave your coat wherever you are asked; wear your gloves and hat.
- When the receiving line, if there is one—and there usually is—has formed, you line up with the other guests and "go down the line." You say nice, sincere things—wish the newlyweds much happiness, comment on what a beautiful wedding it was, how lovely the bride and bridesmaids look—whatever you mean and can say briefly (very little of it will register anyhow). Don't congratulate the bride on securing a husband; give her your best wishes and save your congratulations for the groom. Identify yourself; the bride may be your next-to-best friend, but in the excitement of her wedding day she may forget your name completely. At some weddings there is a professional announcer at the head of the line—a dignified man with the look of a butler. You tell him your name ("Mary Jones," not "Miss Jones") and he repeats it in a loud, clear voice. Or, rarely, an usher may assume this duty. You'll help if you add some identifying tag to your name as you speak to parents and bridesmaids in the line: "I'm Mary Jones. I roomed with Sally."
- After the line you are free to mingle and talk with other guests. If you feel like a total stranger, remember that a wedding reception is the sort of party at which people are extra friendly. Just introduce yourself—"I went to school with Sally, but I'm afraid I don't know a soul here"—and someone will take you under his or her wing. Often an adult can be counted on to find a boy he or she knows and put the two of you together. If you are with your family, of course, you won't feel alone. Don't depend on the ushers to take care of you. Their first duty is to the bride and bridesmaids, and they've probably each been assigned an aged, deaf and easily hurt aunt to watch out for.

- If it's a stand-up reception, you just mingle as you would at any party. At a sit-down reception, you may be assigned a table. Or you may join a group you know.
- At some sit-down receptions, the clergyman who married the couple will say grace. Just to be safe, wait till others start eating before you do.
- When the bride and groom have been seated at the bridal table, the best man may propose a toast. You rise and lift your glass with the others, even if you don't plan to drink your champagne or punch.
- If a fancy, towering white cake is in sight, you can be sure that at another point in the festivities the bride and groom will cut it. This is a high point in the reception, one marked with pictures and a flourish of music. You don't normally take food home from a party, but you should take home a bit of wedding cake, wrapped in a paper napkin (sometimes there are little boxes), and tuck it under your pillow that night. The one you dream of is supposed to be the one you will marry. It's an old custom.
- Toward the end of the reception, the bride and groom will leave to change to their traveling clothes. It is at this moment that the bride tosses her bouquet, and tradition says the girl who catches it is the next to marry.
- After the bride has thrown her bouquet, the reception is more or less over. If you are a good friend, you will want to stay to fling your handful of rice or rose petals at the couple as they dash out the door. Then prepare to leave. The party's over.
- Find the bride's parents and thank them—especially her father, who is often ignored in all the feminine frou-frou of a wedding.
- No matter how close a friend you are, give the bride and groom some privacy after their wedding. A really gregarious pair might welcome your airport send-off, but a shy pair would be thoroughly unnerved by it. And if they are closemouthed about where they plan to go for their wedding night and honeymoon, respect their desire for seclusion.

Should you give a present?

Yes—if you are invited to the reception and have accepted. Or if you have been invited by written note to a small wedding, even if you don't go. Or if the bride or groom is a member of your family or is marrying into it.

If you are invited just to the wedding and not to the reception, you don't need to send a gift. Nor do you if you have been invited to but have declined the reception or when you receive only an announcement of the wedding.

However, if either person is a close friend, you may want to send a present anyway. It's possible that the couple lives in another city and asked only local friends or, because of circumstances (money, a death in the family, family disapproval), had only a small wedding.

How to address and send the present

If you send it before the wedding (and most people do), you address it to the bride under her maiden name and send it to her at her house.

After the wedding, you send it to her and her husband, since they are now one, at their new address. Or, if you lack the address, send it to them in care of the bride's family. If the couple is moving from town after the wedding (they are both going back to college, say), it's often more thoughtful to wait and send the present to their new home, particularly if it's something they are apt to use immediately.

Sign the card with your full name. (They may know several Marys.) You needn't be overformal with your message. "All happiness" is fine, but if you know the couple well, say, "With so much love" or even "Happy days" or, as one of the nicest cards seen recently said, "May you live happily ever after!" Never take a present to a reception unless it's held at the bride's house. It might get lost.

What to give? You'll find ideas on page 175.

CHRISTENINGS

- Behave as you would in church, whether the ceremony is held in church or at home.
- If you are asked to be godmother to a baby, you take on more than a social obligation. Actually you are responsible for the spiritual upbringing of the child, in the event that its parents are unable or unwilling to see to it themselves.
- Present? Yes! Many godparents continue the custom of giving their godchild a present annually, on his birthday, or at Christmas, or on the anniversary of his christening. (Not necessary, though.) It's in keeping with the relationship if the present is occasionally a good religious book, once the child is old enough to appreciate it. It's also very appropriate for a godparent to give her godchild his first Book of Common Prayer or Missal, or whatever prayer book would be most significant in his religion.

FUNERALS

- Unless a death notice, as published in your newspaper, reads "funeral private" or you know, because friends and family have told you, that the funeral is private, you may go to it—and should, if the person who died meant anything at all to you.
- You don't go on to the burial after the funeral service unless you were very close to the person or are very close to his family. The burial, more than

the funeral itself, symbolizes the wrench of parting, and the family may very well want to be alone at that moment. There are exceptions, particularly in the case of a burial which is in a cemetery next to the church. If you do go, arrange your own transportation. The family should not have the added burden of worrying about you.

- If you are advised, again through the newspaper notice or the word of friends and family, not to send flowers, don't send them. Some churches permit only the family's own floral spray at the service. In some faiths flowers are not appropriate. It's often better in any case to send a pretty plant to the family's house or to a hospital "in memory of . . ."—or a small contribution to charity "in memory of . . ." Catholics often arrange with the local parish priest to have a Mass said for the soul of the person who died, either shortly after the death or on a monthly or yearly anniversary of it, and non-Catholics may do the same for their Catholic friends. You go to the priest and make a small offering for his church and he arranges for the Mass.

  You may mention that you have arranged one of these when you write your note of sympathy. Sometimes the church or charity sends a card signifying that "a contribution has been made to the Boys' Club in memory of . . . by . . ." or that "at the request of . . . a Mass will be said for the repose of the soul of . . ."
- If you do send flowers, you write "in sympathy" or "with loving sympathy" on your card. (The card does not replace your note of sympathy, which *must* be written.) Avoid using the word "death" or any synonym for it on your card. If you send flowers to the church, they are addressed to "the funeral of . . ." and the name of the church. And tell the florist the date and time of the funeral, so that the flowers will arrive on time. If you send them to a funeral home, you merely address them to "the funeral of . . ." and the name and address of the funeral home. If the funeral is to be held at the funeral home, you tell the florist the date and time.
- Some funerals are held in churches, others in funeral parlors, others at home. A sexton or funeral director may show you to a seat; if not, find one yourself, remembering that the first few pews or chairs are reserved for the family.
- It is thoughtful to call briefly on the family if you are close to them or were close to the person who died—offering a kind of verbal arm around their shoulders. Depending on the family and its customs, the call is made at home or at the funeral home where the service is to be held or where the body rests until the funeral. If you call at home, say a few words and go. At these occasions friends of all ages will congregate and talk among themselves. This is fine if you talk quietly, but you should avoid turning a wake

into a party. A few generations ago, when most of our ancestors had just come to America from the "old country" weddings and funerals often provided the only opportunities for families to gather en masse. Thus, funerals turned into parties. Today the need for such socializing has passed —and so should the party atmosphere.

- But you should not mouth stilted, sad phrases. Be sincere in your sympathy.
- Your note of sympathy should have the same tone of honest feelings. For suggestions on how to write such a note, which must be written, whether you have visited with the family or not, see page 184.
- One of the most considerate things you can do for a friend who has lost someone dear is to find out ways of helping discreetly during the funeral period and afterward, too, when she and her family may be at loose ends emotionally. Go to her house and stay by the door to receive callers or flowers or sign for telegrams. Or undertake the task of talking to other callers who come and don't seem to know when to leave. Or offer to take little ones to the park or the beach; small children have no conception of death, and at funerals their mothers are often too occupied or too distraught to take care of them.
- For what to wear to a funeral, see page 163.

CONFIRMATION

Although all Catholics are confirmed between the ages of ten and thirteen, not all Protestant churches follow the custom. The ritual varies between faiths, but essentially is a sacrament in which a young person affirms his faith. Those being confirmed are permitted to invite guests, usually limiting them pretty much to family and only closest friends. Relatives (and sponsors in the Catholic faith) usually give appropriate presents—a religious article, religious book, pen, cross, simple jewelry. As a friend all you really need do is send a card. Guests at the church follow the ceremony with the congregation, although, of course, you need not follow any part that conflicts with your own beliefs.

BAR MITZVAH

A boy's Bar Mitzvah is the Jewish counterpart of the Christian Confirmation. The ceremony itself, which involves the boy's reading from the Scriptures, takes place near his thirteenth birthday. (On the birthday or near it, it is always on a Saturday.) Often a dinner is held, after the ceremony, to honor the boy. This is an all-ages party, attended by the boy's family, their friends, his friends, and perhaps their families as well. A special ceremony—it's a matter of custom, not religion—is sometimes made of his birthday cake. A different couple close to the boy and his family lights each of the cake's thirteen candles. The boy's parents light the next-to-last candle and the boy himself lights the last candle.

The boy's friends often give him presents to celebrate the occasion. Good presents are books, a pen, any not-too-frivolous present which might ordinarily be given to him as a birthday gift.

GRADUATION

If you are invited to a friend's graduation, you should respond quickly, since he or she usually has only a few invitations to offer, so that if you are unable to attend, another friend can be asked in your place.

Present? Yes, if you're invited to the ceremony. For suggestions, see page 171.

YOUR OWN GRADUATION

- Wear shoes you can walk in gracefully and comfortably—moderately low heels—and be sure to give new ones three or four long wearings before the great day.
- If your school doesn't require caps and gowns, remember all eyes will be focused on you. Check your stocking seams or wear seamless ones.
- Be sure your hair looks as pretty from the back as the front.
- If you wear a cap and gown, set the cap at a level angle rather than on the back of your head.
- Whatever you wear, your best posture is a must. Will there be steps to maneuver? Practice climbing and coming down stairs (page 13) so you won't crash-land or look clumsy.
- Your manner? One of gentle dignity.
- Watch for your parents and smile at them.
- Invitations are always limited. The order is family first, then your best beau. After that? It's up to you.
- Write prompt thank-you's for graduation presents and telegrams, and answer letters and cards with personal messages as soon as you can.

25. P.S. For The Future: YOUR ENGAGEMENT, YOUR WEDDING

Although you know all about being a guest at a wedding by now, the day will come when you star at your own, and what you will want to know is somewhat different. Your wedding should be consistent with your way of life. Very likely your family will give you any kind you set your heart on—and the choice you make may be the greatest test of your good manners that you'll ever face. Out of kindness to your family, ask for one that is appropriate to the way you live, to your religious beliefs and to your father's income. A wedding is no time to be incongruous. It *is* incongruous for two church members to be married in the city hall or for a family that lives in a modest house with one six-year-old car to have a wedding reception for 300 guests at the country club. It's incongruous to order engraved wedding invitations when you could have the less expensive thermographed ones and fill out your empty hope chest with the sheets and pillowcases you really need. It's probably just as incongruous for you to hold out for a small wedding in the chapel, followed by lunch for the two families, when your mother has the time, money and energy to give you a lavish wedding and your father has his heart set on a big splurge for his only daughter. Do remember that the biggest or the smallest wedding can be equally memorable. A bride can be as beautiful in a pretty pastel suit or in a wedding dress she's made herself as in fifty yards of pearl-embroidered pure silk costing hundreds of dollars. A reception at home may not be as grand as the one your cousin Alison had at the country club, but it might be much warmer and more affectionate.

The details of a lovely wedding are the same; the degrees of formality, elaborateness and expense vary a great deal. In the pages that follow, you will find many details and many variations; choose the ones that will be appropriate—and therefore in the best taste—for your own wedding plans. You'll add to everyone's happiness if you do.

YOUR ENGAGEMENT

Telling the families After you've said "yes," the first thing you and your fiancé should do is tell your respective parents.

- Your father may want to "have a chat with that young man" and vice versa. This isn't as Victorian as it sounds. Both men are deeply, vitally concerned with your future. It's better that they discuss it frankly than leave their questions unasked and unanswered. Leave your father and fiancé alone as they talk. If possible, get out of the house (and take your mother with you!). But come back at a prearranged time, perhaps an hour or two later, to rescue them.

- It is customary for your fiancé's family to call on yours or to be invited over for tea or dinner or the evening if they live in the same town. If they live in another town, your fiancé's mother might write to you, welcoming you into her family. And your mother might write her. The idea behind this is an expression of love for you and your fiancé and obvious approval of your union. But if the visits aren't made and the letters aren't written, no one should feel hurt. These gestures are a custom but are not obligatory.
- Next, tell your friends! If you plan to make an official announcement of your engagement through a notice in the newspaper, your friends may be hurt that they didn't hear first. Tell or write all your relatives, especially the older ones.
- Once the news is out, you may wear your ring (if you receive one) in public, but not before.
- You may wish to tell close relatives and friends individually, then make a more general announcement with an *engagement party*. (Incidentally, there's no set timing for an engagement party; it can be after many friends are told or before, immediately after a newspaper announcement or just before. And the party itself is, of course, not necessary at all.) The party should be given by your family, not your fiancé's, and could announce your engagement in various ways:
- Your mother may issue invitations to a party to "honor our daughter Marjorie and her fiancé, Bruce Webster (this, naturally, lets the secret out).
- The party may be "just a party": midway, your father could propose a toast to "Marjorie and her fiancé, Bruce."
- You may omit mention of the engagement; when the guests see you and Bruce and Bruce's family, they will get the general idea.

If there is a party, your fiancé's family should be invited. Beyond that, you might include close friends of your family, and perhaps of your fiancé's, as well as your contemporaries.

A newspaper announcement is a fine way of spreading the good word, and if you live in a small or medium-size town with a daily or weekly paper, a newspaper announcement may be a time-honored custom. (Large city newspapers don't always have space for every announcement sent in.) Your family issues the announcement of your engagement—just as they announce and give the wedding. To have the boy's family do this would imply that the girl's family does not approve of the match. A possible exception might be if the girl's family were dead and the girl has long been close to the boy's family. But, even in this case, it is better for a relative of the girl to make all necessary announcements and sponsor the wedding, no matter how modest.

How to give the announcement to the newspapers

- You don't make the announcement; your family does.
- The announcement should be written, preferably typed—not telephoned.
- If you want to be sure it's included—or published on a certain day—you or your mother should take it to the newspaper two weeks ahead.
- Its style might follow that of the engagement announcements published by the newspapers in which you would like your announcement to appear. This will vary from town to town, of course, but the essentials are all contained in the sample below:

To: Society Editor [1] For release: SUNDAY, OCTOBER 21 [3]
THE CHICAGO DAILY NEWS [2]

Dr. and Mrs. James Bryant Lowell, of 4856 Astor Street,[4] announce the engagement of their daughter, Miss Elizabeth Macon Lowell,[5] to Mr. Angus Mitchell McFall, son of Mr. and Mrs. Malcolm Douglas McFall, of 333 Bellevue Place.[6]

Miss Lowell is a graduate of the Francis Parker School and of Finch College, New York. Mr. McFall, a graduate of Lake Forest Academy, is a senior at the University of Chicago.[7]

A spring wedding is planned.[8]

Ada S. Lowell
(Mrs. James B. Lowell) [9]

1. If you know the Society Editor's name, use it.
2. Send a separate announcement to each newspaper; a top copy makes a better impression than a smudgy carbon.
3. The release date is important: it binds the newspaper not to publish the announcement until the date specified. If you send your announcement to several papers, give each the same release date. Exception: if you send announcements to morning *and* evening papers, you may time the release in the evening paper for the eve of, or the afternoon after, the morning paper's announcement, depending on what is the custom in your town.
4. If you live in the city where the newspaper is published, you need put only your street, not your city, address. If you live in a suburb or nearby town, you might put street and city address: "8600 Hinman Avenue, Evanston." If it's a small town, just put the town—"Barrington," for instance. Note: your mother *and* father make the announcement.
5. Full name, please—and no nicknames: "Elizabeth," not "Betty."

6. Your fiancé's name, family and address are given in the same fashion as yours.
7. About all most newspapers care to print about an engaged couple concerns their educational backgrounds. (About a *young* couple, anyway.) You may include other information, which the paper may or may not publish, depending on what it considers newsworthy and what it has space for. Examples:
   - your (or your fiancé's) membership in clubs, fraternities, sororities or honorary societies: "Miss Lowell is a member of The Junior League of Chicago" or "Mr. McFall is a senior at the University of Chicago and a member of Phi Beta Kappa"
   - your (or, more probably, your fiancé's) business affiliation—if he is in business rather than in school: "He is with the National Boulevard Bank"
   - your grandparents. For some reason, your grandmother is often more fascinating to a society editor than you are: "Miss Lowell is the granddaughter of Mr. and Mrs. Adam Bede Lowell, of Chicago, and of Mrs. David Wentz, and the late Dr. Wentz, of Cleveland." (A person who has died is always referred to as "the late.") If you mention your grandparents, mention your fiancé's, also, of course.
   - a distinguished ancestor: "Miss Lowell is a direct descendant of General Robert E. Lee."
   - military service (your fiancé's former military service): "During the Korean conflict, Mr. McFall served with the United States Navy."
   - Occasionally a newspaper will mention your father's business affiliation and that of your fiancé's father. If a girl has had a coming-out party, it is mentioned: "Miss Lowell made her debut in 1959 at a dinner dance given by her grandparents, Mr. and Mrs. Adam Bede Lowell, at the Rollingwood Country Club and attended the Christmas Cotillion."
   - Small-town papers always print more information than big-city papers. There's less competition for space.
8. If the wedding date is more or less planned, mention it—a spring wedding, a June wedding.
9. Many newspapers require the signature of a parent of the bride-to-be (usually her mother) if the bride is under 21.

This is all rather cold, but that's the way it's done.

When should you send the announcement? In plenty of time for publication. Some newspapers like to have it as much as two weeks ahead for a Sunday edition. Call and ask, to be safe rather than sorry.

Should you include your picture? Yes, if you have one (your yearbook picture would do nicely, so long as you haven't been out of school too long and the picture wasn't taken in cap and gown), and want it published. Newspapers like large 8″ x 10″ glossy prints of your head and shoulders, not full-length portraits. If you send a photograph, attach an identifying slip of paper across the bottom (tape it to the back): "Miss Elizabeth Macon Lowell, fiancée of Mr. Angus Mitchell McFall." Don't write on the back of the photograph. You'll make it hard to reproduce the photograph well. Never ask the paper to return your picture.

Is a newspaper announcement paid for? No. If, after all this, the newspaper does not print your announcement, don't despair. There simply may not have been space. And you're still engaged, aren't you?

If one parent is dead: "Dr. James Bryant Lowell announces . . . Miss Lowell's late mother was the former Ada Sims." This gives the mother the dignity of more than incidental mention.

If your parents are divorced, your announcement may follow one of these patterns:

1. Your mother makes the announcement and your father is mentioned in the story:
"Mrs. Lombard Brown (if your mother has not remarried and uses a combination of maiden and married names—or "Mrs. Joseph Jones," if she has remarried) announces the marriage of her daughter, Miss Pamela Brown, etc. Miss Brown is also the daughter of Mr. George Brown of Vero Beach, Florida."
2. "Mrs. Lombard Brown, of 25 Ridge Road, and Mr. George Brown, of Vero Beach, Florida, announce . . ."

If your parents are separated—they are still "Mr. and Mrs."

- What applies to the listing of your parents applies also to the listing of your fiancé's parents.

If your fiancé is in the service, he is referred to as "Angus Mitchell McFall, Ensign, United States Navy," or whatever his rank and branch of service, or "Ensign Angus Mitchell McFall, United States Navy." Spell titles out. Let the papers abbreviate them if they wish.

If your parents are dead and a relative makes the announcement:

"Mr. and Mrs. Adam Bede Lowell, etc., announce the engagement of their granddaughter, etc."

The ring

- It's wonderful to have an engagement ring, and wonderful to have the traditional diamond IF your fiancé can afford it. If he gives you a family ring or if you'd both rather save up for a sofa, that's fine too. If you'd prefer a birthstone ring, or a watch or a piece of antique or heirloom jewelry, that's equally fine.
- If your fiancé does want to give you a new engagement ring, you may want to go with him when he picks it out. He can avoid discussing price by asking the jeweler to set aside certain rings which he likes and which are within his budget. Then you can join him to make your choice from that group.
- Keep your wedding ring in mind when you select your engagement ring. The two should harmonize. Matched sets are available. At any rate, make sure engagement and wedding rings are made of the same metal—gold with gold, etc.
- If you plan a double-ring ceremony, you pay for the groom's ring, which he will wear on the third or the little finger of his left hand.

Do you give your fiancé an engagement present? If you like.

Conduct during engagement Remember it's a private romance, so limit public displays of affection. You don't date anyone but your fiancé. You might play tennis with an old friend, but that's about it.

Does an engagement bind you to marry? You make your only firm commitment when you finally say, "I, Elizabeth, take you, Angus . . ." The engagement period is your opportunity to focus more deeply on the man you love and whom, if all goes well between you, you *will* marry.

If the engagement is broken, the ring and costly or valuable presents are returned to your former fiancé. A notice reading "The engagement of Miss Elizabeth Lowell, etc., has been broken by mutual consent" is usually sent to all papers which announced the engagement.

Bridal showers These should not be given by a bride-to-be's family or by the family of the man she plans to marry. The bride's family issues invitations to the wedding, and these imply, although they do not demand, gifts. The groom's family, although they will not be hosts at the wedding, are nonetheless closely involved with it—and in general it just looks a little grasping for a bride to say, "Please give me a present" through a relative. It's far nicer for her to let friends take the initiative. Proper shower-givers are her friends, her fiancé's friends, and friends of their families. (It's rare for a shower to be given by a man's friends, but they might sponsor a joint shower for bride *and* groom.)

Note: When you plan a shower, do talk with the bride (or her family, if the shower is meant to be a surprise) to determine the guest list. It's thoughtless to ask someone to a shower, which is an out-and-out bid for a present, if she is not considered a close enough friend to be asked to the wedding itself. (Exception: small, "members of immediate family only" weddings.) And it's also thoughtless to ask the same friends to give and give at shower after shower. Try to work it out so that different friends are asked to different showers, or consolidate the list of friends and give a joint shower with another girl.

PREPARING FOR THE WEDDING

First of all, decide with your family what sort of wedding you will have. Your fiancé won't really care—he just wants to get married—and your memory of the wedding will be mostly a lovely blur. Here are just a few of the many kinds you could have—in varying degrees of expense:

1. A church (or synagogue, temple or hotel) wedding with many guests, all of whom are invited to the reception. An elaborate dress with a train. Lots of flowers. A soloist or a choir. A goodly number of attendants. A sit-down reception at a club or hotel. A trio playing at the reception. Limousines for the entire bridal party. Engraved invitations, announcements, reception cards, at-home cards. Boxed wedding cake for the guests to take home. A formal engagement portrait, a formal bridal portrait and professional candids of the wedding.

2. The same, but with the reception at home.

3. The same formal church wedding, but with fewer flowers, an organist but no soloist, no choir. A stand-up reception, a piano instead of a trio, a limousine furnished only for the bride and her father (same limousine for bride and groom after the wedding). Thermographed but well-done invitations and announcements. An existing photograph used for the engagement portrait, professional bridal portrait and candids.

4. A formal wedding in church for many guests, a smaller reception for families only, or families and a few guests. In this case there would be a receiving line in the church vestibule. See page 249.

5. A church or chapel wedding for a few guests, all of whom could be invited to a punch-and-cake reception at home. In this case, your mother could issue handwritten invitations.

6. A home wedding, with only a few guests and members of your immediate family present. You in pretty Sunday Best or a going-away suit. Your groom in a business suit. Handwritten invitations. After the wedding, your mother could write other friends to tell them it has taken place and to express her happiness at *your* happiness. Formal announcements are never necessary, but, in their absence, the bride's family should send notes as a matter of good friendship.

Whatever wedding you choose, *consult your clergyman* before you set an actual date. Otherwise he, or the church, may not be available. He will, most likely, want to talk with you and your fiancé at least once before the wedding. Then there may be papers to present (baptismal certificate and such in some faiths). And you will want to discuss what flowers and music are suitable—many clergymen have definite opinions on the subject—whether photography of the service is permitted, if you wish it; when a rehearsal should be held; and other technicalities.

What time of day for the wedding? This varies according to the kind of ceremony, the particular faith and local custom. More about this on pages 216-218.

WEDDING INVITATIONS AND ANNOUNCEMENTS

As soon as you set the date and your family has decided on the number of guests who may reasonably be asked to the wedding, start making your list. By the time you finally *get* married, you will have become very good at making lists!

- More people may be asked to the ceremony than the reception. An invitation to the ceremony alone obligates no one to anything. The guest need not give a present; your parents need not wine and dine the guest at a reception.
- Relatives should, of course, be asked. If you or your fiancé has an enormous family, you'll have to draw the line somewhere, but older relatives should be asked or they'll be hurt.
- What about out-of-town friends who might not come? They'll be flattered to receive the invitation. You may prefer to send an announcement, since many people, though they know a delivered invitation does not obligate them to a present, will want to send one any time they *do* receive an invitation. Whatever you do, be consistent. Don't send an invitation to one faraway friend and an announcement to another.
- In theory, the list is divided equally, with you and your family furnishing half and your fiancé and his family furnishing the other half. In practice,

the larger proportion is usually on the bride's side, if the wedding is held in her home town and her fiancé's family lives in another.

- Who *must* be asked besides relatives? Husbands, wives, and fiancées of everyone in the wedding party. There are no rules concerning your father's partner or your next-door neighbor.

How to draw up the list:

- You consult with your family, your fiancé consults with his family, and as soon as possible both mothers have lists, with verified addresses, in hand. All this plus the actual addressing takes forever, so get people started right away. The simplest way to handle the lists is to transfer them immediately to file cards, so that the names can be filed alphabetically and duplications can be eliminated. Your mother will probably do all this, but you can help. Mark each card "I" for invitation, or "C" for ceremony and "R" for reception, if you plan to invite more to one than to the other, and "A" for announcement. Address envelopes using the cards as reference. As reception acceptances and regrets come in, you check the cards. If you're over your limit on reception invitations, a few names may have to be canceled by both families.

Ordering announcements and invitations

- Do this nine or ten weeks before the wedding. The invitations should be mailed to arrive six weeks before the wedding ideally, and, at the least, three weeks before. The announcements, which have all been addressed, sealed and stamped before the wedding, go out the evening after the wedding or the next day.
- Go to a good stationer. And order simple invitations and announcements on good paper (preferred is ecru, though white can be as good). Those with heart cutouts, gold rings or doves are not in the best of taste.
- Engraved or printed? Engraving can be woefully expensive; thermography is much less so (see page 232). Engraved or printed, your invitations and announcements must be on good paper, in simple lettering.
- Approved lettering styles include a simple script, which is often the least expensive; Shaded Antique Roman; London Script; Shaded Modified Roman.
- *The double envelope custom* Proper invitations and announcements usually have two envelopes. If two are used, the inner one is left unsealed (it shouldn't be gummed anyway) and is placed in the outer so that the writing on it faces the flap. The stationer sends invitations and announcements with inserts of tissue to prevent smudging; *take them out:* the ink will be dry by the time you get them addressed.

- *Addressing envelopes* The handwriting should be neat, the ink black.

<table>
<tr><td>Outer or only envelope: (Use full names, no abbreviations.)</td><td>Mr. and Mrs. James Smathers Gordon
1234 Vail Road
Farmington
Connecticut</td></tr>
<tr><td>Inner envelope, if used:</td><td>Mr. and Mrs. Gordon</td></tr>
<tr><td>Outer envelope to include a daughter:</td><td>Mr. and Mrs. James Smathers Gordon
Miss Nancy Gordon, etc.</td></tr>
<tr><td>Inner:</td><td>Mr. and Mrs. Gordon
Miss Gordon
(for a small boy, put Master Timothy Gordon)</td></tr>
</table>

The point here: Never send an invitation to "and wife" or "and family."

- *Return address?* Yes, if you write it by hand—but don't have it printed or engraved.

Ask the stationer to send the envelopes right away, before the invitations or announcements are ready. You'll be able to start addressing earlier. And order extra envelopes for mistakes. A word of caution: several people may address envelopes, but one should be in charge. Otherwise, there is chaos.

FORMS OF INVITATIONS

Standard invitation to ceremony alone

Dr. and Mrs. James Bryant Lowell
request the honor of your presence
at the marriage of their daughter
Elizabeth Macon
to
Mr. Angus Mitchell McFall
on Saturday, the twenty-third of April
at four o'clock
Fourth Presbyterian Church
Chicago

If there is to be a reception, a "reception card" is enclosed with the above.

This is a stiffer piece of pasteboard, which matches the invitation. The type face should match also.

For a reception at home	*For a reception at a club or hotel*
Reception immediately following the ceremony 4856 Astor Street R.s.v.p.	Reception immediately following the ceremony The Casino Club R.s.v.p. 4856 Astor Street

Standard invitation to wedding and reception (used if you plan to invite all to both)

Dr. and Mrs. James Bryant Lowell
request the honor of your presence
at the marriage of their daughter
Elizabeth Macon
to
Mr. Angus Mitchell McFall
on Saturday, the twenty-third of April
at four o'clock
Fourth Presbyterian Church
and afterward at the reception
The Casino Club
Chicago

R.s.v.p.

If you plan to invite all to both wedding ceremony and reception, you could still correctly use an invitation and a reception card.

At-home card A nice inclusion, particularly if you are moving out of town. This is a small card—the same size, stock and style as a reception card. It reads:

Will be at home
after the fifteenth of May
8800 Vandeventer Place
St. Louis 10, Missouri

If you send at-home cards with announcements, you may add the name like this:

Mr. and Mrs. Angus Mitchell McFall
Will be at home
after the fifteenth of May
8800 Vandeventer Place
St. Louis 10, Missouri

Variations of place (club or hotel for wedding itself; church hall for reception, etc.) can be fitted into the above molds.

Now for variations on relationship:

One of your parents is dead:

Dr. James Bryant Lowell
requests . . . . . . marriage of his daughter . . .
or
Mrs. James Bryant Lowell
requests . . . . . . marriage of her daughter . . .

Your parents are divorced and your mother has not remarried:

Mrs. Sims Lowell
requests . . . . . . marriage of her daughter . . .

or she has remarried

Mrs. Edward Loring Lorimer
requests . . . . . . marriage of her daughter . . .
Elizabeth Macon Lowell . . .

or they send a joint invitation

Mrs. Edward Loring Lorimer
and
Dr. James Bryant Lowell
request . . . . . . marriage of their daughter . . .

Your parents are separated legally Invitations are issued in the names of both parents or of the parent or relative with whom you live. Your mother in this case is still Mrs. James Bryant Lowell.

Your fiancé is in the service See page 230.

Your parents are both dead; a relative is responsible for the wedding

Mr. and Mrs. Adam Bede Lowell
request . . . . . . marriage of their granddaughter . . .

FORMS OF ANNOUNCEMENTS

Dr. and Mrs. James Bryant Lowell
have the honor to announce
the marriage of their daughter
Elizabeth Macon
to
Mr. Angus Mitchell McFall
on Saturday, the twenty-third of April
One thousand nine hundred and sixty-two
Fourth Presbyterian Church
Chicago

PHOTOGRAPHS

A few days before your wedding, possibly a week before, if you're *that* organized, you may want to have a formal bridal portrait made. It's better to arrange it several days before the wedding than to wait until the morning of the big day, when you'll be totally nervous. Many photographers will bring lights and camera to your last fitting for your dress and take your portrait right in the store. Most stores are happy to go along with this arrangement and have special dressing rooms big enough to accommodate you, your mother, the fitter, the cameraman.

- Understated make-up is best for your bridal portrait, as it is for any portrait. And please don't do anything radical to your hair. If you plan a new permanent or a new way of arranging your hair for the wedding, try it out a week before your portrait is taken. Otherwise the total effect will be rather unlike you.
- Some photographers offer a package: your bridal portrait or two of the wedding party (taken the day of the wedding) and candids of wedding-day preparations and the reception. They'll take photographs of the wedding itself, if you wish, and if your clergyman permits. Ask his approval befor instructing the photographer. Professional photographs are a good idea. Some shutter-bug friends can be counted on to take beautiful snapshots at your wedding; others will forget to bring their cameras along.

THE NEWSPAPER ANNOUNCEMENT

This follows the form of your engagement announcement, even to release date (in this case, the day after your wedding) and your mother's signature. Roughly the same information is included, and a bit is added. A sample is given on this page.

To: Society Editor For release: SUNDAY, APRIL 24

THE CHICAGO DAILY NEWS

Miss Elizabeth Macon Lowell, daughter of Dr. and Mrs. James Bryant Lowell, of 4856 Astor Street, was married at the Fourth Presbyterian Church yesterday afternoon to Mr. Angus Mitchell McFall, son of Mr. and Mrs. Malcolm Douglas McFall, of 333 Bellevue Place.

Dr. John L. Martin performed the ceremony. A reception followed at The Casino Club.

Dr. Lowell gave his daughter in marriage (or "escorted his daughter"). The bride wore a gown of antique ivory peau de soie made with a bell-shaped skirt. Her finger-tip tulle veil was fastened to an heirloom coronet of gold and seed pearls, and she carried a bouquet of white hyacinths and carnations.

Miss Anne Kleiner, cousin of the bride, was maid of honor. She wore a dress of turquoise surah silk, with a velvet headband to match. She carried a bouquet of lavender hyacinths and white carnations. The other attendants were Miss Agatha McFall, sister of the bridegroom, and the Misses etc., etc. They wore lavender surah-silk dresses and matching velvet headbands. They carried bouquets of white carnations.

Joseph L. Manciewicz, III, was best man. Ushers were Charles E. Lowell, brother of the bride, and . . . etc., etc.

Mrs. McFall is a graduate of etc. Mr. McFall is a graduate of etc.

(optional) After a wedding trip to Bermuda, the couple will live in St. Louis.

If you include a photograph, again make it an 8″ x 10″ glossy print and attach an identifying caption.

A WORD ABOUT FRAYED NERVES

As The Day approaches, everyone in your family will seem to grow slightly nervous. You may be calm yourself—but more likely you will be the most nervous of all. So when your father insists on leaving his easy chair in a living room cleared for the reception or your mother becomes upset because the announcements aren't addressed a week ahead of time, keep your temper. The chair can always be whisked away at the last minute, and somehow the announcements do get done.

All weddings seem to evoke the same amount of tension. And one of the nicest pre-wedding presents ever received was a note from a recently married friend. It began: "Now calm down. It will all be over in a week. And then, what bliss!"

BACHELOR DINNER, BRIDESMAIDS' LUNCH

In some areas, these are vanishing customs, but they are still nice. The bachelor dinner is basically a stag dinner given by the groom for his ushers. It should be held a few days before the wedding. The bridesmaids' lunch or dinner, at which you entertain your attendants, should also be held a few days ahead, so that the last two or three days before your wedding are free for rehearsal, rehearsal dinner, chores—and time with your family.

FLOWERS for the church should be discussed with the sexton. The best plan is for your mother, the florist and the sexton to meet at the church so they can discuss the flowers in the setting in which they will be seen.

- Your own bouquet should be white—although if you wear a pale pink or beige or blue dress for your wedding, your flowers might be colored. The general effect should be pale and fragile.

MUSIC

You go with your mother to make arrangements for music, soloist, choir, or whatever you wish, with the organist or musical director of your church. The organist is perfectly capable of arranging his own musical program, but he'd like to know what you prefer.

WHO WEARS WHAT WHEN?

Bride:

wedding dress, usually long:	white or cream; or pastel blue, pink or green; or brocade with gold or silver.
fabric:	silk, satin, peau de soie, faille, taffeta, velvet, chiffon, malines; in summer, organdy, lawn, piqué, linen
wedding veil, long or short:	to match or complement color of dress
fabric:	lace, malines, chiffon, organdy

matching silk or satin slippers
matching gloves

Groom:

morning coat or cutaway	black or very dark gray
striped trousers	black or gray stripe
double-breasted waistcoat	buff or pale-gray woolen, or white linen
stiff white shirt, wing collar	
ascot or four-in-hand tie	light-gray minute-patterned silk
spats	to match waistcoat
black silk socks	
black shoes	

Customs, as always, differ; some areas forget about spats, prefer a white dress shirt and four-in-hand to stiff wing collars. (Unless he wears a military uniform—acceptable at any wedding.)

Best man, ushers, fathers of the bride and groom wear what the groom wears. Ushers, however, should wear matching ties and gloves, usually given to them by the groom.

Maid of honor wears a dress exactly like the bridesmaids' but in a different color—or one in the same color in a different style. Her gloves, slippers and headdress are like the bridesmaids'; flowers may be different.

Bridesmaids dress alike, wear long or short dresses, carry flowers.

Mother of the bride wears an afternoon dress, with sleeves, in a pretty color; a dressy hat; matching gloves and shoes. She wears flowers or pins them to her bag.

Mother of the groom wears the same kind of dress, accessories.

At an evening wedding the groom, best man, ushers and fathers of the bride and groom wear full evening dress—white tie, tail coat, evening waistcoat, pumps.

In cold weather when wraps are needed the bride wears a cape or a stole; the groom, best man and ushers wear dark coats, gray mocha gloves, usually a silk hat.

At a small church wedding or an informal home wedding, the groom, best man, ushers and fathers of the bride and groom might wear dark-blue suit, white shirt and gray silk tie, black socks and shoes.

The bride may wear a long or short wedding dress (in a simple style) or a pretty street-length dress with a headdress or a little hat.

See page 163 for what to wear when you're a guest at a wedding.

More things to think about when selecting a wedding dress:

- Find something that is your type. If you're most at home in sweaters and skirts, choose a simple style.
- Remember it takes four to six weeks for the sample dress to be made up in your size.
- If you know a good dressmaker, why not have your dress made? It will probably be less expensive.
- If you sew and love to, make it yourself.
- Is there a lovely dress of your grandmother's on a shelf—or your mother's? If it can be made to fit, it adds a nice touch of sentiment.
- Have your wedding dress fitted over the underthings (waist cinch, corselet or whatever) you plan to wear with it.
- If you have your dress ready three weeks ahead, fine. But try it on again a few days before the wedding. Many brides lose weight in hectic prenuptial weeks, and a dress that fit three weeks earlier could hang like a tent on your wedding day.
- Don't walk down the aisle in shoes so new you'll slip and fall. Wear them a few times so you'll get the soles scratched for traction—and so the shoes will be thoroughly comfortable.
- And of course—wear something old, something new, something borrowed, something blue.
- And a final thing: your gloves. If your dress has very short sleeves and the effect you wish necessitates long gloves, you'll have to slit the underseam of your ring finger for the ceremony. Better solution: short gloves, which can be easily pulled off at the altar. You don't put them back on once you're married; just give them to your maid of honor and she'll carry them out under her bouquet.

ATTENDANTS

You and your groom will each need one, as a witness. Beyond that, it's up to you. Usually, the more formal the wedding, the more attendants, but there is no firm rule.

Selecting attendants Brothers and sisters are chosen first; your sisters should attend you; your fiancé's brothers should attend him. A sister is usually maid or matron of honor; it looks unfriendly to have a best friend serve as maid of honor while your sister ranks as a mere bridesmaid.

- If a groom hesitates to choose between his college roommate and an Army buddy as best man, he often asks his father to serve. (Thoughtful solution.)

- Bride's usher and groom's bridesmaid: It's nice to ask your groom's sister or favorite cousin to be a bridesmaid and to have your groom ask your brother or a favorite cousin to be an usher. It emphasizes the joining of the families.

Duties of attendants

- *Maid or matron of honor* You may have both, but choose one for your ranking attendant.
- She is usually your witness.
- She helps you manage gloves, train, veil, flowers, prayer book, etc., during the ceremony.
- *Bridesmaids and junior bridesmaids* look pretty. That's all they *have* to do, but most bridesmaids offer to run errands, etc., before the wedding.
- *Best man* really works for his title. Among his duties:
- He is usually a witness.
- He is responsible for seeing that ushers get to rehearsal and ceremony on time.
- He acts as guardian to the groom before the wedding: gets him to church; waits with him before the ceremony; takes charge of the ring, which he keeps in his waistcoat pocket or, better, on his little finger, until asked to produce it during the ceremony. (In a double-ring ceremony your maid or matron of honor is responsible for holding the groom's ring.) He carries the clergyman's fee (in a small envelope) and gives it to him after the ceremony.
- He sees that before the ceremony your going-away clothes, and those of your groom, are safely at the place where the reception is to be held. If you are spending your wedding night at a hotel before leaving on your wedding trip, he takes luggage for both of you to the hotel, registers you (Mr. and Mrs. Angus M. McFall), gets the key and gives it to the groom.
- He makes sure the car you're leaving in is in running order and not *too* decorated with old tin cans and ribbons.
- He is toastmaster at the reception and the rehearsal dinner.
- *Ushers* do what their name implies: they usher guests to their seats. As guests enter the church, the ushers go up to them, offer their right arm to women, merely half bow to men, and ask where they wish to be seated. The guests tell the ushers that they are friends of the bride, or of the groom, and are seated on the appropriate side (in most churches, the left side, as you face the altar, is the bride's and the right is the groom's). They escort the bride's and groom's families in *and* out; other guests, unless they are "special" (e.g., those older ladies whom you've called "Aunt" all your life), leave the church unescorted.

- At the reception, ushers may help serve punch, or announce guests in the receiving line or otherwise prove useful.
- Often a groom may appoint a "head usher" to lead the others into line while the groom himself, and his best man, wait in the vestry for the ceremony to begin. The head usher directs the other ushers, lines them up for the processional, etc.

Presents

- It's custom for you to give presents to your attendants and for your groom to give presents to his (presents for maid or matron of honor are exactly like those given bridesmaids; presents given best man and ushers are also alike). Suggestions: something in silver which can be engraved with the attendant's initials and, if you are going all out, your maiden initials, your groom's initials and the date of the wedding (4-22-62 will do). Stamp boxes, charms, bracelets, etc., for the girls. Penknives, bill clips, tie clips, etc., for the men. Or unengravables: evening purses for the girls, wallets for the men. The present chosen should be something lasting.
- It's also the custom for attendants to give the bride a joint present and for best man and ushers to chip in on one for the groom. Again, anything engraved makes a wonderful remembrance; many presents, such as silver picture frames, cigarette boxes and trays, can be engraved with facsimile signatures. Often the group present can take the place of individual presents.
- Presents are usually exchanged at a bridesmaids' luncheon or bachelor dinner or at the rehearsal dinner.

YOUR TROUSSEAU

- Naturally you'll want pretty nightgowns, peignoirs, slippers, slips, bras, girdles—the works. If you're lucky, relatives will give you a nightgown or two as engagement presents. In buying your trousseau, save money for a few dresses, shorts or whatever to wear on your wedding trip and things to wear at home in the evening after you're married. If your typical at-home costume has been, up to now, blue jeans and one of your brother's shirts, this is the moment to change!
- You'll need some sort of going-away ensemble—a travel dress or suit. It's nice if it's new—but not at all necessary.

WHAT WOULD YOU LIKE FOR A PRESENT?

As soon as the invitations are out, people will begin to ask you, your mother, and possibly your groom and his mother this happy question. Technically, all presents are given to the bride, because she is the homemaker. If you say, "Oh, just anything," that's probably what you will receive. It's really more considerate all around if you have an idea of what you'd like to have given you. Then you or anyone else who's asked can make light suggestions to suit pocketbooks of all degrees of fatness and slimness: "Aren't you nice to ask! What I really need is a cookbook . . . or a pepper grinder . . . or a toaster." Don't forget practical presents—frying pans, etc. If you've registered at a store, people can be referred there. See page 175.

A basic list of trousseau "treasures" may help you and the gift-givers:

for your table	*you need*
china or earthenware place settings—dinner or luncheon plate, butter plate, salad or dessert plate, cup and saucer	at least four place settings; eight is even better
sterling or silver-plate flatware—knife, fork, teaspoon, cereal or soup spoon, butter spreader, salad or dessert fork	at least four place settings; eight is ideal
glassware—iced tea glass, water glass, juice glass, sherbet dish and small plate for salad or dessert	at least four place settings—and hope for eight

for your linens	*you need*
bed linens per bed	
6 sheets	1 comforter
3 pillowcases per pillow	2 mattress pads
1 winter blanket	2 bedspreads (one washable)
1 summer-weight blanket	1 electric blanket (if you like)
bath	
12 each of bath, hand and guest towels	2 bath mats
12 washcloths	2 shower curtains, plastic liners (especially for fabric shower curtains)

- Get one of those "Wedding Gift Record" books and enter presents as they arrive. (Some shops give you a book if you order your wedding dress or register for china, etc., there.) Most books come with perforated sheets of gummed numbers; when present No. 1 arrives, you open it, note it in the book, and paste sticker No. 1 on the back or bottom of the present. This may seem like the height of foolishness or commercialism, but it makes sense. At first you think you'll always remember who sent you that marvelous gravy ladle. But by the time you've unwrapped the ninth ladle . . . The books look like this, and this is how you write in them:

No.	Name	Address	Description	From (store)	Date rec'd	Acknow.
1.	Mr. & Mrs. Gary Todd	301 E. 91 St. N.Y. 28	Teak Steak	B. Altman	4/10	

It's useful to list the store, because you might wish to exchange the gift.

(You could easily make a similar book and buy numbered stickers at the stationery store.)

- *Thank-you's* must be written, even if you have thanked the giver of a present in person. Try to write thank-you's as the presents come in before your wedding. And although no one would expect you to write thank-you notes on your honeymoon, people do expect to hear from you shortly after your return home. So keep at it. Make a job of it. Write the relatives and friends of your groom's family first. (That will make your in-laws glow as they hear "How nice that girl is; she wrote us such a lovely letter—and so soon!") Then start on your family's friends, and write the older ones first. Older ladies get especially hurt if they don't get a prompt thank-you. Then do your relatives and, lastly, your own friends. They know you best and can understand why you had to write others first.
- *Displaying presents* Many brides like to display their presents in a room at home. If the reception is given at home, people can run up to the guest room and take a look. If the reception is held away from home, people can stop by on their way home. If this custom seems ostentatious to you, forget it. But remember that many of your friends will like to see what you have received, and, if you're moving out of town after your marriage, this may be their one chance.
- The presents should be neatly arranged on tables or sawhorses and planks pushed back against a wall and covered with white or matching pastel sheets or tablecloths. (If the cloths hang to the floor, you can store boxes beneath.)
- Remove the cards from presents; there is no point in calling attention to the fact that one person gave you a silver teapot while another gave you only a dish towel.
- Arrange the gifts so that the inevitable duplications will be hidden. If you receive four electric skillets, space them about; don't line them up, warehouse-clearance fashion.

- Make a place setting of your china, silver and glass. If you receive a set of glasses or plates, put out one sample and leave the rest of the set in its carton.
- Checks, gift certificates, bonds: If people give you these, you might write, on a folded sheet of note paper, "These people gave Betty and Angus checks, savings bonds, gift certificates." List the names (never the amounts) and prop the note paper up among the other presents.
- Saying your thanks for presents at your reception is thoughtful, if you really remember what people gave you. Your mind is apt to be a bit confused at this point, though, so it's best not to trust your memory. Just say, "We loved your present" and let it go at that.
- If you'd like to display presents but feel shy about doing it on your wedding day, you can always have them arranged for your friends, or friends of your family's, to see a few days before the wedding.

Do bride and groom exchange presents? Yes, if they wish. The groom usually gives his bride jewelry; she may give him anything from good cuff links to a watch or a desk set. To be avoided: "intimate" gifts (night clothes, for example).

THE REHEARSAL is usually held in the evening a day or two before a wedding. All in the wedding party should assemble at the church at whatever time the clergyman specifies. The processional and recessional are rehearsed, but the words of the ceremony are never used. The bride doesn't take part in the rehearsal but stands on the side lines watching while a friend, or the groom's mother, or an aunt (at any rate, someone who's not in the wedding party) stands in for her. It's supposed to be bad luck for a bride to rehearse her own wedding.

THE REHEARSAL DINNER often follows the rehearsal. Once, a bride's family was supposed to act as host for the rehearsal dinner, but now the groom's family, or a close relative, often assumes the role (and bill). The best man serves as toastmaster.

- All members of the wedding party are invited, with their husbands or wives if they are married. Friends or relatives who have come a long distance for the wedding are often included. And, often, so is the clergyman (who almost as often declines).
- Toasts are given by the bride's family, the groom's, the ushers, the best man sometimes by maid of honor and bridesmaids. The groom toasts the bride, his family, her family. The bride doesn't rise to toast anyone. As well as being beautiful, brides are supposed to be shy and demure.

- The rehearsal dinner ends at a reasonable hour so that everyone can get some sleep.

THE WEDDING DAY

- Bridesmaids and maid of honor gather at your house and go from there to the church. (Your family, incidentally, is responsible for transporting them from your house to the church and to the reception. Limousine, cab, private car—it doesn't matter which.) If you have space, you might have the attendants dress at your house so that you know all their dresses, shoes, gloves, headbands, etc., are safely in one place. You give them their bouquets at your house. If your house is too crowded, have the attendants meet at church—but make them swear to be *there* fifteen minutes before the wedding.
- Ushers meet at the church an hour or half an hour before the ceremony, depending on what the best man has told them. (Your family is responsible for their transportation from the church to the reception.)
- Best man calls for the groom and escorts him to the church, where they wait in the vestry. You do not see your husband-to-be before the ceremony.
- Your mother goes to church with the bridesmaids, or a relative or a friend, and you and your father go together. This is symbolic; from now on you will be another man's love and worry. Your father will want to savor this last little-girl moment. And so will you.

"Giving the bride away" Traditionally, a father gives his daughter in marriage. If your father is dead, you may ask an uncle or older brother to assume the honor and escort you down the aisle. Or if your mother is remarried and you are close to your stepfather, you might ask him.

- Even if your parents are divorced, your father would give you away.

SEATING PEOPLE AT CHURCH

The bride's family sits in the first few pews on the left in most churches, the groom's family on the right. Aunts, family friends who have come a long distance and other special guests are given reserved seats just behind the families. Before the wedding, tell these favored people, "We'd love to have you sit in the fourth pew" or "fifth"; when they arrive at church, they will tell the ushers who seat them. Sometimes pews on the center aisle are roped off with satin ribbons to reserve seats for special guests. Ask the sexton and your florist.

- Occasionally a groom's family—because they come from out of town—will have fewer friends at the wedding than will the bride's. In this case, ushers will seat some friends of the bride and her family on the groom's side to even things out.

- After guests, the families are ushered to their seats. Next to the last to be seated are the groom's parents. The head usher escorts the groom's mother; the groom's father walks a step or two behind. Then the head usher returns to the vestibule for the bride's mother and escorts her to her seat.
- Then the church doors are closed. No one is seated after the mother of the bride.
- The canvas carpet, if any, is unrolled at this point. This is used to protect the bride's long dress (and train) from any dust which might be on the aisle. The canvas carpet is rolled on a huge spool and may be unrolled from the altar steps or the vestibule door. It remains down until all guests have left the church after the wedding. A florist or the caterer who supplies a canopy if you use one, usually furnishes this canvas.
- The ushers and bridesmaids assemble (see page 215 for order); the maid or matron of honor takes her place behind them; the bride and her father stand behind the maid of honor. The wedding-procession music is begun, the groom and his best man walk to the spot where they will await the rest of the party, and—HERE COMES THE BRIDE!

AFTER THE WEDDING

- The bridal party leaves the church (see page 216 for order); then the ushers scurry back to escort the bride's mother to the door first, then the groom's mother, then the other occupants of the first pew on either side, then the second or third pews, until all members of the immediate families have left the church. Guests do not leave their seats until after the families have been escorted out. (If there are ribbons, they can't until the ribbons are rolled back.)
- Or if you have invited more guests to the wedding than to the reception, you may wish to receive them in the vestibule of the church. You and the groom, his mother, and the bridesmaids stand next to your mother, who is always first in line. (If the groom's mother is from another town, she stands next to your mother, who will introduce guests to her before they move on to greet you and your husband. If the groom's mother is not a stranger, she stands a little beyond the bridesmaids.) The father of the bride may or may not stand in line; more often, he circulates in the neighborhood of the receiving line. The father of the groom is free to chat, like any other guest.
- Otherwise, you, your families and your wedding party go as quickly as you can to the place where the reception will be held, so that you can have your formal group picture taken (if desired) and form a receiving line without delay.

THE RECEPTION

What follows on the next few pages applies to receptions held at home as well as to those held in clubs or hotels. And of course it's warmer, and less expensive, to have a reception at home!

- At a *formal* home reception, you would have a receiving line if there's room for one.

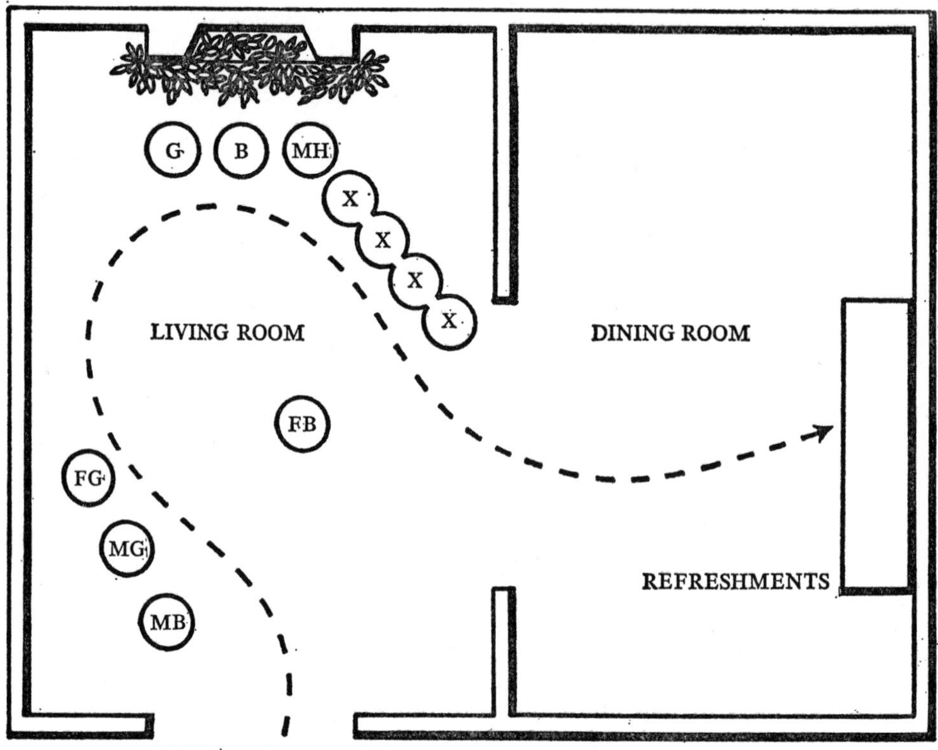

MB—Mother of the Bride
MG—Mother of the Groom
FG—Father of the Groom
FB—Father of the Bride

G—Groom
B—Bride
MH—Maid of Honor
X—Bridesmaid

- If your home is small (or small in view of the size of the party), stand-up food should be served. Special tables for the bride and groom and the parents might be exceptions.
- The cake is cut, of course, with all due ceremony.
- There may or may not be dancing, may or may not be music. Music is never

really necessary, but a strolling accordionist, or a pianist, or even a record player spinning light, happy tunes makes things gay.

- The bouquet is tossed and all other procedures are as they would be at a reception outside the home.

AT THE RECEPTION

The receiving line is arranged like the diagram (page 250). The bride's father may stand on line too but, as host, may prefer to mingle with guests.

- If your mother is dead, your father might choose a relative to act as his hostess in the receiving line. He would head the line then and, as guests come along, introduce them: "This is Mrs. Clark, Betty's aunt."
- There is no sit-down eating or dancing until all guests have been through the line (except at extremely large weddings), and the bride's mother, as hostess, leads the group from the line to the bridal table and the parents' table or tables. Of course, the guests do get some punch or champagne.

The book This is an old southern custom—often observed in other parts of the country as well. A small table is placed just at the end of the receiving line and an honored female guest (usually a relative who wasn't in the wedding party) presides over a guest book, which each guest signs.

The bridal table At most formal weddings there is a bridal table, set with the cake in front of the bride and groom. The bride sits at the groom's right, the maid of honor at his left. The best man sits at the bride's right. Ushers and bridesmaids alternate around the balance of the table.

- The wedding cake, if there is to be one, is the chief decorative feature of the bridal table.

The parents' table might be arranged like this:

Friends	Groom's father	Mother of bride	Clergyman	Friends
Friends	Clergyman's wife	Bride's father	Groom's mother	Friends

Tables may be round or long banquet tables.

- At a sit-down reception, guests find their own places with friends at tables scattered about the room. It's thoughtful at a stand-up reception to have a few tables and chairs in the corners for the older people.

- Most clubs and hotels will automatically seat guests at vast tables for ten or twelve unless you persuade them to do otherwise. The disadvantage of the big tables is that they crowd the room and tend to keep people put through the entire reception. If guests are seated at smaller tables for four or six, they are more apt to mingle, there is room saved for dancing, and a girl's friends will have a chance to meet those handsome ushers! With this arrangement, a few people will wind up eating off coffee tables or their laps in an anteroom. But these people are, usually, the younger ones, and they will crowd to the door when the bride cuts the cake, throws the bouquet, etc.
- As soon as punch or champagne is served to the bridal table, the best man should propose the first toast to the bride. Best men have been known to forget, but an alert usher may nudge him—or substitute if he's tongue-tied or suddenly missing. Other toasts may follow.
- Cutting the cake is the climax of the feast. The bride rises to her feet, all men at the bridal table rise with her, the guests gather round, and bride and groom cut and eat the first slice together. Often, the first slice is cut beforehand but not removed, so the bride just pretends to cut and then removes the slice to a plate. Someone else cuts the rest of the cake.

Dancing If there is to be dancing, the bride and groom start it. They dance together, with the floor to themselves. The groom's father usually asks for the second dance and the groom dances with the bride's mother. Then the bride's father cuts in. Then the wedding party and other guests dance.

During the reception While a bride is in her wedding dress and veil, she should look and act dignified. No calling across the floor or enthusiastic waving, no matter how good a time she is having. *No smoking*. It looks unbecoming, and the veil might burn up, along with the bride.

- It's nice to make a circuit of the room with your groom, talking with all your guests. You'll be able to talk more informally and at more length than in the receiving line.

THE BOUQUET is tossed just before the bride and groom leave the reception to change. See page 240 for more about the bouquet.

GOOD-BYS should be said to both sets of parents before you leave on your wedding trip. Your own mother will, of course, crowd into the room with your bridesmaids as you dress, and your father will appear as soon as you are dressed. But your groom's family may feel shy about invading a roomful of ushers to see their son, and they will definitely be reticent about walking into your room. So send a bridesmaid to find them and bring them up when you are dressed. A point should be made of this; it's easy to forget in all the flurry. (Bride and groom change in separate rooms, of course.)

It's a nice custom as you leave to be pelted by paper rose petals, confetti or rice. The best man organizes the send-off.

HOME WEDDING

If both wedding and reception are held at home, the guest list may be large or small, depending on, among other things, the size of your house. You could limit guests for the ceremony to your families and invite other friends for the reception.

- If you are married at home, you will probably want to be married in front of a window with a pretty view or the fireplace. If there is room, ushers will escort friends and family to folding chairs and you will make a dramatic entrance with your bridesmaids. Or you might simply walk into the room with your father, once everyone else has assembled.
- At most home weddings, the recessional and reception line are nonexistent. You and your groom merely turn and greet your guests, after you have received the clergyman's congratulations. However, it is correct to have a recessional and reception line, if you wish. Put the reception line in the hall, so that guests can go through it and on to a larger room (the dining room, probably) for refreshments.
- The wedding cake and other refreshments should be set on a prettily decorated dining table pushed against the wall. Guests should gather round for toasts, cake-cutting and the tossing of the bouquet; the rest of the time they mix and mingle as they please.
- It's lovely to have both wedding and reception in a garden if the weather is nice. But be prepared to use the house in case of emergency. It might rain!

RECTORY WEDDING

Usually, only members of the families, and perhaps a few friends, are present. The bride is dressed simply—not in a wedding dress. There is no processional, no recessional and no receiving line. A small, informal reception might be held later at home, in a friend's apartment, in a club, at a hotel. There would be toasts, and perhaps a cake, but, again, no receiving line. The bride's mother would greet guests, but she need stand in no particular spot to do so.

WHO PAYS FOR WHAT

The bride's family pays for

- invitations and announcements
- the bride's wedding dress, veil, etc., and trousseau

- decoration of the church (flowers, canvas carpet if any, etc.)
- fees of church organist, soloist (if any) and sexton
- the reception—flowers, music, food, drink, etc.
- transportation of the bridal party (for ushers, this means only from church to reception)
- wedding photographs (portraits and candids)
- the bridesmaids' and maid of honor's bouquets (and, usually, gloves and head pieces) and their presents from the bride
- flowers for both mothers
- boutonniere for the father of the bride
- the bride's bouquet, although the groom can—and may want to—pay for this
- The bride's family pays for accommodations of the bride's attendants if they come from out of town. (Naturally they pay their transportation to the town in which the wedding is held.) This could mean having them stay with friends or putting them up at a hotel—with a married woman as chaperon if they are young

The groom pays for

- the engagement ring
- the marriage license
- the bride's wedding ring
- his boutonniere, that of his father, and those of his ushers and best man (For other flowers, see above.)
- the ushers' gloves, ties and (if necessary) collars
- his gifts to the ushers
- the contribution to the clergyman—to be given after the wedding
- his own wedding clothes
- the car in which he and his bride leave the reception (if it is necessary to hire one)
- the wedding trip, the new home, and its major furnishings
- The groom pays for the accommodations of his out-of-town attendants

The maid or matron of honor and bridesmaids pay for

- their dresses, shoes and underpinnings for the wedding
- a share in a joint present to the bride

The best man and ushers pay for

- the clothes they wear for the wedding, with the exception of what the groom furnishes—ties, gloves, and sometimes collars
- a share in a joint present to the groom

Anyone may pay for

- the rehearsal dinner

PROBLEMS OF THE DIVIDED HOUSE

One of the functions of an etiquette book is to offer a tactful way out of a difficult emotional situation, and since divorce does exist, and can mar plans for a wedding, these suggestions may help.

If the parents of the bride are divorced:
Invitation and announcement See page 237, earlier in this chapter.

Giving the bride away The father of the bride gives her away unless father and daughter have been completely estranged for years and the father will not be present at the wedding. In that case, a devoted stepfather, uncle, grandfather, older brother, sister's husband or older male family friend substitutes.

Where the father of the bride sits during the wedding In the second or third pew on the left side of the church; if he has remarried, he may be accompanied by his new wife. She is invited to the reception if all are on civil terms. Neither she nor the bride's father stands in the receiving line.

Does he sit at the parents' table? No; he is very much a guest.

Solution if he doesn't go to the reception: He might give a wedding supper to which his family and friends are invited—which the bride, groom and attendants, still in their wedding clothes, attend immediately after the reception itself.

United action like this would make the wedding happier for a bride who loves both parents:

- Mother and father issue invitations to the wedding and reception and send out announcements jointly:

  Mrs. Edward Loring Lorimer
  and
  Dr. James Bryant Lowell (etc.)

- One parent gives the rehearsal dinner; the other gives the reception; but invitations to each are issued jointly. (The groom's family, if they wish, could be hosts at a small party before the rehearsal dinner.)

- The father gives the bride away. If he's unmarried, he could join the mother in the front left-hand pew while the stepfather sits with an aunt in the second pew. If the father has remarried, he should sit with his new wife in the second or third pew.
- Father and mother stand in the receiving line, while the second spouse (or spouses) mingles with the other guests.
- Parents' table: Have two (one for the mother, the groom's family and the clergyman; a second for the father and a few friends).

If the groom's parents are divorced:

The wedding ritual, fortunately, doesn't point this fact up. Usually they should not be seated together; the mother and someone she chooses sit in the first pew; the father sits in the third. Or the bride might simply ask the groom how he would like his parents seated.

The hardest problem of all is when an engaged couple finds that one or more of the parents is bitterly opposed to the marriage, for whatever reason—differences in background, education, finances, social position, religion, or just plain dislike of the fiancé or the other parents. Sometimes the real reason is that the parent secretly feels no one could be good enough for his/her boy or girl. Sometimes it is that the parent would resent anyone's taking first place away from him/her. Sometimes the proposed marriage signals the end of a parent's cherished ambition for a boy to become a doctor, a girl to marry "well" (meaning a boy with a better future, better position, or better income).

One thing you will discover fairly quickly is whether you love the person you're engaged to enough to weather the storm. If you do, proceed with your wedding arrangements as determinedly and peacefully as you can. Try to win the support of other relatives; hope for the support of your love's family. Curiously, you may find your best help comes from unsuspected sources—his brother's wife or her stepmother, people who are in a neutral emotional position and are able to be concerned with *your* happiness. More often than not, the bitterest parent will control his feelings and be pleasant on the day of the wedding.

The thing you won't discover for a while is that all the excitement will be forgotten once you are married. There's little point in continuing to argue about an accomplished fact; suddenly the parent will be less concerned with having gained an unwanted son or daughter and more interested in not losing you. On your first wedding anniversary, they too will wish you, as we do, a lifetime of happiness.

26. A Treasury Of Entertaining Ideas

everything about parties . . . food, fun, games, table setting and all the trimmings . . . what to say from the first invitation to the last good-by

INVITATIONS

There are about as many ways to invite people to a party as there are kinds of parties.

You may give your invitations in person, by telephone, by writing little notes, by sending cards you either make or buy. If you have folded visiting cards called "informals," you may use them. When you ask anyone in person or by telephone, it's a good idea to follow up the invitation with a reminder.

The important thing is to include all the information in your invitation—the date, the time to come and your name and address.

Plus extra information, such as "Sweet Sixteen Party for Marilyn Baxter" or "Buffet dinner before the dance."

Plus information on what to wear—"blue jeans," "black tie," "bring your bathing suit."

Plus "R.s.v.p." and your telephone number, to make answering your invitation easier. If you're having a large party, you may want to put "Respond regrets only, please" instead of "R.s.v.p." * Or simply include in your message, "We'll be counting on you; let me know if you can't come."

A chart showing various ways to handle invitations appears on the following page.

---

* *Répondez, s'il vous plaît*—French for "Please answer."

INVITATIONS

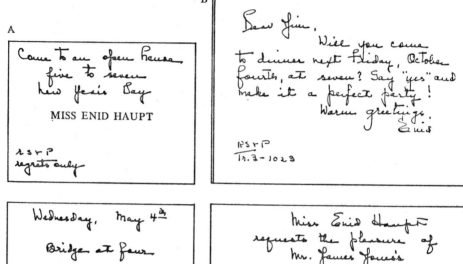

A

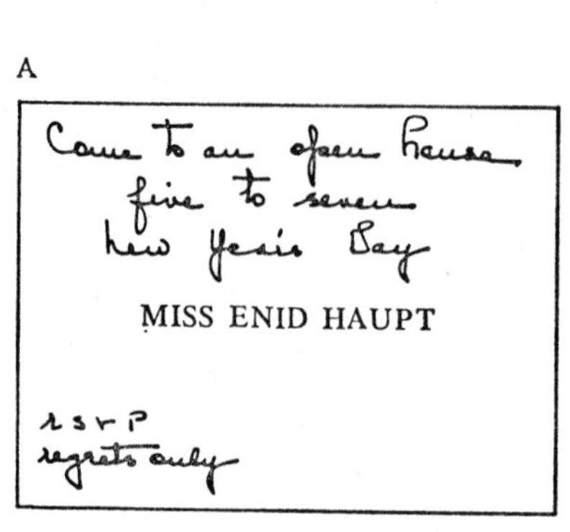
Come to an open house
five to seven
New Year's Day
MISS ENID HAUPT
RSVP
regrets only

B

Dear Jim,
Will you come
to dinner next Friday, October
fourth, at seven? Say "yes" and
make it a perfect party!
Warm greetings,
Enid
RSVP
TR.3-1023

Wednesday, May 4th
Bridge at four
MISS ENID HAUPT
RSVP
TR.3-1023

A

Miss Enid Haupt
requests the pleasure of
Mr. James Jones's
company at a small dance
at nine o'clock on Monday,
the third of October, at
Two Garden Place
black tie
RSVP

C

A—On visiting cards or informals
B—On note-size paper
C—On a correspondence card, size of a penny postcard, with envelope to match or note-size paper

GOOD PLANNING

- Ask only as many people as you can entertain comfortably in your house, kitchen, garden or wherever the party is to be.
- Ask only as many people as you can afford to entertain.
- You can invite people any way you choose—with a date, without a date—just so you have an idea of the prospective boy-girl ratio. (To be safe, you might ask one or two of the stag boys to bring a friend. Just a few, though: a wealth of boys is not necessarily a blessing, since boys tend to herd.)
- You can invite girls to come by themselves—or arrange for boys on your list to call for them and take them home.

- You can invite girls only—and ask each to bring her own beau. (Unless your party is very casual, it's a nice idea to confirm the invitation by sending a card or note directly to the boy too.)
- Invite your guests ten days to two weeks before the date of your party.
- To prevent hurt feelings, avoid talking about your party in front of those who are not invited. Above all—even if you've been trying to catch up with her for days—never, never ask Sally to a party in front of someone you're not planning to ask.

(*More than above all—take care not to talk about Sally's party in front of anyone else, unless you're sure that person's been asked too.*)

Plan your party so you can be one of those confident hostesses who have as much fun as the guests. Your menu should be the kind that's either fixed before the party or cooked with the guests watching and helping (waffles, hot dogs, hamburgers). New recipes, difficult recipes should be tried in advance.

A check list is a soothing bit of organization. Here's a sample:

BUFFET DINNER BEFORE THE DANCE—for twelve

menu
Swedish meat balls
noodles baked in sour cream
tossed salad
hot *croissants*
mixed fresh fruit
squares of frosted cake
milk
coffee

china
12 dinner plates
12 dessert dishes
12 glasses for milk
12 coffee cups and saucers

silver
12 dinner forks
12 dessertspoons
sugar tongs
12 spoons for coffee
serving spoons, forks—four sets

decorations
flowers for the dining table
flowers for the living room

serving things needed
electric serving tray
large casserole
large baking-serving dish
large salad bowl (or two?)
serving dish with napkin
glass (or silver) bowl that can go in refrigerator to chill
cake plate with doily
large pitcher
coffeepot, creamer, sugar bowl

linen
tablecloth
12 napkins

wraps
girls' in my room
boys' in hall closet—six hangers available?
hand towels
new cake of soap
cleansing tissue
safety pins and bobby pins

Once it is planned, get your party prepared as early as you can. Food and flowers can be bought the day before; food can be cooked or partly cooked in the morning; the table can be set as soon as your family is willing—all with the idea of giving you time to bathe, dress, even nap. One of a hostess's pleasures—if she's planned right—is the leisurely inspection tour of the food, the table, all the little details before the first guest arrives. Very contenting.

QUESTIONS ABOUT PARTIES AND THE ANSWERS . . .

We don't know all the answers—in fact, we don't even know all the questions!—but here are the ones most often asked by readers who write in to SEVENTEEN. The answers to these (and to most questions involving success with people) follow the tried-and-true formula of just being nice people.

Q. *There are always a few boys who manage to arrive half an hour ahead of the party. What can a hostess do with them? At our age they are staggered by this kind of mistake and they shrink into an embarrassed shell.*

A. Early-comers do require special handling. Best technique we know is to put them to work (much more relaxing than a long chat with your father or little sister). If you plan to have dancing, save rolling up the rug for the strong-armed early-comers. Ask for advice: get them to go through your records and help you select the evening's musical program. Important rule is to keep a boy busy; he'll forget to be self-conscious.

Q. *Some girls have a talent for getting parties off the ground. Mine just don't seem to launch well. What am I doing wrong?*

A. Possibly what's wrong is your thinking that you're doing something wrong. The hostess sets the mood of every party, so start yours enthusiastically—mostly by making every single guest feel that his (or her) arrival has made your life complete.

Q. *Should I get a friend to answer the door so I can stay with the other guests?*

A. Do whatever makes you feel most confident. The one who does handle the door—a brother, a sister, a friend—should direct the girls first, then the boys, to the places you've planned for them to leave their things. Usual greetings go something like this: "Hi, Mary! Hello, John. Good to see you! Mary, will you leave your things in Lucy's room—head of the stairs on the left? John, let me put your coat here in the hall closet."

Q. *How do I introduce strangers so there isn't that thud of silence following their names?*

A. Some appropriate scene-setting remark can form the basis for a babble of conversation: "Mary, this is John Jones, who knows all about skiing—"

Q. *I find it's very hard to get one person introduced all around a group. Is there a trick?*

A. Well—no. With luck and a small number of guests, you may be able to command a moment's silence and proceed to introduce the group to a girl, or a boy to the group. (If the newcomer is a girl, you say, "This is John Jones . . . Edna Williams . . . Jerry Jackson . . ." And then, to the group, you say, "Mary Baxter." If it's a boy, you say to the group, "This is Gary Smith," and then you say to Gary, "Edna Williams . . . Jerry Jackson . . . John Jones.") But if you've got a large gay group chattering away, just introduce the newcomer to people in one corner.

Q. *I plan my parties in detail, really organized; they're always fun, but somehow my plans get shelved halfway through the party. Should I try to be more of a cruise director?*

A. Stay as you are—flexible. Party plans are primarily to get the social ball rolling. Once the party's in motion, you're quite right not to insist on following a rigid schedule. If you've planned games or dancing and everyone's having a great time telling anecdotes about what happened last term in gym class, don't break the spell. Just ponder happily about what fun your friends are. Spontaneity is one of the real pleasures of a party.

Q. *Our house just doesn't have enough chairs, and my sister and I long to have a big party. Should we ask our parents to rent folding chairs?*

A. Unless you really need them for a sit-down meal at many bridge tables—or you're planning a colossal game of musical chairs—don't spend your money hiring chairs. Most young people really prefer sitting on the floor.

Q. *My best friend is a problem at parties; she just sits the party out in a corner, waiting for people to come and talk to her. I can't not invite her, but she never budges.*

A. Actually it's part of your job as hostess to budge the shy ones. Draw her into a game that's being organized or get someone else to. Give her a job to do—greet people at the door, pass pretzels, make the waffles—or, best of all, ask her to make a point of helping another shy person (preferably a boy) have a good time.

Q. *It may sound foolish, but I honestly worry about what to do when there's one of those horrid lulls in conversation—especially when it's my party.*

A. Keep some controversial topics of conversation in the back of your mind for such emergencies. Comment about a popular movie or song. Start a discussion about school politics or the *real* trouble with the football team.

Ask someone about a planned trip or an exciting summer job. The point is not to do the talking yourself but to stimulate others to talk.

Q. *My mother says a good hostess makes everybody feel at home. Please, how do I do it?*

A. Mix, dance, talk with all your guests. If there's a boy who's too bashful to ask a girl to dance, ask him yourself—your privilege as the hostess! Get your date to dance with a girl who's miserably shy—and get your brother or someone to cut in. If a few couples seem determined to dance only with each other, arrange double cuts—or a circle switch of partners. (And, however much you prefer to cling to your best beau, you can't be that exclusive when you're the hostess—and, since he in a sense is the host, he can't either.)

Q. *The most embarrassing thing is to have a friend who wasn't invited call when we're having a party. (I have two sisters, so we can't invite all our friends every time.) My mother says I can't take time from the party for a long chat—but how do I cut the call short without letting my friend know she was left out?*

A. It's part of growing up to understand you can't be asked to all parties (or all clubs, societies, committees, etc.), and if your friend hasn't learned this yet, she'll have to soon—or be an overly sensitive, unhappy grownup. But, to answer the immediate question, just say, "Oh, Mary, I so want to talk to you, but we have guests. May I call you tomorrow morning?" If Mary is ruffled or hurt because she wasn't asked, be as bland and noncommittal as you can. And ask her to the next party.

Q. *At a party, when the boys huddle together by themselves, is it all right for a girl to go over and talk to a boy she likes?*

A. Yes—but make it casual by asking another girl or two to go with you. That way, the other boys won't find a splendid opportunity to tease the one you like.

Q. *I want to give a Valentine party but can't think of any boy to ask as my date. Should I give up the idea?*

A. No, no, no. Ask your friends as individuals rather than as couples. This is a perfect way to get to know members of the opposite sex, who—as you know by now—are really very shy.

Q. *I would like to give a surprise birthday party for a boy. Is this proper? What should I do about presents? Most of the boys will give them to him anyway, but the girls wouldn't ordinarily. Should I say no presents on the invitation—or say 25-cent funny presents only—or get one myself and have everyone sign the card?*

A. Your idea is very proper indeed—and a wonderful way for a girl to "treat" a boy! About presents—the funny, inexpensive ones are always fun. If you think your friends would want to give the boy something grander, perhaps solve the problem by collecting a small sum from each person and buying the birthday boy something you know he wants.

Q. *If you're having entertainment at a party, when do you have it?*

A. If you're having a dinner party, the planned entertainment should take place after dinner. If it's an evening party with the food last (sandwiches, cake, coffee), you'd have the entertainment first.

Q. *How do I go about getting guests to go in to dinner or refreshments?*

A. If there are boys present, the best way is to flatten yourself against the wall to avoid the stampede once they hear there's food. Usually you just say something like "Supper's ready. Let's go in, shall we?" If your party is a large one, ask a few friends to help you circulate the word that the food is ready.

Q. *What do I do about parents at my party?*

A. Ask them to help greet your guests. Once everyone's arrived, they can—and probably will!—disappear to another part of the house.

Q. *How* do *you handle crashers?*

A. If they're friends and there's room, you might ask them in—obviously not to a sit-down dinner! Objectionable crashers are another matter, and that's when you need parents or an adult to help. They can ask the crashers—privately and one at a time—to leave. If it's not practical for them to join your party, just tell them the simple truth: "I couldn't be sorrier, but I can't ask you in because we already have quite a crowd. Next time!"

Q. *How can I avoid having a party wind up as a make-out session? My parents are furious when they find the lights low and a lot of smooching going on.*

A. *Food,* dancing, *food,* cards, games, *food,* table tennis, *food.* Be sure not to start the romantic proceedings yourself. And do have some fast-paced or funny records on tap for emergencies. People get that springtime feeling to slow, dreamy music—never to one or more comedians or some chipmunk song.

Q. *Help! I can't seem to get my parties to end—and this is bad news for me with my parents and for my friends with theirs.*

A. Success is not always sweet! Your best bet is to arrange with a few friends to enforce the curfew by gathering up coats and saying, "Everyone, *come;* you can't party forever." Other aids: play a record such as "Good Night, Irene"; turn the lamps on full and dispense with the mood lighting. If all fails, get your parents to come down to say good night.

TABLE TALK

Of course you're a good cook (or an expert with frozen prepared foods!), but a point for any hostess to remember is that even indifferent food tastes better served attractively—and delicious food becomes superb in a pretty setting. If you think of each table you set as a picture, the result will probably be more imaginative. (One shy but very creative girl we know pretends she is setting the table for *someone else's* party; somehow this small fool-the-mind device unleashes her imagination—and the results are charming.)

Any table needs balance—balance of plain and patterned silver, china and linens; balance of bright and soft colors; balance of textures; balance of excitement and serenity; even balance of different periods of design.

Color is your friend or foe, depending on how you use it. Too many colors are confusing; too few are dull. If your china has a colored pattern, play up the colors in linens and centerpiece. A plate with a design in gold, rust and green would be delightful on an olive cloth with gold napkins—with a centerpiece of gold and orange pompons and marigolds. Supposedly, pale colors are more formal, but that's a rule to be broken. A rich red cloth and napkins with gold-rimmed china, cut crystal and scrolled silver brims with as much elegance as a silver-gray cloth with rose-bordered china and a centerpiece of pink roses and white freesia. By varying the colors and textures in linens, you can make the same set of china, glass and silver look formal or rather casual. As an example: violet-patterned china on woven blue mats—*informal;* same china on a white lace cloth—*very formal.*

You have to strike a balance with the varying, though; a wild plaid cloth, perfect with contemporary white china, would be a miserable partner for the violet-patterned china even if the plaid were basically violet—just as the same cloth would be ideal for a barbecue and very much out of place for an engagement party.

a too-serene setting—one with everything so overmatched it looks homogenized—is dull. A relatively simple pattern, if repeated throughout, can bore the eye. You can add excitement by teaming plain plates with patterned bread and butters or by adding checked napkins to a solid cloth. Too much excitement is equally bad. To explain: one floral pattern is plenty; if china is flowered, simpler glass, linen and silver are more attractive with it.

an all-one-period setting can be dull too. Simple modern china might be much more interesting with gaily colored Early American glasses—and classically patterned English china might be more interesting with stark contemporary glasses than with the traditional cut crystal. All pieces should share the same degree of formality, though—no chunky mugs with fragile china.

set your table for an informal sit-down meal like this:

As you see, all the silver *up to the dessert course* is placed in the order it is used. If soup is to be served, soup cups and saucers are placed on the service plates and soupspoons are at the far right. If you plan to serve fruit instead, substitute teaspoons for the soupspoons; if your first course is to be salad, put salad forks to the left of the luncheon forks and omit the spoons.

At a more formal meal eliminate the butter plates, always add salad forks if salad is to be served, and you might find it convenient to place the dessert silver like this when the table is set for the first course (that small fork to the left is for seafood cocktail; as usual, silver is placed so you work from the outside in):

Here are some tips for the placement of various objects at a sit-down meal:

- When a roast is to be carved at the table, the carving set goes to the right of the carver, just above his place setting—the idea being that when the roast is brought in, all the implements will be to the right of the platter.
- Jellies and condiments are put on the table with their serving spoons to the right of them (or on their plates) rather than placed in the goodies. The first person taking the jelly, or condiment, inserts the spoon. If the spoon is relatively clean after use, it is returned to the plate; otherwise, it is returned to the jelly.
- Iced-tea spoons are placed at the right of the knives. Regular teaspoons do not go on the table except when they are used as substitutes for soup or dessertspoons. When served with hot tea or coffee, teaspoons are placed on the saucers.
- Coffee cups appear on the table from the start at breakfast and sometimes at lunch. At dinner they should stay out of the picture until dessert. Small after-dinner cups normally appear only in the living room, but, occasionally, if you are pressed for time (an eight o'clock curtain for the class play), they are brought to the table.
- Butter plates are used at breakfast and lunch and informal dinners—never at formal dinners, even though hot garlic-buttered bread or *croissants* may be served. (You put the buttery bread on the edge of the dinner plate.)
- Place cards may be perched either on a folded napkin centered on the plate at each place or just above the place setting.

- Plate patterns, napkin monograms should go right side up when seen from the chair behind the place setting—in other words, no flowers or figures standing on their heads!
- In deciding what serving implements are needed, choose a fork and spoon unless the food to be served can be managed easily with a spoon—peas, for example. Incidentally—a soup or punch ladle is a big help in serving casseroles; most serving forks and spoons slither to the bottom of deep dishes.
- Mats or tray cloths go on trays only when a meal is to be served on the trays. They are not for iced drinks, coffee or tea.
- Table "separates" are more interesting than peas-in-a-pod sets—but they should be harmonious rather than disorganized in effect. And dinner plates should match, although butter or salad plates need not match dinner plates.
- At a sit-down dinner, people should be seated not too near and not too far. If eight or ten crowds your table, serve the meal buffet-style. And if four people are lost at a vast dining table, group them at one end.
- Seat people so that they are spaced boy, girl, boy, girl. This way:

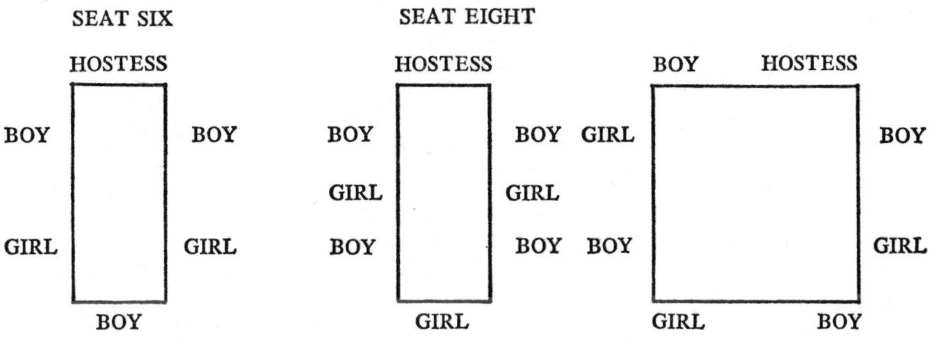

- The male guest of honor sits at the hostess's right, the female guest of honor at the host's right. All girls? Then the guest of honor sits at the hostess's right.
- Merry idea when you have a crowd for a sit-down dinner (Thanksgiving, Christmas, pre-prom) is to seat some at the dinner table, some at one or more bridge tables. For dessert, have some of the bridge-table eaters change places with the dinner-table group. This keeps the bridge-table guests from feeling left out, gets the tables cleared and gives everyone a kind of seventh-inning stretch.
- Centerpieces needn't always be flowers; figurines, antique bottles, a paper creation made for a special-occasion party are just as decorative.

Here is a simple way to serve a sit-down meal:

- Have your first course on the table when you bring in your guests. If you're having heated crackers to go with soup, have them at your right so you can start them around the table.
- When the first course is finished, remove the soup cup and saucer (or fruit dish) from the left, leaving the plates at each place. Carry out two cups and saucers at a time. If you have five or more guests, plan for one of the girls to help carry out and serve dishes.
- Bring in the serving dishes that hold the main course and set them in front of your place (on mats to protect your table). Then bring in the heated plates on which you'll serve the main course. As you pass each filled plate to the girl who's helping you, she will—starting with the guest of honor—remove the place plate with her right hand and set the filled plate, which she holds in her left hand, in front of the guest. If you have fewer than five guests, you simply pass the filled plates down the table; some helpful soul will make a collection of the place plates.
- After the main course, remove all the dishes, the salts and peppers, and all but the dessert silver. (At a formal dinner with maid service the dessert plates would be brought in with a dessert fork and spoon placed in the center of each plate, a finger bowl partly filled with water on a small doily on the plate. Each guest removes the silver, places the fork on the left of the plate and the spoon on the right; then the guest removes the bowl and doily and places them to the left of the dessert plate.)
- Then bring in the dessert; serve the plate at your place and pass it to the guest of honor, who will trade plates with you. Fill that plate and have it passed down the table, saying, "This is for Joan . . ."
- When you've finished dessert, you leave the dining room and forget about clearing the table. If it's evening and you've used candles, ask someone to put them out—but *you* go with the guests and bring the coffee once they're settled.
- *A simpler way to serve a sit-down meal would be to omit the first course and the service plates. Have a dish or small bowl of salad at the left of each place and the main-course serving dishes in front of your place, ready to be served when your guests are seated. Fill your own plate and exchange for the plate of the person sitting at your right—and so on around the table, till all are served. Forget the finger bowls and, after clearing the first course, bring the dessert and stack of dessert plates to your place to serve.*

Set your table for a buffet breakfast, lunch or supper like this:

- Place everything so it's easily accessible to the guests as they go round the table helping themselves to china, silver and food. Make the order progressive, so they won't have to backtrack or reach around the centerpiece.

- Be sure to give your arrangement plenty of "breathing room."
- Group like pieces neatly in units—plates, napkins and silver together; hot dishes together; salad apart from these.
- Pitchers of milk, ice water or punch (with glasses), hot drinks go at the end of the table.

Set your tea table like this:

- Cover the table with a cloth; but use no doilies or mats on the trays that hold the tea and coffee services.
- On the tea tray set a teapot, hot-water pot (on an alcohol warmer, if you have one), tea strainer in a little dish, sugar, cream and a plate of thin lemon slices.
- On the coffee tray set the pot, more sugar and cream.
- Arrange cups and saucers, spoons, napkins along the sides of the table, cookies and sandwiches in the center. Some hostesses like to omit the saucers and place the cups on tea plates (salad plates, really).

JUST LOOKING, THANK YOU

Choosing your own table appointments You'll be wise to do a lot of looking before you start making this important investment. Look with interest at every table you sit down to—asking yourself if this is the china, silver, glassware of your dreams. Think of patterns in terms of the kind of furnishings you like best—contemporary, traditional, English, French. Think of the colors you like—strong citrus shades or delicate blues and grays. Consider whether the patterns you plan to buy will go with all that glassware your grandmother gave you when she closed up her house—if you love the glassware, that is. (It may not fit in at all with your present tastes. However, if it's old and lovely, do keep it until you've been married a few years; tastes change or it might go beautifully with china from your husband's family that he will want to use.)

With proper care, your silver, china and glassware will always stay just as beautiful as when new—and you certainly don't need to keep them unused in your treasure chest until you're married. Those first tiny scratches on your silver are not a cause for distress; they'll increase with use and give your silver that desirable soft mellow finish known as a patina.

When you wash dishes—as soon as you can after meals, so food particles don't have a chance to harden—use hot, *not* scalding, soapy water. Do silver first, and rinse it in clear hot water; dry it with a clean soft linen towel while the silver is still warm. (Wait till it's cool to put it away.) Do glass next in mild soapsuds and water that's just comfortably hot to your hands. A rubber mat or a dish towel in the bottom of your dishpan or sink cuts the chance of chipping. If your glassware has a cut or pressed pattern, you can use a soft brush to reach into the crevices. Rinse glassware with fairly hot water and stand it in a rubber rack to drain. Dry it with a soft linen dish towel—the sooner the better, to avoid spotting. Follow same procedure for china—washing it separately from the glasses, as you have gathered.

If you have a dishwasher, follow the manufacturer's directions on choice of a detergent; one that's too strong can hurt the finish on your china.

Polish silver about once a month with a cream or liquid polish. Rub each piece with a lengthwise motion. Wash in hot soapy water, rinse and dry. Then bring up the surface luster with a soft flannel cloth.

Hints: Tumblers stuck together? You can part them without breakage just by putting cold water in the inner glass and holding the outer one in warm water. Pouring hot liquid into a glass containing ice? Place a spoon in the glass first, so it won't crack.

About storing your table treasures

- Keep silver in a clean, dry place. For daily use, keep it in a lined, tarnish-resisting chest or drawer. Pieces used less often should go in tarnish-preventing bags or chests.
- Never use rubber bands around silver; they contain sulphur and will cause tarnishing.

- Don't crowd, never stack glassware. Place glasses side by side with rims up.
- If a tiny nick mars your glassware, you can smooth it by rubbing carefully with fine emery paper.
- Stack china plates according to size—largest on the bottom and no more than twelve plates high.
- Separate each plate from the next with a thin pad of felt or paper to protect the pattern and the glaze.
- To protect cup handles, place cups on the shelf individually. Or, if space is limited, use cup hooks.
- Wrap table linens in tissue paper and store them in a cool, dry place. (Many linens now come with their own protective plastic cases to keep them fresh and clean.)

FIFTEEN IDEAS FOR PARTIES THAT ARE EASY AND FUN

PINK PLAN FOR A PERFECT PARTY

Here is an omnibus theme which is as applicable to a Special Sweet Sixteen Party as to an eighteenth-birthday fete, the ideal choice for a graduation or a confirmation party, an engagement celebration or a bridal dinner, a shower for a bride—or a baby-to-be.

Everything will come up roses for the girl who gives a Pink Party where cupcakes bloom with frosting roses (pink, of course), pink posies bloom on centerpiece and place cards, splashes of rose water lend fragrance to the punch bowl.

Invitations bloom if you pen your message on small white cards, each with a baby-pink rosebud glued to the corner, painted on, or fastened with a ribbon streamer. Use the same idea for place cards—tiny white card plus tiny pink bud.

Concentrate on pink in your decorating scheme Use pink linens for your party table if you have them; otherwise, search party and novelty stores for pink paper accessories. If you're creative, get in the pink by making a tablecloth of two layers of pink tulle, underlaid with a sateen runner. Catch up the tulle in puffs around the table; secure with tiny roses, "quick"-stitching to plant them securely.

Create a colossal centerpiece by baking a cake or making a floral arrangement. If you're clever in the kitchen, prepare an eye-catching three-tiered cake; frost it in white and garnish with roses. Be a kitchen florist and "grow" roses from a pastry tube—or, if you'd rather put your trust in honest-to-goodness buds, garland the cake with real pink roses. Another tier idea: if you have a three-tiered compote dish, adopt this as your centerpiece. Deck it lavishly with roses, using various shades of pinks and reds on all three layers.

Pink nights are made for candlelight, so add an extra touch of rosy glow via a pair or a row of slender pink tapers arranged in your prettiest holders. For double glow in the same space, stand candlesticks on mirrors.

Borrow your family's prettiest silver and china for this extra-special occasion. If the family is not permissive, an attractive effect can be had for the price of rose-patterned paper plates. (If you're serving in the basement or out of doors, these might be your best bet anyway.)

Plan a pink menu for feasting that's festive. Your cue for refreshments: treats that look too pretty to eat but too good to pass up. Tickle your guests' appetites pink with rosy cupcakes . . . heaps of vanilla or strawberry ice cream, with berries as an accompaniment . . . cherry thumbprint macaroons . . . fancy in-the-pink sandwiches, such as shrimp-cucumber rounds, checkerboard or ribbon shapes filled with ruby-toned fruit jelly or pimiento-cheese combinations . . . a sparkling bowl of punch sparked with rose water (buy it at the drugstore).

What you do will depend on what your party celebrates. For a shower, there'll be gift-opening and girl-to-girl chitchat; do invite the boys in later, though, to enjoy the refreshments. For a birthday or graduation party, dancing would be fun (if space permits). If you like the dancing idea, add this special touch: make a little program for each guest, decorated with a tiny pink rosebud much the same as your original invitations and place cards. The cards may help to encourage mix-match dancing and will provide one and all with a perfect memento of your perfect Pink Party.

AUDITIONS PARTY Make your invitations like newspaper announcements: Joan Palmer and Katie Marsh announce that auditions will be held at Two Sycamore Drive from 8 till 11, Friday evening May 9th. There will be ample opportunity for dancers (solo, couples or groups), singers, musicians, puppeteers, comedians, actors and actresses to demonstrate their skills. A typical actors' midnight supper will be provided by the sponsors of the auditions, Mrs. Joseph Palmer and Mrs. Alonzo Marsh. Please call Liberty 3-1235 if you will be present.

The midnight supper—served at ten o'clock, but everything is exaggerated a bit in the theater—might be spaghetti, hot French or Italian bread and salad

. . . or Welsh rabbit . . . or "Broadway" sandwiches of corned beef, pastrami or salami on rye bread with dill pickles. Serve cheesecake for dessert with milk and something hot to drink.

TREASURE HUNT ON WHEELS Ride your bikes for this one and stage the hunt from 5 to 7, followed by a cookout at your house.

TOWN TREASURE TOUR Plan a walking tour to notable spots in your town—not necessarily to the best-known ones. The library, your history teacher, the town's historical society or one of the patriotic groups can help you work out interesting places to see. Send your groups off in small numbers, four at the most, each group starting at a different point of interest. You'll need to give each a map to follow or written directions. Good souvenir: paste the map and a page of information about the places on the tour inside a folder of colored paper. Follow up the tour with the kind of lunch or supper that might have been served in the early days of the town.

GARAGE GAIETIES Fill the driveway with little tables and chairs, set up a soft-drink bar and turn your garage into a gay room for dancing. The walls are no problem: cover them with jackets of dance records secured by masking tape or with travel posters. The ceiling is easily decorated with crepe-paper streamers or strings of Japanese lanterns. But you will need to dust the garage floor with sand to blot up oil and grease spots, then sweep it clean. Next cover it with an old rug and have a sock hop; better still, cover it with a sheet of linoleum or a linoleum rug you might borrow. On the tables put little vigil-light candles or citronella candles in chunky little glasses.

If your parents like dancing too, you might persuade them to give a dance on Friday night and have yours Saturday—to get more use out of your decorating efforts and some financial aid toward buying the trimmings.

SNOW-CHASERS' COOKOUT This is a garage party too, but held in the winter after skating, skiing or just making snowmen who look like your friends. Set up all the summer outdoor-cooking gear and terrace furniture in the garage. You'll think you're in Sun Valley!

SPOOK PARTY Not necessarily for Halloween, you understand, but very appropriate then. Masks are a must, and the best kind for this party is made from a pillowcase with slits cut for eyes, mouth and breathing space—very scary with no face marked on at all, possibly very funny if you mark one with felt-tipped ink pens, and very pretty if you add glitter for eye shadow, upholstery fringe for eyelashes, sew on beads for earrings and a necklace. Add a hank of thick black cotton rug yarn and you could be Cleopatra.

Have a cauldron of water bubbling in the fireplace, on a grill or on the kitchen stove to cook frankfurters in, and let each guest spear his own with a long-handled fork or sharpened branch. Relishes, hot-dog rolls, baked beans and other yummies team with the witches' brew of cider or orange-cranberry punch.

Ghost stories (if you're low on these, try the library), bobbing for apples carved with the initial of your true love's first name, and fortunetelling add to the fun. If one of your friends has the gift of fast, comic patter, he might be the fortuneteller; or you might write simple funny predictions in plain old milk on slips of paper and let each guest pass his slip over a candle flame to read the message. (Messages? "You will be asked to baby-sit next Thursday." "Riches await you." "You will own a basset hound before you are 30." "There is a cloud in your life at present, but it has a silver lining." "Within seven years a sports car will be made with your initials on it." "You will get through high school by the time you are 25.")

A good game to play is "Which Witch Is Which?" Hang a sheet across a doorway, allowing just enough room for feet and ankles to be seen. Each girl appears barefoot—one girl at a time. The one who keeps the boys guessing the longest is the winner.

SQUARE DANCE You might arrange to have this at school, the "Y" or in a church hall. If no one in your group knows how to call the dances, check your library for one of the excellent books on square dancing. Have the girls bring box suppers, and follow the old tradition of having each boy pick out one of the boxes to find his supper mate. Idea: start a square-dance club to meet every second Friday night.

PANCAKE PARTY Boys love to cook—and eat—pancakes. Borrow an extra electric griddle if you can, so two chefs can flip away. With bacon and sausages kept warm in a covered dish, a casserole of scalloped tomatoes, milk and a trayful of sirup, honey and hot blueberry preserves, you have a delicious meal that couldn't be easier to make.

COME AS YOUR HERO Or heroine! Give each guest a list of the boys and girls you've invited and ask them all to guess who's the hero or heroine the guest is supposed to be. This kind of costume party is one everyone enjoys, because it isn't hard to dream up the costumes. Obvious choice of food: hero sandwiches—at their best when each guest makes his own.

JAPANESE HIBACHI SUPPER This can be indoors or outdoors, but you'll need something to cook on for each group of four—hibachi grill, charcoal grill, or any electric grill you can put a skillet on—or an electric skillet! Give each group (who, ideally, would be seated on cushions on the floor) the fixings for sukiyaki and directions for cooking this quick Japanese dish of vegetables and beef. Most cookbooks have the recipe. If your library has a record-lending division, you might borrow Japanese records to play. Appropriate favors for the girls would be Japanese fans or chrysanthemums, wired to combs, to tuck in back of each ear.

Tea, rice, kumquats and rice cookies would round out the meal. No rice cookies available? Just "import" Chinese fortune cookies.

WRITE YOUR OWN FORTUNE COOKIES

Type the fortunes on small slips of very thin paper, tuck them inside little turnovers made of packaged cookie dough.

To help you get started writing fortunes for your party, here are some suggestions: Your secret ambition may soon be realized, but don't trust all to luck. . . . An interesting stranger is coming into your life. . . . You will soon have humble honor of doing dishes. Not all fortune good, cookie! . . . Sudden wealth, not necessarily money, is headed your way. . . . There's a Ford in your future. . . . Your heart line may soon become tangled, but there's a happy ending. . . . Some hidden capability is about to bring you good fortune. . . . Look for some unexpected money. You probably won't find it, but keep looking! . . . What you have been wishing for lately will soon come to pass. . . .

CRAZYBURGER TASTE-TESTING Serve miniature burgers—each with a numbered flag on a toothpick—made of different ingredients: tunaburgers, lambburgers, chickenburgers, turkeyburgers and real hamburgers. Let everyone try to guess which is which. Little ones cook quickly, so if it's too cold to cook outdoors, you can make them inside on an electric grill or skillet or on the kitchen stove with all the guests gathered around.

Try the same idea another time with hot dogs. Varieties could include *Bratwurst,* knockwurst, Polish and Italian sausages and the frozen franks that are made with tuna instead of meat. Since these can be recognized easily by their looks, you might blindfold the testers.

APRIL FOOL PARTY Also called a Drawkcab Ytrap, meaning a backward party. Girls ask the boys to this one—and, with luck, you might even get some good-sport brothers to give the party and provide the food. Until everyone arrives, have records of "Good Night, Ladies" and "Auf Wiedersehen" playing and everyone dancing. Next the appetizers are served—and at an Ytrap party, they're dessert, of course. If the brothers want advice about this course, suggest doughnuts split in two, filled with ice cream and topped with fruit preserve. While you're waiting for refreshments—the main course, really—you can go on with the dance, with the boys being the wall-weeds and the girls doing the cutting in. Or play that old Chinese game Tsohg, which is ghost with the words all spelled backward. Foolish but delicious main course: fat knockwursts instead of franks. Split each of them like a frankfurter bun and insert a third of a slice of bread. Best place to serve these would be the kitchen. Eat the knockwursts with a fork, of course. At the end of the meal, serve little glasses of tomato juice.

TREE-UNTRIMMING PARTY This is a good, though untraditional, finish to the merrymaking season, and New Year's Day might be the time to have it. Ask old friends and new to come help take down the tree and suggest that they dress casually. Have enough cartons, paper and string for storing and wrapping delicate ornaments and lights; boxes for icicles that can be used again; extra ornament hooks; several wastebaskets for the damaged items; a thick crayon or ink marker to label the boxes. Heavy string is useful to tie the spreading branches into a tight bundle, and you'll need a dustpan and brush to round up stray pine needles. Guests are bound to be starving by the time the tree is down, so have a hearty buffet of platters of sandwiches, coffeecake and stuffed dates as well as the expected bowl of eggnog. Guests won't eat and wander off if you have a few games in mind. Here are two resolution games: First, give each player a paper and pencil so he can jot down a serious or humorous resolution for the new year. Put all the slips of paper in a hat and, as the host or hostess reads them off one by one, let the others guess who wrote each one. Second, give each guest a list of 15 letters of the alphabet. He must use these to write a resolution, beginning every word with one of the letters, in their given order. Allow 15 minutes for this. Current Events is a good seasonal game too: ask each player to write a list of 10 important events that took place in the year just finished. The first completed entry wins. Let other players read items on their lists which don't duplicate the winning ones.

COME-AS-YOUR-FAVORITE-SONG PARTY Classics, old-timers and the newest tunes on the hit parade are all good sources for costume ideas. An easy one would be "Greensleeves," "Roses Are Red, My Love," which ought to be very pretty indeed with all those hearts and flowers. A boy might be the gunslinger who killed Liberty Valance or somebody's Funny Valentine.

PARTIES FOR GIRLS ONLY

Then there are times when you want to give parties for girls only. Here are some:

PAJAMA PARTIES can be a very special kind of girl-fun. Start the evening with nibble food—pretzels, potato chips, crackers (with a spicy dip), lots of ginger ale and fruit-flavored soda. Just about the time you're down to salty crumbs in the pretzel bowl, someone's bound to ask, "Well, when do we eat?" That's your cue. Bring out a pretty tray heaped with the makings of hearty Danish open-face sandwiches. Next serve a selection of fresh fruit, neatly trimmed, lightly sugared to bring out its juicy goodness. Sound tempting? The best is yet to come—a spectacular chocolate pie with a graham-cracker crust and topped with toasted almonds.

For fun and games, get out your camera (with flash attachment), keep it popping. If a tape recorder is available, have it on (but hidden) when the girls arrive. Later, play it back and let everyone hear herself as she really sounds. You can shop for inexpensive favors, which you pick because of each girl's special foible (a toy pigskin for a girl who worships a football hero, a pretend watch for a girl who's always late), and have everyone guess which guest is described before she receives her gift. You might tell fortunes with cards . . . and at bedtime, word games and ghost stories can spin out the fun a bit longer.

SHOWERS are a special, wonderful world of fun and dreaming (who will be next?). The omnibus Pink Party is ideal for this occasion. So is a brunch or a bridge-tea.

If you plan the shower as a surprise party, check the date and guest list with the mother of the bride. She can help make the "Surprise!" perfect. Invite your friends early, so they'll have time to gift-shop. For good gift ideas, see Chapter 21.

AT ANY TEEN GATHERING

GAMES, GAMES, GAMES GET A PARTY GOING

Here is a roundup of different kinds of games you might have at your parties. By planning a few for early in the evening, you can keep dancing as the climax of the evening—and also as a big reserve if things get sticky. If the thought of directing a game is sheer horror to you, ask a friend who's good at game-organizing to take over for you.

ACTING AND QUIZ GAMES

Charades: Divide your guests into two teams. Decide on a subject, such as book or movie titles, slogans or proverbs. The teams go into separate rooms, and all players help think up a title or phrase for each member of the opposing team. Write the selections on slips of paper. All return to the same room. Each team's slips of paper are distributed to the opponents. Each player must individually act out in pantomime his phrase or title so that his own team can guess it. Time each player. The team doing the fastest guessing job wins.

Who Am I? Pin the name of a famous personality on the back of each guest. He must try to find out who he is by asking the other guests questions which can be answered "yes" or "no": "Am I dead?" "Am I an actor?" "Am I a political figure?"

Find the Pairs: Write out a list of things that are usually paired with other familiar items—ham and eggs, pen and ink, needle and thread, and so forth. Copy the first half of each combination on blank cards—one for each guest—and hide the second half of each combination somewhere in the room. Next to the egg, the bottle of ink, the spool of thread or whatever, write a number. Each guest is given a card and told to find the mates for all the objects—but not to let the others know of his discoveries. Instead, he writes the correct identifying number next to each item on the card.

SIT-DOWN GAMES

Ghost: The players are seated in an informal circle. The first player calls the first letter of a word of more than two letters which he has in mind. The second player thinks of a word beginning with that letter and adds the second letter. The third player adds the third letter, and so on. Each player must be very careful that the letter he adds does not complete a word. For example, the first player calls "T," the second "R," the third "O." The fourth player, unable to think of any word but "Trot," is forced to add the "T" and complete the word. For this, he becomes a "half-ghost." Anyone who speaks to a half-ghost becomes a half-ghost. The next player then starts another word. Any player whose mistakes make him a half-ghost twice becomes a ghost. Anyone who speaks to a ghost becomes a ghost. Ghosts are out of the game but still remain in the circle and attempt to draw the players into conversation with them.

A player must always have in mind a word of more than two letters when he calls a letter. Frequently a player, in a tight spot and unable to think of a word from the letters passed on to him, will attempt to bluff and call a letter anyway. Any player suspecting that this is the case may challenge the player to state the word he has in mind. If he is unable to do so, he becomes a half-ghost; if he does name a legitimate word, the challenger becomes a half-ghost. For example, let us suppose that the letters so far named are TRINIT.

The next player names the letter "A." One of the other players, who expected the player to add "Y" and complete the word "Trinity," suspects the player of bluffing and challenges him. The player names the word "Trinitarian" and the challenger becomes a half-ghost.

Buzz: Your guests, seated in a circle, count off. The player who begins says 1, the player next to him says 2, the third player says 3, and so on around the circle, each player in turn calling out the next highest number, except when a 7 or any multiple of 7 comes up—and that is where the fun comes in. No player may say 7 or a multiple of 7; instead, he must say "buzz." So counting would be like this: 1, 2, 3, 4, 5, 6, buzz, 8, 9, 10, 11, 12, 13, buzz, 15, 16, one buzz, 18, 19, 20, buzz, 22, 23, 24, 25, 26, two buzz, buzz, 29, 30, 31, 32, 33, 34, buzz, 36, three buzz, etc. The counting should be as rapid as possible, and anyone who fails to buzz at the right time is eliminated from the game or has a point charged against him. The survivor or the one who has no points against him wins.

Magic Circle: You need an accomplice to get this started. You announce that you're about to put on an amazing demonstration of telepathy or magic or what have you. You say that you will create a magic spell and that whenever somebody feels he has it too, he can take part in the demonstration. Then you stand up in the center of the room and go into an incantation something like this: "Around this room I weave a magic circle; don't anybody move until you feel the magic." After a bit, someone is bound to say "What gives?" or something—at which point your accomplice will hop up and announce she "has the magic spell." Tell her to leave the room. After she's gone, go over and shake hands with someone. Tell the guests that if she really has the magic, she'll be able to tell which person you shook hands with. Then call her back in—and she'll go unerringly to the person you shook hands with. The trick, of course, is that you've agreed with her beforehand that you will shake hands with the first person who says something after you've said the magic incantation. Keep this up till some smart ones catch on and announce they have the magic feeling too. Then let them test out their powers by going out of the room themselves. Eventually everyone will get it, but you'll be amazed how long it takes some of the brightest people to figure this out.

Consequences: Have everyone write an adjective at the top of his sheet of paper, then fold the paper over and pass it to the person on his right. Now everyone is told to write down the name of a girl. Papers are folded and passed again, and the next question calls for another adjective . . . then the name of a man . . . the place where they met . . . when they met . . . what he said . . . what she said . . . what he did . . . what she did . . . the consequences (what happened) . . . and what the world said. Read the papers out loud, putting in the connecting words "met," "she said," "the world said," etc. The narratives will be masterpieces—of nonsense.

ACTIVE GAMES

Apple-Chin Relay: Divide the guests into two opposing teams and get them to stand up in two lines. Now tuck an apple under the chin of the first person in each line. He must turn to the next in line and, without using his hands, tuck the apple under his chin. If the apple is dropped, it goes back to the person who dropped it.

Lifesaver Relay: Another variation of the same theme. For this each person gets a toothpick to hold in his teeth. A candy lifesaver is passed from toothpick to toothpick. This is particularly funny when a very tall boy stands next to a short girl.

Hold That Ball: To play, set goal lines about eight feet apart. Then line up in teams, with two or three couples on each team. The lead couples are given a small ball, which they must hold between their foreheads while running sideways from start to goal line and back again. The only time they may touch the ball is when it falls (which is often). It is then passed to the next couple—who start for the goal line, and, with luck, may get there to win the prize.

Balloon and Broom Relay: This calls for two or more teams, with four to six players on each team. Your props are colored balloons—a different color for each group—and a broom for each team. Give the first player on each side a broom and a balloon and stand by with extras, in case of breakage. The first person sweeps the balloon (or tries, anyway) to a goal line and back, then hands broom and balloon to the next in line and takes his or her place at the end of the row. First team to finish the sweep wins—a toy broom for each member.

Pack and Run: Prepare two weekend suitcases in advance: cram them full of various things—anything that could possibly be draped or attached to a human frame. Throw in everything from lace-fringed scarves to earrings—the more, the better—but equalize the contents of the two bags. Guests line up in two teams. The first person on each side picks up the bag, runs to a given destination, opens the bag and puts everything on, picks up the empty suitcase, and goes back to the starting point. Then he takes everything off, hands the repacked bag to the next person on the team, and the performance is repeated. The "winnahs" deserve more than a prize, but maybe they'll settle for a packet of safety pins to help meet similar situations with greater aplomb.

Beat the Pan: Bring out an old kitchen pan and a big wooden spoon. Send one player out of the room while the rest of you decide upon something for him to do when he comes back—pick up a certain magazine, turn off a lamp, kneel in the middle of the room or what have you. When he comes back in the room, he is "directed" by another player, who taps softly on the pan. He taps more loudly when "it" gets nearer the object he's to touch. The tapping gets soft again if he moves away. No words are allowed; but you'll be amazed at how much the pan can say in its own way.

MIXER GAMES AND DANCES

Match Mates: Get your party off on the right foot by mixing and matching couples from the very beginning. Tear small sheets of heavy, colored construction paper into jagged pieces; put half the pieces in one bowl and the other halves in another. As guests enter, have each of them take (girls from one bowl, boys from the other) a card. After everyone has arrived, each must look for the mate who has the matching half of his card. Couples stay together for the first game or dance.

This game can be varied to suit the season, the occasion. For example, at a Valentine party your cards could be broken hearts. For a costume or personality party, write the names of the male and female members of famous couples on separate cards (Romeo and Juliet, Hamlet and Ophelia, Mickey Mouse and Minnie, etc.). Each guest must find the other half of his famous pair.

Cinderella Dance: Have each girl drop one shoe in a big box. Shuffle the shoes and cover the box with a big sheet. When the music starts, each boy must walk by the box, grab a shoe without looking, find the girl it belongs to and claim her for his partner.

Broom Dance: Divide the group into couples, but leave one volunteer without a partner. Instead, supply him with a broomstick. When the music starts, everyone must dance, including the gallant lad with the broomstick. The minute the music stops, he drops the broom and claims the nearest partner for the next dance. Everyone must switch partners, and the guest who is left wins the broom. This goes on until everyone has had a chance to dance with everyone else. Vary the length of the musical interludes so guests won't know when to expect the break, but give them a long enough time to get acquainted with each new partner.

Big Bang: With about two feet of string, tie an inflated balloon to each girl's ankle. Announce that a boy can cut in on a couple only after he has stepped on and broken the girl's balloon. It is perfectly legal for a boy to try to protect his best girl from an approaching male by using some fancy footwork.

Grand Right and Left: Boys circle the room one way, offering first their right then their left hands to girls as they approach, circling the room the other way. Each starts dancing with the nearest partner when the music begins.

Man Hunt: Let the girls be the aggressors with an all-out "man chase." Blindfold all the girls, give them a twist or two just to confuse them, then turn them loose. Their object: to catch a partner for dinner, the next dance or game. The boys walk into this one with their eyes wide open.

TWENTY FAVORITE PARTIES FROM SEVENTEEN

ZODIAC BIRTHDAY PARTY wouldn't be a party without ice cream and a cake with candles (to wish on!), gay decorations, favors and games. But though the traditions of a happy birthday never change, the food—and fun—become more grown-up and sophisticated as *you* do. Invite your guests for eight, the fashionable come-for-dessert hour. Serve a pretty pink birthday cake, pink sodas. For a surprise, design a Zodiac Tree centerpiece to bloom over your pink-is-for-girls paper tablecloth. The Zodiac Tree may be any sizable leafy potted plant, to the branches of which you can tie Fortune Apples—one for each guest. Each "apple" is decorated with the appropriate sign of the Zodiac and the guest's name. A "fortune" is inside, an astrologist's view of your friend's personality, gleaned from the books on astrology you'll find in your public library. The tree is simple to arrange, just shape tissue paper into ball-shaped forms, enclose the "fortune," and tie with ribbon at the top. Then tie the "apples" to the tree with ribbon. The Zodiac Tree takes advance planning, but adds a delightful bit of table-talk your guests will love. After cake and soda-sipping, clear the table for games—bridge, or whatever is most popular with your crowd.

PREDICTION FOR SWEET SIXTEEN: A Pink Cake and A Rosy Future. Turning sixteen is so special it calls for a party. Since presence demands presents, limit your list to close friends. Invite them for coffee and cake and the game of Predictions: you and your guests each write a funny ten-years-from-today prediction for every other guest; then you read the end results aloud.

SHARE-A-RECORD PARTY Feel like dancing to Bob's and Susie's and Tony's records as well as your own? Give a Share-a-Record party and ask everyone to bring one or two of his current-and-choice—name-tagged to prevent mix-ups. (Cut invitations in the shape of records from black construction paper; in the center of each place a bright-red legal seal from the stationery store.) If your walls can take it, tape or tack up record jackets; otherwise, pin them on the draperies. Make it a costume party, with all comers dressed as songs. Or play the game of "Who Am I?" Pin the name of a singer, composer or instrumentalist to each guest's back; make him guess his identity by asking questions of fellow guests, deciphering their mysterious answers.

BIG SPLASH SWIMMING PARTY!

If you're lucky enough to have a pool in the family's back yard—make it a poolside picnic. If there's a private pool in the neighborhood, pool your resources and get in the swim! Of course, a picnic's a party anywhere—by a mountain lake . . . near a lazy rippling river . . . on a sandy patch of beach by the sea. The fun is where your friends are. Choose an accommodating menu—one you can serve anywhere, hot or cold, any time—for lunch or dinner! Blessing in disguise is the kind of food you can make a day ahead, with no last-minute fuss the morning of your party. First make a check list of the things you'll need; you may have some of them, such as paper plates and napkins, in the house already. If you're picnicking away from home, include a vacuum jug—to keep punch icy cold—and insulated bags to keep perishables safe. When you've finished your shopping, invite one or two of the girls on your guest list over for K.P. (that's Kitchen Party). While you're frying the chicken to a golden turn, they can whip up the potato salad, fix the radishes and celery sticks. Don't forget to pack the corn muffins, cake and lots of fresh fruit for in-between nibbling. Ready? Then get set to go—out to the pool, off to the beach, wherever your fancy takes you.

POST-EXAM POST-MORTEM

Exams over? Toast your term papers . . . in effigy. Take advantage of the slight lull between semesters to invite other members of the Bored-of-Education. For entertainment, spring a crazy quiz that's a parody of the ones you've just survived; stack new records on the player and spread a table with the makings of heap-'em-yourself hero sandwiches.

A SKATING PARTY

The ground's blanketed in snow and the thermometer has taken a nose dive. A setting like this calls for a party—at the lake or pond (or indoor rink). Telephone your friends—three couples and someone for yourself; let them know there's a party in the wind.

If you're holding your party outdoors, advise everyone to bundle up warmly and bring a pair of skates. You bring the record player, the paper cups and napkins—plus the food: a vacuum jug of hot apple cider; another of soup (canned minestrone teamed with sausage bits); buttered onion rolls, kept oven-warm in an insulated bag; apples on the stick. If you're holding your party at a rink, take your guests back to your house and serve them buffet-style, with dancing and a songfest afterward.

HAVE FUN, RAISE FUNDS—How to fill the till for school, church or charity

Draft workers from your class, divide them into teams of four or six and offer to rake leaves, mow lawns, shovel snow (depending on the season) for citizens of the community. Charge a set fee and let it be known that proceeds earned will go into the fund.

Start a community car-wash day. Arrange for the use of a large public area, such as a municipal parking lot or a schoolyard, near an adequate water supply. Set up an assembly line with separate teams to wash and rinse cars, sweep out interiors.

Auction off the services of eager volunteers at a simple record dance. Samples: a taxi ride to school (in a wheelbarrow), term-paper typing, a week's service as table waiter in the school cafeteria. Offer some silly, some practical services.

Charge one toy or a game as admission to a dance for the local children's home. Hold the dance in an undecorated gym to keep the expenses down; let records supply the music. Or make the fee food or clothing for a charity package.

Plan a "Pound Prom." Set up a scale at the ticket booth and charge each boy a penny for every pound of his date's weight. (For scale-shy females, set a dollar-and-a-half limit). Decorate in theme with calorie guides and diet charts. Refreshments: poundcake and dieter's punch!

Let class cooks whip up a batch of their favorite cakes or confections to be sold at a public cake sale. Wheedle a convenient spot to set up your wares—in the lobby of the local bank or City Hall or the school gym. Earn pin money by selling typed copies of recipes.

Vary the usual bridge-party format with an all-games party. You set up chairs and tables for expected customers and supply the refreshments. Let guests bring their own games (cards, Scrabble, Monopoly) and pay to play. Ask local merchants to donate door prizes.

Stage a gala carnival. Let school clubs compete in setting up novel booths and award a prize for the most original. Ringtoss, darts, weight-guessing are old favorites. Try a funny portrait booth. Paint comic pictures (amusement-park style) for people to pose behind. Snap them with a picture-in-a-minute camera.

HAVE A DANCE FOR UNICEF Celebrate UN Day, October 24

Want to have a "big-name" recording star at your next dance? Want to have your favorite disc jockey act as emcee? Teen-agers in Pittsburgh, Pennsylvania, one year discovered a way to do both and at the same time raise $1,121.48 for UNICEF (United Nations Children's Fund). Their formula: Penny Proms.

Penny Proms began because Pittsburgh teen-agers wanted to celebrate UN Day and Halloween (which are both in October) all at once. They decided to give a record hop and donate the proceeds to UNICEF. They chose the name Penny Prom because of an astounding statistic: with one penny UNICEF can provide enough milk to take care of one underfed child for a week.

Disc jockeys in Pittsburgh offered to emcee the Proms, bring their records, their friends. Neighborhood merchants donated pop, cookies, games, door prizes, flags and crepe paper. The idea has spread to other cities.

A Penny Prom can be any kind of record hop; in Pittsburgh it started with a carnival air. There were dart games, ringtoss games, penny-pitching games: all cost pennies to play. Girls paid 50 cents to dance with the disc jockey; the boy with the biggest feet forfeited five pennies.

Think up your own ideas for a Penny Prom theme or (if you're stuck) write to U. S. Committee for UNICEF, United Nations, New York.

A KRISS KRINGLE PARTY is the most satisfying kind of pre-Christmas get-together you could plan. It's the kind of party where everyone has fun by working—making or refurbishing toys for needy children.

Invite three couples (plus a co-host) to join you at your workshop one afternoon. Ask each guest to come armed with a hearty appetite and a toy or the makings of a toy. When the last package has been wrapped and the last morsel of food devoured, tote the gifts to your favorite community organization for distribution on Christmas Day.

MENU

Dagwood Sandwiches
Carrot Sticks and Cauliflower Buds
Raspberry Sherbet Float
with Ginger Ale

WRAP-A-PRESENT PARTY Serve yourself a double dip of fun while you fill a Christmas stocking.

Here's a gay holiday party to wrap up a season's worth of cheer for you and the children in your local hospital or children's home. Ingredients: a few friends, reams of ribbon and wrapping paper and presents, presents, presents! Approach hospital authorities and tell them you would like to contribute some gifts for their children's Christmas. They will tell you the types of toys needed. Biggest hits are inexpensive blocks, coloring books, oversized beads to string. Pass the information on to your guests when you invite them and ask each to bring a few gifts to your wrap-a-present party. It's best to set a limit (a dollar buys a lot) and let them see how good they are at bargain-hunting in the dime store or their own attics. You supply the wrappings and food. Cocoa and cookies are good: the guests can nibble while they work. For atmosphere, play carols on a phonograph. Remember, children are more impressed by lots of crazy packages than by fancy bows. Wrapping a set of jacks? Tie each separately and string together. Bundle lumpy things in colored tissue or crinkly kitchen foil; garnish with jingle bells or a lollipop. Decorate flat packs with faces made of candy canes and peppermints. You'll have as much fun thinking up silly wraps as the youngsters will in opening them.

DINNER PARTY ON THE MOVE. Co-hostesses make a party more fun, less work. A wonderful way to keep a party going is to keep it going from place to place: guests on the go never wonder, "What do we do next?" And a "progressive" dinner party gives not one but three hostesses a chance to shine, sharing the fun (and funds) of entertaining.

Here's how this party works: the crowd gathers at one house for appetizers, moves to the next for a main course, has dessert at a third. Each hostess prepares her third of an easy dinner early enough to leave her free to join friends in trooping from house to house. So that no girl pays more than another, expenses are totaled, then split three ways.

EAT YOUR WAY AROUND THE WORLD New idea for a progressive dinner

Some people will go anywhere at the drop of a hat. We go at the drop of a spoon (which means friends are coming too!). How about you? Like to travel—in gay company, of course? Then assemble your friends, choose your itinerary and go—around the world via a United Nations party! Your passport to fun: exciting (yet easy-to-make) conversation-piece dishes.

Where would you like to travel? For a buffet party, with a guest list of six couples or so, we suggest a round-the-world tour. Your route, starting with appetizers, might include, among others, England and Sweden, then sunny Spain perhaps, Italy and Mexico, with stop-offs for salad and sweets in such faraway places as Indonesia and Romania. This *is* a Cook's (and diners') Tour—and one which increases international understanding as it pleases the palate. It's easy with recipes translated into simple American terms. Special travelers' aids: canned foods—including Swedish meat balls, Scotch broth, ravioli and beef stew—that need only a quick heating before serving time.

Decorations: If there's someone artistic in your crowd (you?), make posters to hang around your party room by cutting out travel pictures and travel-ad headlines (like "Getting there is half the fun") and pasting them together in a collage. Other decorations: UN flags; colorful foreign stamps, to scatter on a crepe-paper tablecloth; a UN building to tower as the centerpiece of your table.

Entertainment: Start your party off with a scavenger hunt. When you make up your "hunting" list, include each of the countries on your menu. Your list might read, for example: find something French, something English, something Russian. Some suggestions (for you, not for your guests!): the "something French" might be a poodle or a bottle of French perfume; the "something Russian" could be a Russian novel, such as *War and Peace;* the "something English," imported marmalade, perhaps.

SUPPER BEFORE THE GAME What better way to put your crowd in a cheering mood than to serve a buffet supper before you all go on to a Friday-night game? Handsome décor—pennants and construction-paper megaphones sprouting glossy green leaves—is simple; the food is easy to fix partially the night before, partially after school the day of the party. And an all-in-line buffet table makes serving very easy, too. Guests can collect plates, forks and napkins at one end; fill their plates; pick up glasses and begin eating without having to backtrack or wait for one another. Don't plan to play games at this party (you won't have time), but do practice school cheers and songs if there's a piano somewhere about.

AFTER THE GAME MIDNIGHT FEAST

What better way to celebrate victory (or forget defeat) than by having after-game get-together in your kitchen? Set your "table" on the counter; serve quick-to-fix cocoa and cake; let guests start munching the minute they come.

FAREWELL DINNER PARTY Dressy clothes, soft candlelight and a picture-pretty table are in order when you plan this sophisticated feast for someone departing—say, a boy who's going into the service. Invite a few couples and ask them to bring inexpensive presents to heap for a centerpiece. (Your contribution: a book of snapshots of the crowd.) Happy chatter and a delicious dinner will keep everyone busy enough, but you might, for fun, play the game of Predictions. Let each guest write a five-years-from-today prediction for every other guest—the more fantastic, the better—and read it aloud. Save these prophecies to see, later, how close they came to being true. For sentiment's sake, capture the fun with your flash camera and send the snaps to the guest of honor when he's at camp.

BOSTON TEA PARTY

A hop, snack and open house: that's the party formula dreamed up by Boston teens. It's a tea dance—with a difference. The new time for dancing (to records) is four o'clock in the afternoon. The day for a get-together is (surprise!) Sunday. Even the menu is different (though tea still heads the list).

REFRESHMENTS

Hot Tea Iced-Tea Punch
Cream Cheese and Date-Nut Bars
Ham-Asparagus Rolls Open Hearts
Chinese Chicken Sandwiches
Lobster Puffs
Pound Cake

If Sunday is a nothing-ever-happens day, here's just your cup of tea. Invite your friends—some old, some new—set up the buffet, put on some records and dance. Since all you need is stand-up room, you can invite as many people to a tea dance as you can comfortably squeeze into your room or budget. And don't be afraid to invite the football-team captain if that's whom you're secretly giving your parties for these days. Boys are boys in Boston too, and *they* love the tea dance. And you'll love it; one of the best things about a tea dance, from the giving side, is that all you do at party time is Have fun! The cake can be made ahead and frozen. Some night at the end of the week you can frost the cake and bake the lobster puffs. With friends to help on Sunday, you can waltz through the rest of your party preparations in three-quarter time.

Tuning up for a tea party First, make arrangements for three of your very best friends to help you the day of the party. Well in advance, bake the cake. Assemble the silver and china you will need. The day before the party, buy all necessary groceries, frost the cake, do advance preparation for the punch and make the cream cheese and date-nut bars, and bake the shells for the lobster puffs. The morning of the party you and your crew can follow this plan: No. 1 Girl: Make creamed-lobster filling; refrigerate. Fill puffs, arrange on trays. Wrap and refrigerate. No. 2 Girl: Make and wrap the sandwiches, place on tray, refrigerate. The No. 3 Girl and You the Hostess: Roll up the rugs for dancing and stack records. Set the table. A white or lace cloth is traditional; so are flowers, candlesticks. Just before the guests arrive, put the tea service at one end of the table, punch bowl and cups at the other. The cake, with a server, should be in the center; plates of sandwiches can be right in front. Let guests help themselves or ask one of them to serve the punch and another to pass sandwiches.

Tea trimmers When you serve hot tea, offer guests milk (not cream, which spoils the flavor), wedges of lemon and sugar—in tiny cubes or granulated. For fun, try cinnamon-stick stirrers. Whenever you serve iced tea, provide wedges of lemon or bottled lemon juice, superfine sugar. Nice changes: orange juice, fresh or concentrated, to sweeten and flavor; lemon-lime soda (no sugar is necessary).

SERVE A SUNDAY SPECIAL JUST FOR THE FAMILY A family that's nice enough to let you give a party deserves one of its own. So why not turn the tables on your family and play hostess to them, at a long, lazy Sunday breakfast? Start with fruit-topped cereals; follow up with a main course that doesn't force you to do a vanishing act in the kitchen. (One good suggestion: waffles cooked right at the table.) Finishing touch: you do the dishes! For fun, vary your scene: if you eat weekday breakfasts in the kitchen or dining room, move to the living room on Sunday. Set your table in a sunny window; use a teacart to make serving easier.

WANT TO MAKE NEW FRIENDS? GIVE A BRING-A-STRANGER PARTY Some day soon add new faces to your crowd with a Sunday open house to which each guest brings a friend unknown to most of the others. (Let a girl bring another girl, a boy bring another boy, if you like; just be sure to ask plenty of each!) Afraid people will be shy? Team charades, group singing and occasional nibbling will keep them too busy.

SHARE CHRISTMAS TREE-TRIMMING AND GIFT-WRAPPING AT AN OPEN HOUSE

The holidays: a breathlessly gay, frantically busy time when you shop for gifts, help decorate the house, trim the tree, wrap your presents. It's party time, too—but how can you fit in time for a party you give yourself? Easy: have an open house! Combine the fun of getting ready for Christmas with the warm, generous hospitality of the season. Have a tree-trimming party or gift-wrapping party. For invitations, send your guests shopping bags to tote their gifts and wrappings in; you provide plenty of scissors and sealing tape. You can sing carols, dance and play games at your open house. You'll have time to enjoy your own party too, because you serve delicious, Christmasy refreshments that take just a few precious holiday minutes to fix: hot, spicy cider; thick, creamy eggnog; crackers and sharp cheese; coffeecake, light angel food cake, cookies, stuffed dates, candies, nuts. Just take all these elements, arrange them cozily around the glowing candles and pine-fragrant evergreens on your buffet table and gather around. In this hospitable season, it's a good feeling to be able to say, "Come to my holiday open house!"

A NEW YEAR'S EVE PARTY

Welcome the New Year with a gala celebration for ten couples. For invitations, print the vital statistics (time, place, etc.) on narrow colored streamers. Roll each tightly, tuck deep inside a deflated balloon, place in envelope and mail. Each person must blow up his balloon and break it to get at the invitation.

Have noisemakers and confetti on hand for the magic midnight hour! Serve some bubbling mock champagne earlier in the evening while guests compete in a party-hat-making contest. Provide guests with crepe paper, feathers, pins, and tape. The couple creating the maddest hat wins a prize. Dancing plus a fortunetelling séance at dessert time rounds out the evening.

PARTIES FOR PLENTY

To end on a lavish note—what about parties for plenty . . . crowd parties, such as the Junior-Senior dinner or your church youth group, where you're asked to be in charge of food? If you can cook for eight, you can cook for eighty! But you must multiply both the food and the number of hands needed to help prepare and serve it. And since it's usually a club or class party, use organization to line everything up. Consult your home-economics teacher for good simple menus and ask her help in locating good cookbooks. Next, line up your refreshment committee. As to shopping, let each of your "chefs" be responsible for the necessary ingredients for her own particular specialty (and remember: it's "cheaper by the dozen," so buy in quantity when you can save). If you plan a meat dish, such as barbecued chicken (quick to do, filling and luscious to look at), assign three girls to prepare the birds and the barbecue sauce, one to take charge of a quantity salad, another to prepare a hot vegetable (a casserole would be better than a vegetable that must be cooked and served instantly), and three to prepare a dessert (such as pie, which can be done in quantity and not suffer). Eight belles, and all's well!

Index